CARE WORK

D1355614

The quest for security

CARE WORK

The quest for security

Edited by Mary Daly

INTERNATIONAL LABOUR OFFICE • GENEVA

Daly, M. (ed.)
Care work: The quest for security
Geneva, International Labour Office, 2001

Child care, elder care, care of the disabled, informal care, social service, developed country, developing country

02.09

ISBN 92-2-1114023

ILO Cataloguing-in-Publication Data

Printed and bound in Great Britain by Biddles Ltd, www.biddles.co.uk

PREFACE

This study is one of the first to stem from the International Labour Office (ILO) InFocus Programme on Socio-Economic Security, and is devoted to a topic that has received relatively little attention in mainstream economic and social policy analysis. As emphasized in the introduction and elsewhere in the following chapters, we believe legitimizing, compensating and giving voice to those doing care work is a fundamental part of a decent work agenda, which the ILO has set out to promote in the twenty-first century.

The ILO's InFocus Programme on Socio-Economic Security has a philosophical foundation, which is that the Good Society of the twenty-first century should ensure basic security for all its citizens as the fundamental principle of distributive justice, and that this requires basic income security and sufficient voice. In promoting these two forms of security, income and voice, other forms should not be neglected, but the trade-offs and other types of security depend crucially on these two forms. And in developing policies and institutions, two policy decision rules should guide reformers.

The first of these is what might be called the Security Difference Principle, following John Rawls' famous proposal, which was not couched in terms of security. As we postulate it, this states: A policy or institutional change is just if, and only if, it enhances the security of the least secure groups in society.

The second decision rule is what might be called the Paternalism Test Principle, which is fundamental to liberty and a Good Society, but which is sometimes forgotten by even the most liberal reformers. This states: A policy or institutional change is just if, and only if, it does not impose controls on some groups that are not imposed on the most free members of society.

These two rules and the fundamental principles underlying the Programme are highly relevant to care work and those required or wanting to do it, in all its various forms. Care workers have been society's forgotten citizens for too long: undervalued, under-appreciated, under-paid, and typically only seen in the breach.

This study is a small contribution to the debate about how to compensate, legitimize and regulate care work. It certainly does not cover all aspects of the debate. However, it marks out a sphere of work on which the Programme will build. In preparing it, thanks are due to several people, for editing and commenting on the drafts. Gratitude is due in particular to Sukti Dasgupta, Bridget Dommen, Julie Lim and Jacinta Tierney. For their participation and comments, we also thank Robert Anderson, Alejandro Bonilla-Garcia, Susan Davis, Cleopatra Doumbia-Henry, Jo-Jo Dy Hammar, Mireille Kingma, Lena Lavinas, Anna Ricciardi, Adriana Santa-Cruz, Michael Sebastian, Pascale Vieille, Mike Waghorne and Jane Zhang.

This work represents a first step, not a final contribution. We will continue to assess policies dealing with care work, and develop more specific policy and institutional recommendations over the course of 2002-03. Undoubtedly, care work will be one of the major areas of social protection policy over the next decade, and we will do our best to ensure that it is not overlooked in the reformulation of the ILO's general re-orientation to its decent work agenda.

Guy Standing
Director
InFocus Programme on Socio-Economic Security

CONTENTS

Preface v

Notes on contributors xiii

List of abbreviations xvii

Introduction, *Mary Daly and Guy Standing* 1
  The time squeeze 6
  The need for voice 6
  The future of care work 8
  Structure of the study 9

PART I: Care as decent work 13

1.   Care work: Overcoming insecurity and neglect, *Guy Standing* . . . 15
  Introduction 15
  Care, identity and citizenship 17
  Care work: A framework 19
  Compensation: From gift to market 24
  Income security: The role of the State 26
  Conclusion 31

2.   Care policies in Western Europe, *Mary Daly* 33
  Conceptualizations and definitions of care 34
    The evolution of care as a concept 34
    Care as a social policy analysis tool 34
    Policy parameters of care 36
  Provision for care in European welfare states 39

General outline of trends in provision 39
Public policies on care in European welfare states 41
Models of managing care in European welfare states 43
Evaluating alternative ways of compensating for care 47
The different features of care as a policy good 47
Considering the likely effects of different policy measures 50
Overview 53

3. **Legitimizing care work and the issue of
gender equality,** *Jane Lewis* 57
The crisis in care 57
Care and the erosion of the male breadwinner model 59
Anxieties about growing individualism and the
implications for care 65
The nature of care work and an ethic of care 69
Policy implications 72

PART II: Care in developing countries 77

4. **Development, freedom and care: The case of India,**
Umadevi Sambasivan 79
Introduction 79
Individualism and care in industrialized countries 80
The familial self in India 82
The self and child-care practices in India 84
The elderly in Indian society 87
Conclusion 89

5. **Early childhood care and development in India:
Some policy issues,** *Rekha Wazir* 91
Introduction 91
The case for ECCD 91
ECCD in the Indian context 94
ECCD indicators 96
ECCD programmes 98
Key policy issues 100
Conclusion: the need for dialogue 104

6. **Child care as public policy in Brazil,** *Bila Sorj* 105
Introduction 105

Profile of the supply and demand for crèches and
pre-school nurseries 107
    Types of pre-school 109
    Pre-school management 111
Child care as a social good 112
    Social struggles 113
Public policies 116
    Child care as a "right to education" 117
    Tensions and ambiguities 120
Conclusion 123

7.   **Social support for home-based care in the Russian
Federation,** *Liana Lakunina, Natalia Stepantchikova and
Tatyana Tchetvernina* 125
Introduction 125
The background to social protection policies as they relate to care . . 125
Privileges to workers providing care for family members 127
System of state support for persons in need of care 129
    Income benefits 129
    Social-service-related assistance to the elderly and
    the disabled 132
Efficiency of the social protection system 136
Reforming the social protection system 138

PART III: Care in industrialized countries 141

8.   **The politics of social care in Finland: Child and elder
care in transition,** *Anneli Anttonen* 143
Introduction 143
The Scandinavian social care regime 144
Finnish child-care policy: Universalism and pluralism 147
Elder care in transition 151
Support for informal caring: the system of home-care allowances . 154
Conclusion 157

9.   **Care work: Innovations in the Netherlands,** *Trudie Knijn* 159
Introduction 159
    Welfare state and care discourse 159
    The care-gap discourse 160

Substitution of formal by informal care discourse 161
The care and work discourse. 161
The care and citizenship discourse 161
The ethics of care discourse 162
Care as a dimension of the "Combination Scenario" 163
Do women gain? 168
Care work: Another private solution. 170
Conclusion 174

10.   Accounting for care in the United States, *Nancy Folbre* 175
Introduction. 175
Defining care. 176
The care labour force in the United States 179
The decline of home-making 180
Time-use surveys 181
Employment in care occupations 182
Employment in care industries 184
Three care industries 184
    Health care 184
    Child care 185
    Elder care 186
Public support for care in the United States 187
    Support for child rearing 187
    Child care 188
    Elder care 190
Conclusion 191

PART IV: Representation for care work 193

**11.   From private carer to public actor: The carer's
       movement in England,** *Marian Barnes*. 195
Introduction. 195
The National Council for the Single Woman and
    her Dependants 195
    "A stronger voice". 198
The Birmingham Community Care Special Action
    Project (CCSAP). 200
Consolidation 202
Informal care and the State 202

What do carers want from community care? 205

Conclusion 209

12.   **Caring for carers: An example from Ireland,**
      Eddie Collins-Hughes 211

Introduction 211

The Carers' Association of Ireland 212

Lobbying and advocacy 213

Providing for the needs of carers 215

The future 217

13.   **Creating unions, creating employers: A Los Angeles**
      home-care campaign, *Jess Walsh* 219

Introduction 219

The home-care industry and labour market 221

Creating a union of independent providers in Los Angeles 223

The emergence of the public authority model 225

Establishing a public authority in LA County 226

Home-care workers and consumers emerge as a political force 228

Back to the State: Reforming home-care funding in California 230

Conclusion: Security of care, security of work 231

Bibliography 235

Index 253

List of tables

2.1   Universe of provision for care 38

2.2   Clustering of European countries on the basis of their
      provision for children 44

2.3   Clustering of European countries on the basis of their
      provision for the elderly 46

2.4   How policy provisions rate in relation to different objectives 51

3.1   Labour force participation as a percentage of population
      from age 15–64 61

3.2   Part-time employment in 13 OECD countries ranked by
      part-time employment as a proportion of female employment
      (1979 and 1995, percentages) 61

5.1   Child survival and development 97

7.1   The most widespread social benefits and allowances for child care
        (Russian Federation) 131
7.2   Evolution of home-based social services 135
7.3   Ratio of minimum social guarantees to the subsistence
        minimum (1996–98). 137
8.1   Publicly funded day care for children in Finland, 1965–98 149
8.2   Care of children under age 3 in Finland, 1985–98 150
8.3   The primary sources of help among people aged 65+ in Finland
        in 1994 155
8.4   Care service provision for older people in Finland in 1998 157
9.1   Types of families with children, 1998 (percentage of families
        where parents are aged between 20 and 50) 168

List of figures

1.1   The social process of care 23
3.1   Patterns of male and female paid work and arrangements
        for care 63

NOTES ON CONTRIBUTORS

Anneli Anttonen (Ph.D.) is Senior Lecturer in the Department of Social Policy and Social Work at the University of Tampere, Finland. She has written widely in the field of women, citizenship care and social services. Moreover, one of her interests lies in comparative social policy analysis. Currently, she is co-editing the book *The young, the old and the State: Social care systems in five industrial nations* (to be published in 2001).

Marian Barnes is Reader and Director of Social Research in the Department of Social Policy and Social Work at the University of Birmingham. Much of her work over the past 13 years has been on user involvement and user self-organization in the context of health and social care. Her publications on this subject include: *Care, communities and citizens*; and *Taking over the asylum: Empowerment and mental health* (with Ric Bowl). She is a member of the national Health Action Zone (HAZ) evaluation team, focusing on community involvement and inter-agency partnerships, and is leading a project on public participation and social exclusion in the Economic and Social Research Council's (ESRC) Democracy and Participation research programme.

Eddie Collins-Hughes is Director of the Carers Association of Ireland. He is a member of the Working Group on Needs Assessment for Carers; the Consultative Forum on Health Strategy of the Department of Health; and the Pre-Budget Forum of the Department of Social, Community and Family Affairs, as well as a number of voluntary organizations. He represents Ireland's Carers in the European Union EU as a Board Member of the European Association of Care and Help at Home (EACHH).

Mary Daly is Professor of Sociology at the School of Sociology and Social Policy at Queen's University Belfast. She has held research and teaching positions in Germany, Italy and Ireland. Among the fields on which she has published are poverty, the welfare state, gender, family and the labour market. Much of her work is comparative, in a European and international context. Her most recent book, *The gender division of welfare*, undertakes a comparative analysis of how the British and German welfare states affect gender inequalities. She is a member of a number of European networks and boards on topics related to social policy, family and gender.

Nancy Folbre is Professor of Economics at the University of Massachusetts at Amherst, and staff economist with the Center for Popular Economics. Her academic research explores the interface between feminist theory and political economy. In addition to numerous articles published in academic journals, she is the author of *Who pays for the kids? Gender and the structures of constraint* and an associate editor of the journal *Feminist Economics*. The books she has co-authored for a wider audience include: *The ultimate field guide to the U.S. economy*; and *The invisible heart: Economics and family values* (forthcoming). She is co-chair of the MacArthur Foundation Research Network on the Family and the Economy and a recent recipient of a five-year fellowship from the Foundation.

Dr Trudie Knijn is Associate Professor at the Department of Cross-cultural Studies of the Faculty of Social Sciences at Utrecht University, the Netherlands. As a researcher, she is a member of the Amsterdam School for Social Science Research and of the Interuniversity Centre for Social Science Theory and Methodology. She is also founder and coordinator of the *European Network – Women, Welfare State and Citizenship* group (since 1991). She is one of the leading researchers of the Netherlands Kinship Panel Study and has published many articles on gender, care and the welfare state, mothers' care and work and on transformations in public services such as home care and child care.

Liana Lakunina gained her Ph.D. in Economics at Moscow State University in 1981. She is currently a senior researcher at the Centre for Labour Market Studies, Institute of Economics, Russian Academy of Sciences (IERAS). She is also a member of the Scientfic Board of the Department of Social Policy and Labour Market, Institute of Economics, IERAS.

Jane Lewis is Barnett Professor of Social Policy at the University of Oxford. She has a long-standing interest in gender and social policies and her most recent publications include: (ed.) *Lone mothers in European welfare regimes*; (ed.) *Gender, social care and welfare state restructuring in Europe;* with K. Kiernan and H. Land, *Lone motherhood in twentieth century Britain*; and *The end of marriage? Individualism and intimate relationships.*

Umadevi Sambasivan is Professor and Head of the Department of Economics at the University of Kerala, India, and Director of the Cost of Cultivation Scheme, as well as a member of the Governing Body of the Centre for Development Studies in Trivandrum. She has served as Director of the Centre for Women's Studies at the University of Kerala and as Vice-President of the Indian Economic Association. She has taught at the University of California at Berkeley and at Harvard University. She is currently working on "globalization, human development and gender concerns", with the support of the Vanguard Foundation. In addition to numerous articles published in academic journals, she is the author of *Evolution of economic thought and theory*; *Economic theory and methods of reasoning; Women, work, development and ecology*; and *Plantation economy of the third world.* She is co-editor (with Krishna Ahuja Patel) of *Women and development.*

Bila Sorj is Professor of Sociology at the Federal University of Rio de Janeiro (UFRJ), Brazil. She has a doctorate in Sociology from Manchester University. She was co-editor of *Estudos Feministas*/UFRJ. She has contributed numerous articles to academic journals and has edited several books on home-based work, gender and work and ethnic identities.

Guy Standing is Director of the InFocus Programme on Socio-Economic Security of the ILO. He was previously director of the ILO's Labour Market Policies Branch and director of the ILO's Central and Eastern European team, based in Budapest. He is chairman of the Basic Income European Network (BIEN). He has worked with many international governments and bodies, including the Governments of Malaysia and South Africa, the Russian Federal Employment Service and the Commission of South Africa. He has written or edited several books and articles on labour economics, labour market policy, unemployment, labour market flexibility, structural adjustment policies and social protection policy. He is on the editorial boards of several academic journals. His latest book is *Global labour flexibility: Seeking distributive justice.*

Natalia Stepantchikova is Senior Researcher at the Centre for Labour Market Studies, Institute of Economics, Russian Academy of Sciences (IERAS). She has participated as a researcher in several projects and surveys including: analysis of labour relations in the Russian Federation transition period; analysis of enterprise restructuring and employment of the redundant workforce; individual and collective conflicts and disputes at the enterprise level; dynamics of trade union activity under economic reforms; analysis of different aspects of the formation of a social partnership in the Russian Federation; collective bargaining and agreements; analysis of the current social protection system in the Russian Federation; and the legal status of women in a transition economy. She has written several publications and monographs in these areas.

Tatyana Tchetvernina is Director of the Centre for Labour Market Studies, Institute of Economics, IERAS. She received her Ph.D. in Economics from IERAS in 1986. She is the author of several publications on the Russian labour market, social protection systems in transition countries, the unemployment insurance system in the Russian Federation, and active labour market policies. She is also the editor of *Labour in the Russian Federation* (1999) and *Living standards in the Russian Federation* (1998, 1999).

Jess Walsh is completing a Ph.D. in Urban Planning at the University of Melbourne. She researches union strategies for organizing and regulating low-wage service-sector work. Her recent research on the home-care organizing of the Service Employees International Union (SEIU) was facilitated by an appointment as SEIU Fellow at the Economic Policy Institute in Washington, DC. She has also spent time at the Johns Hopkins University, as an International Fellow in Urban Studies, where she studied Baltimore's living wage movement and related labour issues.

Rekha Wazir is co-founder and co-director of International Child Development Initiatives (ICDI), based in the Netherlands. ICDI is an international development support agency specializing in programmes, policy and research for marginalized children and youth. She has a broad range of research interests that span issues such as education, child labour, child abuse and child care and she has considerable international experience in these areas. Her recent publications include *Child sexual abuse: What can governments do?*, co-edited with Nico van Oudenhoven, and *The gender gap in basic education: NGOs as change agents*.

LIST OF ABBREVIATIONS

AOC	Association of Carers
AWBZ	Algemene Wet Bijzondere Ziektekosten (General Law of Specific Health Costs)
BIEN	Basic Income European Network
CCSAP	Community Care Special Action Project
CDM	Consumer Directed Model
CHCA	Child Home-Care Allowance
CNA	Carers National Association
CPCA	Children's Private Care Allowance
CRC	Convention on the Rights of the Child
EACHH	European Association of Care and Help at Home
ECA	Statute of the Child and the Adolescent
ECCD	Early Childhood Care and Development
EEC	European Economic Community
EITC	Earned Income Tax Credit
ESRC	Economic and Social Research Council
EU	European Union
FIM	Finnish Mark
FORCES	Forum for Crèche and Child Care Services
GAO	General Accounting Office
GDP	Gross Domestic Product
HAZ	Health Action Zone
HCA	Home-Care Allowance
HIV/AIDS	Human Immunodeficiency Virus/Acquired Immune Deficiency Syndrome

HMO	Health Maintenance Organization
IBGE	National Census Bureau, Brazil
ICDI	International Child Development Initiatives
ICDS	Integrated Child Development Services
IERAS	Institute of Economics, Russian Academy of Sciences
IHSS	In-Home Supportive Services
ILC	Independent Living Center
ILO	International Labour Office/Organization
IMR	Infant Mortality Rate
IP	Independent Provider
IRAPS	IHSS Recipients and Providers Sharing
Local 434B	LA Homecare Workers Union
MSWR	Minimum Standard Wage Rate
NCCED	National Council for Carers and their Elderly Dependants
NCSWD	National Council for the Single Woman and her Dependants
NGO	Non-governmental Organization
NHS	National Health Service
OECD	Organisation for Economic Co-operation and Development
OMEP	World Organization for Early Childhood Education
ONS	Office for National Statistics
PA	Public Authority
PCO	Medicare Personal Care Option
PNAD	Pesquisa Nacional por Amostras de Domícilios (National Household Sample Survey)
PPV	Pesquisa sobre Padrões de Vida (Research on Living Standards)
RLMS	Russian Longitudinal Monitoring of the Economic Situation and Health of the Population
SCP	Social and Cultural Planning Bureau
SEIU	Service Employees International Union
SIF	Social Insurance Fund
STDs	Sexually Transmitted Diseases
U5MR	Under-Five Mortality Rate
UFRJ	Federal University of Rio de Janeiro
UNDP	United Nations Development Programme
UNESCO	United Nations Educational, Scientific and Cultural Organization
UNICEF	United Nations Children's Fund
WHO	World Health Organization

INTRODUCTION

Mary Daly and Guy Standing

The International Labour Organization (ILO) is committed to the development of a strategy to promote decent work in the twenty-first century, in every part of the world. A claim underlying this book is that there can be no "decent work" agenda in any country of the world where the needs of those providing care to their fellow human beings are neither recognized nor protected. Care work is real work and, as succeeding chapters suggest, it deserves to be fully integrated into the analysis of work. Its neglect in mainstream statistics, economic analysis and social policy in the twentieth century was deplorable.

This study has several interrelated themes. To begin with, there is, or should be, a human right to receive care, which means that there should be a right to provide care. This in turn means that there must be a right to adequate income, both for those providing care and for those in need of it. There must therefore be real freedom for caregivers and care receivers, which means having access to the mechanisms of defending and enhancing the same rights as those enjoyed by all other groups of workers and citizens in society. The picture is more complicated still. The right to give and to receive care is underpinned by a right not to be obliged to provide care – a cry of oppressed women throughout history. This is not a plea for social irresponsibility; it is an assertion that care is precious, and therefore suffers if it is treated as something close to forced labour.

Another of the study's themes is to argue the case for considering care as work, just as much as wage labour or "self employment". It should be considered generically, covering the work of caring for anybody, not just those conventional life cycle or ill-luck contingencies of childhood, illness or disability and old age. Care is a part of our basic needs. It should be seen as an abiding part of life for all of us, not something akin to unpredictable risk. This point is developed in the next chapter and elsewhere in the book.

1

This should not be taken to imply a call for the commodification of care. On the contrary, it is a plea to policy-makers to find ways of enabling people of all kinds to provide and to receive care as they choose. Thinking about care should prompt concern that, in modern societies, we are in danger of bringing every aspect of human existence into the "cash nexus". We do not want to value care in terms of monetary exchange. But neither should we want to penalize or exploit and oppress those providing care by denying economic security. Those who preach that care is a gift or a moral act neglect the fact that for most people there is not much choice, which negates any sense of giving or morality. Real decommodification can only come from real freedom, which is precisely why some of us assert the need for basic income security as an unconditional right of a "Good Society".

Several other aspects of seeing care as work need to be kept in mind and they bring care into the public sphere. The frame of reference shifts from regarding care as "wholly private" to "partly private/partly public". A shift of location may also be involved, to be seen most clearly in the spreading concern for child care on the part of public authorities. And, in order to appreciate it as work, care should be placed in a broad international framework. Up to now, care has mainly been considered from a European or an American perspective, and only a sparse literature has examined it from a world comparative framework. The merits of a broad comparison are numerous, including a realization that care plays a more integral role in some societies and cultures than in most industrialized countries. The contributors to this volume cumulatively demonstrate that care, however culture specific it may be, involves issues transcending national and international boundaries.

The study also seeks to consider care for children together with care for the elderly and other adults. There has been a tendency to treat these groups separately in policy and research. While we do not claim that they are identical, and have no wish to undermine the particularity of each type of care, we consider there are significant advantages in treating them as related. To make the connection explicit, the nature of the activities involved in caring for adults and children are rather similar. So, too, is a tendency to privatize both forms of care, although the extent to which this is the case varies across countries. A further commonality is that the carer is usually a woman and that the care work is not paid and, indeed, is often regarded as an obligation. While we do not see the two types of care as synonymous and identical, it is useful to treat them together as they involve relatively similar issues for public policy-makers. This is especially the case if one focuses on emerging developments. Increasing longevity, growing female participation in paid employment and the changing meaning of family and community solidarity portend a growing role for public authorities in regard to care of the elderly and of children. Care is one of our basic needs.

In addition, looked at from within a larger frame of reference one can see a relationship between care provision and poverty. Recognizing and respecting care can be a tool in the fight against poverty and social exclusion. For example, if child care is conceived of and promoted as a good for children, as it has been in some European and South American countries, it can act to counter and overcome the barriers faced by children in disadvantaged neighbourhoods and communities. Similarly, many adults are impoverished by the financial consequences of care. Just as some people are unable to take up paid work for care-related reasons, others are financially handicapped by the costs associated with purchasing care. Hence recognizing care as a primary human need and social exigency has a role to play in national and international struggles against poverty.

A key policy challenge in the next few years will be to resolve the debate on the relative roles of the State, the market, the family and those "civil society" networks that seem to be playing a growing role in many industrialized countries in particular. This and related issues underlie most chapters in this volume. Where is the divide to be drawn between care as a "public" or "private" activity? How should we redefine social norms and obligations at a time when changes in underlying values and ideologies spell a growing disenchantment with the merits of collective provision?

Undoubtedly, the various strands of feminism have brought care work towards the mainstream of social thinking and policy formulation. This is partly because women do most of the care work, partly because women's higher labour force participation has meant a more visible squeeze on time available for child care and for the care of elderly relatives, and partly because women comprise a majority of the electorate in a growing number of countries. The fact that this time squeeze has become more critical for "middle-class" women (and for some role-model affluent women in the public eye) has also surely contributed to the increased attention.

Another theme raised by considering care work from an international perspective is that of quality. The meaning of quality is something which remains to be worked out in almost all national contexts and there is certainly no agreement internationally on what constitutes quality in the provision and receipt of care. The primary emphasis seems to be on getting access to the services of a care worker; issues of quality come a poor second. One must also be conscious of the possibility that there is a trade-off between universality and quality. It may be that as access to care labour or services becomes more prevalent, resources are stretched and so have to be spread more thinly. Issues of class become vitally important here.

The changing position of women has been critical and their dominant role in care has been universal. But four demographic developments have also been altering the terms of debate. The first of these concerns family roles. Around the world, notions of family and household have been in a state of flux, with the demise of extended family systems in some cultures, the nuclearization of households in others, and the growth of fluid, atypical household forms in others. The modern era of globalization is an era of generalized mobility, behavioural flexibility and resultant precariousness. There may be greater stability than popular accounts suggest but the anticipation of instability has become pervasive. Household flexibility has brought many tendencies to the fore. There appear to be many more "female-headed" households, more single-adult households, more precariousness in personal relationships between adults of the same generation, and more fragile relations between the generations.

In such circumstances, old norms of behaviour, expectations and reciprocities cannot be taken for granted. Increasingly, the claims we make on each other lack a sense of "natural" reciprocity (even if many had traditionally been foisted on people as a form of oppression). In a European and American context one can see a general movement towards individualization and privatization of action wherein the law of the market and of individual choice are the everyday norm. In this context, we look more to contractual bargains, opportunistically perhaps. The adage of modernization that contract replaces compact has enormous implications for the pattern, reliability and quality of care we give to each other. In this respect, we must reflect more on the needs of different types of household and different types of relationship. Among these are gay couples, elderly married couples, and HIV/AIDS-afflicted and HIV/AIDS-affected households.

A second global demographic development is ageing. Research highlights the rapid growth in the number of people aged over 60 in various parts of the world, and the dramatic growth in the number of very old women, particularly in Europe. Yet ageing is not just about numbers or the "dependency ratio". There also seems to be a challenge of "active ageing", in that more of those in the supposedly old-age bracket are in good health, able and willing to play a social role, often involving work of some kind. This is posing one of the many challenges to policy arrangements, and pension systems in particular, and to the desired flexibility of support systems in general, including the provision of care.

By contrast, there has been an international tendency, associated with health-care privatization, to reduce the length of stay in hospital or formal care, which means that there is a greater and growing demand for post-hospital, quasi-medical care, of a type that is relatively high-intensity and requires delicate skills. Public policy has not dealt with the burden placed on women by shorter medical stays and the need to look after mentally or physically ill relatives.

The ageing process also influences family dynamics. There are numerous reports of women being caught in a lifetime time bind, no sooner finishing a period of childbearing and child caring than being put under pressure to look after elderly relatives. For some women, the claims on their time may overlap, which is why the peak care-work period comes for women in their 40s.

The image propels us to a sense of inequity. However, although for many it is a burden, we should not fall into the trap of depicting care purely as a burden. The most important issue is one of freedom of choice: to be able to select from a menu of options how much care to give or receive, and who should care for whom. The ageing of society should bring this issue into the centre of our thinking.

Care is an area of policy development that is concerned with the complementary attractions of home-based and community-based care, as well as those of various forms of institutional care. It is also an area of considerable interest to the ILO and the World Health Organization (WHO). There is a widespread feeling that there is insufficient information on the living conditions and needs of elderly people – and about what they want. Dignity, comfort and a sense of autonomy are surely high on their agenda.

A third demographic development is migration. There is nothing new in this. Yet the debate about care in the twenty-first century should be linked to changes in the role and levels of migration. There is a tendency for migrants to be used to fulfil the role of carer. Many carers worldwide are migrant women and there is a chain of care stretching from the less developed nations to the industrialized countries. Many of the care workers in the West have left their own care responsibilities and work in the hands of other women in their countries of origin. Young women from different parts of the world seem to be drawn increasingly into a chain of care relationships. Some move from isolated villages to a distant city to care for strangers, some go abroad to care for middle-class households, yet others go to labour in institutions providing care for the frail and elderly. In the Philippines, for example, care work is the country's prime export. This raises political, legal and social concerns. In all cases, those providing the care have to struggle with potential oppression and exploitation that is uncomfortable to contemplate, even for those of us far removed from the scene.

The fourth demographic development is the spread of the pandemic of HIV/AIDS. The main link with care work and the insecurities associated with it is the devastating effect on family structures, above all in large parts of sub-Saharan Africa. In this region, the incidence of deaths from HIV/AIDS and related complications has created a growing phenomenon of orphans having to attach themselves to households of relatives, often placing a heavy burden on already burdened people. The United Kingdom charity Christian Aid in 2001 estimated that there were 12 million orphans in sub-Saharan Africa as a result of HIV/AIDS. The following chapters do not deal with this huge challenge. But it will no doubt figure strongly in the ILO's future work on the links between HIV/AIDS and social protection policy in general.

The time squeeze

Because of its low status, care work tends to be squeezed to the margins of many people's lives. While some people are burdened by the demands of care work, preventing them from doing what they would wish to do, others come to the point where they neglect to care. Unlike other forms of work, many people can avoid doing care work with relative impunity, in the sense that there are no immediate penalties or sanctions for doing so. The consequences are longer term or intangible. How many fathers look back in regret at not having spent more time with their children? How many of us regret not having cared for our aged, frail parents? The tragedy of care is that it is not valued by a market society geared to the maximization of income, expenditure and consumption.

The time congestion and the harried nature of modern life should induce more debate on how people, particularly in affluent societies, can acquire control over their own time and be able to free up time to give greater space for care work of all types. It should be part of our education, to learn why care is so crucial to human security and development.

The need for voice

The sense of crisis that surrounds care provision largely reflects a threat of insecurity for care providers and care recipients. But there is also a sense of opportunity, if organizations to represent the interests of care providers and recipients can be created and strengthened. A question here is whether or not fledgling organizations should act like trade unions or like community or citizenship action groups. There is no consensus on this and, as the chapters by Barnes, Collins-Hughes and Walsh demonstrate, different models have been successful in different parts of the world.

One obvious problem is that more often than not there is no "class" bargaining involved or that the class interests and identities are blurred. This may change though as market services in care, which are based on low-income workers working predominantly for richer clients, often mediated through firms, become increasingly widespread. But in most cases, people providing care for other people do not see themselves as workers in the traditional sense of the term. There are always elements of the gift relationship, even if there is financial remuneration. For some observers, there is also a sense that this is a "middle-class" issue, in that the poor or those in the working class have to provide care without thinking and do not have the luxury of considering how it could be otherwise. All the issues of recognition, time squeeze and sense of duty affect women in all social strata, but working-class and poor women have had the least effective representation in most societies. So their needs have been ignored. This may change, making it potentially easier to create strong alliances between professionals and community groups at the local level. However, there is another obvious difficulty for those wishing to organize carers, which is the lack of a common workplace. Jess Walsh's chapter is insightful about how the Service Employees International Union (SEIU) overcame this problem in Los Angeles County.

It is moot whether it would be an advantage for carers to be depicted as workers in the traditional sense of the word. But how can respect be generated for those providing care, rather than sympathy or, worse, pity? As George Bernard Shaw so memorably put it, "Pity is akin to contempt." Care providers must have respect. Without respect, their needs will be treated as peripheral to public policy, as outside society even. Trying to find the language of decent care work that is respectful of each person's activity remains a challenge. Avoiding the word "informal" would help, since that suggests something casual and outside the ambit of public concern.

In thinking about organizing carers, and ensuring that their needs are respected, it helps to reflect on the nature of modern democracy and how the practice of democracy can be harnessed in the struggle to represent the interests of those involved in care work. In the case of Ireland, the Carers Association has gained strength in part because it has included various differing types of care. An underlying strategy was to enable the membership base to be as large as possible, not least so that the votes of Association members in a general election would be taken seriously. The effectiveness of this kind of strategy is considerably enhanced by the nature of recent electoral politics in Ireland, which has meant that few members of parliament have safe seats.[1] But there is a general point to be recognized here, which is that the degree of influence which carers can have on public policy is related to the extent to which they are organized and lobby effectively.

Another lesson confirmed by the Irish experience is that policy change often comes from mobilized anger. The Carers Association perceived that the Government, implicitly at least, was continuing to regard women's labour as belonging to men, in that the carer's allowance was means-tested on the

---

[1] This prompts an interesting hypothesis, which is that in countries with large constituencies there is less likelihood that politicians will give high priority to the income-security needs of minorities or marginal groups in society.

husband's income. Sensing the anger among women carers, the Association decided to become more militant in this regard. Carers could not strike because there was no direct target and the only persons who would have suffered would have been those requiring care. So, the carers, feeling that they were being "blackmailed", retaliated by drawing the media into homes to depict the drudgery and long hours of work being done by them. Information, organization, pressure and voice gradually inform public perceptions and change social policy.

As discussed in the chapter by Marian Barnes, the carers' movement in England also gave high priority to the construction of the political identity of carers. Action started around issues of single women having to give up paid work in order to look after elderly parents. The Association of Carers (AOC) saw this issue as expanding the perspective beyond the conventional terms. Taking on elderly parents was an unexpected burden, whereas looking after children and sick or disabled husbands or children was seen as part of the moral obligation to care "in sickness and in health".

Governments have also come to realize that the growing number of elderly people requiring care represents a potentially huge financial burden. And so it seems that policy has evolved to try to strengthen the family's capacity to care. But this is not enough. There is still a need to move away from a paternalistic model, in which the potential recipients of care are depicted as "dependent" and their carers as "obliged". The independence of those needing care has been epitomized in the campaign by those with disabilities to have the right to an independent living. The model of caregiver and care recipient has also been challenged, because it is often not clear who is the carer and who the recipient. Indeed, the activities of the disabled movement have demonstrated that two people can survive through caring for each other in complementary ways. The acknowledgement of reciprocity is a key part of the emergence of a strategy to demand negotiating capacity, rather than better categorization.

However, one cannot take for granted that there is a unity of interest between the provider and recipient of care. Indeed, almost all political mobilization around care has focused on particular sets of interests rather than the panoply of interests involved. Divergence in the rights of caregiver and receiver is much more likely in the case of care for adults than it is in care for children. The disabled rights movement, for example, campaigns primarily for the well-being and interests of those receiving care.

The future of care work

In the West a discourse of crisis tends to surround care. Governments express concern about the shortage of care facilities and at the decreasing willingness of family members to care for each other. It is important in the general discourse to think of care and resources relating to it in a positive way as well. Care is part of our identity, and the resources allocated to care within communities represent a form of institutional support.

The role of public policy is vital. European policy tends to respond selectively to care and one can see a tendency for countries to choose between one kind of policy and another. We need to recognize that some policies are better than others. A policy to give money to the care recipient may be good for the recipient but bad for general equity as well as gender equity because it tends to privatize care. We have to identify both the strengths and the weaknesses of policies and how these can and do vary across national settings. Taking an integrated approach to care is also important. This means thinking not just in terms of individual policies of support, but locating care within an integrated framework of economic and social policy. We need to integrate notions of the market into our analysis. Within and across nations, companies are becoming increasingly involved in care and the principles of market provision are encroaching on the organization of care work. However, in regard to marketization we need to register differences between regulation, financing and provision.

The analysis and policy debate around care work is in itself in a state of transition. As many of the chapters in this study emphasize, there is no going back to seeing care work as lying in the shadow of "real work". How will carers obtain income security? This is the first great question before us. In civilized democratic society, that security will come only when care recipients as well as care providers have income security. There is an inter-dependency involved. And those two forms of income security will only be achieved when caregivers and care recipients are represented by strong, democratic and accountable organizations ensuring that their interests are taken into account. We should be optimistic that in the next few years great progress will be made in all these respects.

Structure of the study

The three chapters which comprise Part I of the study establish a framework for understanding care. Guy Standing offers a philosophical perspective within which to view care, setting it especially within a framework of rights. His chapter makes the point that care is part of our identity and that the universality of caring has been widely neglected. Mary Daly's chapter outlines care as an exigency for public policy and examines the various ways in which European countries have developed policies for care. Using a broad framework, considering the interests of both the care receiver and the caregiver, she analyses the strengths and weakness of those policy responses. Jane Lewis continues the theme of care and public policy, focusing on the ethical and gender equality issues. Concentrating on emerging trends in English-speaking countries, she argues for care to be treated as work and for policies to promote the capacity of both women and men to engage in and share it.

Care is a term that varies in meaning and significance in different cultures and languages. We have therefore encouraged contributors to identify both the meaning attached to the activity and relations of care and the way in which care is understood for purposes of political or policy action. For this and other reasons, Part II includes chapters on care in various parts of the world. In her chapter on India, Umadevi Sambasivan contrasts different value systems around care and production. She makes the argument that the pursuit of inner freedom and a society which values care are not possible in an economic system based on large scale production, given its urge for constantly increasing productivity. Rekha Wazir also focuses on India, this time from the perspective of the care needs of children. To illustrate the shortcomings of existing provision and the potential for a different way forward, she utilizes the inclusive concept of Early Childhood Care and Development (ECCD). Bila Sorj's chapter on Brazil shows that child care is at the forefront of political mobilization and policy transformation in that country. However, while pre-school provision has been extended, this is happening through the partial privatization of the service, which means that the pre-school may reproduce rather than reverse the situation of deprivation in which many children live. The final chapter in this section considers the situation of the Russian Federation. What this shows is that while care-related provisions have a long history and indeed have been strengthened in recent legislation, care is in reality a hugely under-resourced area, with most people providing for their own care without state assistance.

Part III is again concerned with Western Europe and the United States. Anneli Anttonen documents and analyses the situation in Finland, one of the most developed welfare states in Europe. This case study shows that it is possible, even in very developed welfare states, for policies to treat different forms of care differently. Hence, in Finland, the principle of universalism is far more developed in relation to child care than to care for the elderly. The Netherlands offers a somewhat different constellation of events. What Trudie Knijn's analysis shows is that marketization of care is advanced there, both in terms of the encroachment of market principles into care and of the market as provider. Nancy Folbre's chapter, which completes this section of the study, is a detailed analysis of the situation regarding the provision of care for children and the elderly in the United States. An issue brought up by her analysis is the need for better accounting systems for care provision.

Part IV turns the spotlight on political representation and mobilization. Under the theme of "voice", it offers case studies of political organization among carers. In the first, Marian Barnes charts the trajectory of collective action and organization among carers in England. As well as showing the diversity of their political engagement, her analysis indicates that carers want more from public policy than financial support. Eddie Collins-Hughes, Director of the Carers Association of Ireland, outlines the different services provided to carers in Ireland as well as the political strategies followed by the Association. In the last chapter, Jess Walsh analyses how 74,000 home-care workers became part of the SEIU in Los Angeles County in 1999. Tracing the subsequent activities of the Union and members, the story is told of how the SEIU created a union, as well as an employer, and how it wrote new rules for organizing low-wage personal assistance work. It is an encouraging note on which to conclude the first phase of our work.

Guy Standing

PART I

CARE AS DECENT WORK

CARE WORK: OVERCOMING INSECURITY AND NEGLECT

1

Guy Standing

Introduction

Who is the more insecure, the giver or the receiver of care? Probably, the answer most of us would give is the recipient. But it is not as obvious as it might seem, nor is it by any means always the case. The neglect of care work by mainstream policy-makers, economists, statisticians and the social sciences generally was a shameful failure for most of the twentieth century. A few social scientists focused on it, but their work was relegated to the margins and footnotes. Feminists demanded that it should be taken seriously, as did some Marxists in debating productive, unproductive and "reproductive" labour. The literature on the subject became vast in the last quarter of the century. But still the subject retained a marginal existence. Talk to a typical labour economist about it and he or she is likely to adopt a glazed look and react by saying (or thinking) that it is a subject for sociologists or "the welfare community". Even lobbyists for inclusion of "informal" work in economic activity have tended to regard the work of caring as non-work.

Reflecting this marginalized appreciation, statisticians have made little attempt to measure the extent or incidence of care work, let alone its economic or social value. Implicitly, policy-makers in the twentieth century were inclined to allow care work to decline, because of the way economic growth was measured, and because economic growth was regarded as the primary objective, followed by "job creation". People doing unpaid care work were reducing economic growth and the number of people in "jobs". The great nineteenth-century economist, Alfred Marshall, appreciated the anomaly. He pointed out that if he hired a housekeeper national income went up, but if he married her it went down.

Positioning care work has not only been a source of difficulty for economists. The difficulty starts with linguistic ambiguity. "To care for someone" has several meanings that blur into one another. "I care for Jane" may mean no more than I care about her, that I hope all goes well for her. Or it may mean I am taking responsibility for looking after her well-being. Or it may mean that I take care of her, through tending to her needs, perhaps because of a disability or frailty. This multitude of meanings has surely contributed to the neglect of care work in general social analysis and in the measurement of work.

Another contributory factor to the neglect is the universality of caring. To some extent, almost all of us have done something we would call care work, and barring those who are ill, frail or disabled, we all think we could do it, if necessary or if we wished to do so. This perception of near-universal capacity or the belief that we can all perform it has surely contributed to its under-valuation. It is nothing special, or so the conventional view would claim. This is most unfortunate, because the skills in most forms of care work must be as great as in most other forms of work, and the capacity to perform it well is undoubtedly acquired through experience and training as much as in many other forms of "skilled" work.

Another cause of neglect is that care work conjures up an image of a widely differing intensity of work. It may mean no more than being a presence, available in case of an accident or an untoward development requiring support. Or, at the other extreme, it may mean almost constant attention to a person in degrading circumstances, as in giving assistance to a bed-ridden invalid scarcely able to function as a human being. The sheer range of intensity makes it hard for policy-makers and for statisticians to have a clear concept of care work.[1]

Whatever the causes of the twentieth-century neglect, care work will be far more important in the twenty-first century, in part because of the changing demographic patterns, the deconstruction of extended families and even nuclear families and households, the changing social and economic status of women, and the overhaul of welfare states. But there is a more important reason that transcends all those standard pressures. Care work will be part of our identity, and unlike the dominant images of the past, the performance of care work will be part of real freedom and our sense of occupation. The image that typically predominates in our minds today is of harassed mothers scurrying between crying infants, the kitchen and the market or shops. Or, increasingly, it is a picture of a middle-aged woman trying to cope in caring for an elderly relative or a sick husband. It is an image of what Richard Titmuss called the "gift relationship", distinct from the market with its social attractions and financial rewards. But this is changing.

---

[1] Nancy Folbre and others have differentiated between care work as "primary" and "secondary" activity, and primary into "developmental" versus "low intensity" time.

What may do more to elevate care work to the social and policy-making mainstream is that the middle classes around the world are increasingly seeing the need to perform care work themselves, for elderly relatives and for their children (to give them a competitive edge, inter alia), seeing the prospective need to receive care themselves in old age, wondering whether their relatives will be around or willing to provide it. One may regret the nature of the pressure, but the opportunistic demand of the "median voter" may do more to legitimize care work than all the philosophical, economic and sociological reasons for legitimizing it.

Care, identity and citizenship

The twentieth century was the first one in human history to elevate the performance of labour to a social right. In the nineteenth century, the right to employment would have seemed a peculiar idea to most social observers. But then gradually, the performance of wage-earning labour became something to be maximized, in jobs and full employment. With the celebration of labour came the political linkage between working, or at least the demonstrated willingness to work, and entitlements to state transfers and services. At least in industrialized countries – and as a long-term objective elsewhere as well – you could only expect state aid if the labour conditions were met, or if you were of the very young, the sick, the disabled or the elderly and frail. To labour became an obligation, in the name of being a right.

In this historical context, care work was not only invisible in the global statistical picture of social and economic reality. It also came to be seen as an impediment or a barrier to norm-based social entitlements, a "barrier to work". For one's own economic well-being (as well as social status), care work became something to be minimized, so that we could indulge more in the great fantasy of the age, the performance of labour. At the same time, the very real negative aspects of care work were heavily emphasized – the squalor, social isolation, burden of responsibility, drudgery, oppression and so on. It was as if none of these was characteristic of most forms of labour. To be doing care work became not just a source of low social status, but one of pity. And as George Bernard Shaw so pithily put it, "Pity is akin to contempt".

The negative side of care work exists, and should not be minimized. However, this one-sided perspective does all of us a disservice. To give care is a valuable part of the human condition, just as much as the need for care is part of it. In a sense, care work defies easy definition. But we should try to provide one.

Care work may be defined as the work of looking after the physical, psychological, emotional and developmental needs of one or more other people.

Care work has more dimensions than many other forms of work, and has a distinctive structure. It may be useful to think of it as having the following dimensions:

Care work = Time (Actual + "stand by") + Effort + Technique + Social skills + Emotional input + Stress (fear of failing the recipient + fear of failing observers and regulators)

One of the peculiar features of most forms of care work is that the time required may be much greater or much less than the time spent on the actual work. Quite often a person simply has to be available in case of need. Similarly, the effort may be highly variable and unpredictable, and ultimately a matter of personal discretion. As for the techniques required, they have rarely been adequately recognized, and require a relatively high degree of "social skill". The emotional input is also likely to be much greater than in many other forms of work, implying a cost or disutility of the work. The same could be said of the two forms of stress mentioned, to which one might wish to add a third – the fear of failing oneself.

Is there, or should there be, a right to care? One may feel, as this writer does, that everybody has a human right to be cared for. However foul or undeserving we are, we should receive care *in extremis*. This last caveat is the primary difficulty, because being in need of care is subject to gradations of meaning. A need may be little more than a wish or, at the other extreme, a dire necessity. The need to be loved is part of the human condition. It is a right only in the breach. In practice, we fall back on societal norms. A frail elderly woman may have lost the capacity to look after herself. Surely, we say that her right to dignity requires care by others. But should that be based on some administrative test of her capacity to look after herself? If one says yes to that, it opens the door to moral hazard – i.e., the person could have an interest in behaving in ways that would demonstrate to discretionary adjudicators that care is needed.

If one makes it a categorical right, for instance, that all those reaching a certain age can have care provided in some form, then those not actually requiring care might take advantage of the facility. Because such moral hazards exist, the only practical solution seems to be a pragmatic rule involving a mix of categorical entitlements, such as all children under age x, all elderly people over age y, all people with registered impairments, and so on.

The other side of care would seem even more problematical. Is there, or should there be, a right to provide care? The provision of care might seem to be a matter of morality. But a society faced by extensive family dissolution, for instance, might wish to give an incentive to potential care providers, beyond giving compensation directly to those needing care. This way of looking at care is usually ignored. Because there are so many incentives and pressures on people to do other forms of work, one could conclude that care "giving" is discouraged systematically. Yet caring for others, regardless of any demonstrated need, has potential value to the giver as well as to the receiver, and for those not directly involved. The positive externalities for society mean that there is a case for subsidizing personal care work. To some extent, this is being recognized by the spread of parental leave, a rationale for which is that it will strengthen family bonds (particularly, but not only, paternal responsibility) and strengthen a culture of caring.

Provisionally, we may conclude that, as the twenty-first century progresses, the right to care will advance, as will a right to receive care when there is a demonstrated need. The notion of need itself will become broadened to include more and more contingencies, until the absurdity of any boundary will be recognized in a perception of universal need. One predicts that the debate on what should constitute need will be one of those gurgling undercurrents of social policy in the next decade, subject to all sorts of arbitrary and discretionary interpretations. However, lagging behind this debate will be one on the right to care perceived as the right to provide or give care.

The ILO could do a service by taking a lead in this respect. The right to do care work should be an integral part of the ILO's "decent work" strategy, and not be either ignored altogether or relegated to a patronizing footnote.

In this regard, it might be useful to reflect on the concept of occupational security that we are advocating in the ILO's InFocus Socio-Economic Security Programme – the opportunity in all types of society for people, with all levels of education and competence, to pursue a sense of occupational career, bundling different types of work and work status at the same time and sequentially, without oppressive controls or intolerable insecurity. We need to think of society as encompassing a diversity of lifestyles within a context of communal responsibility, not unbridled individualism and competitiveness; to recognize that part of our identity is caring for those around us, and that this requires an institutional set of social arrangements. Only if we think like this will we rescue the notion of decent work from becoming yet another euphemism for the global promotion of labourism.

Care work: A framework

Let us return to the basics. It is a truism that care work is infinitely variable, and that we need distinctive policies and institutions for the several types of care.

Even so, we can define the ideal types of care recipients and care providers fairly easily, and then depict the societal structure of care work.

The types of care recipient, or care needer, are conventionally identified as: infants, children of school age, the sick, the disabled and the elderly. I insist on adding "You and Me". Societies have tended to favour different forms of care for each of these categories, usually making infants and the elderly primarily the responsibility of the family, whereas they have been more inclined to support institutions and commercial forms of care for the chronically sick and disabled, seeing these as social risk contingencies requiring a redistributive response by the state.

"You and Me" have tended to be squeezed out of the need list, and one can argue that this was a cardinal folly of the twentieth century. The "macho" nature of labour meant that the softer, recreative caring side of work was systematically neglected.

It is important to note that the conventional classification of care recipients is more arbitrary than most observers presume. Thus, for example, in the second half of the twentieth century in industrialized societies the age up to which infants were deemed by policy-makers to require care by their mothers probably declined. Whether this was justified or not, it was an implicit or explicit reaction to the fact that more women wished to take or return to jobs or were put under more pressure to do so. Similarly, at least for a while, there was some widening of the definition of the sick and disabled deemed to "merit" care, and greater recognition that the elderly should receive care from outside their families.

In more recent years, there has been a tendency to narrow the definitions of care need categories. Undoubtedly, this owes much to the ideological shift in the last quarter of the twentieth century in favour of cutting back social spending. This shift reflected the global influence of libertarianism and the belief that all forms of support to the needy induced the moral hazard referred to earlier. We will come back to this.

Familiar types of care provider include public and private health services, state regulated or paid social workers, public or private care-provider agencies, enterprises of employment, voluntary and community organizations, and relatives.

The potential range of care providers is very wide, although in practice societies have traditionally relied extensively on only a small portion. Clearly, some types of care provider can perform certain functions for definable groups that others cannot. But the degree to which one type of provider can be substituted for another is considerable. A checklist of all the advantages and disadvantages of each type would be useful. In this introduction, just a few issues will be mentioned that relate to the socio-economic security of care recipients and care providers.

Some types of carers have greater formal qualifications than others. Modern society gives great weight to so-called "human capital" defined in technical terms. But thinking of care work should be a useful antidote to this technocratic way of designing and evaluating policy. We know that formal caregiving can provide a marvellous social service, and that those working to provide such care are among society's most decent citizens. We also know that most of us do not or would not want to rely either wholly or partially on formal care providers if we could avoid it. Why not? Of course, financial and status reasons are part of the response. However, another consideration is that care work is intrinsically a social relationship, in which moral sentiments such as affection, altruism, mutual respect and dignity and deeply meaningful reciprocities come into play.

For the care recipient, there are also more pragmatic considerations, whatever the type of care provider involved. Particularly if one were to pay for formal care, one is likely to have several sources of anxiety or insecurity:

a) fear of care provider's incompetence;
b) fear of phoney expertise (i.e., misleading formal qualifications);
c) fear of unreliable delivery of care specified (contract failure);
d   fear of non-provision of anticipated care (compact failure);
e) fear of regulatory failure;
f) fear of cost escalation or unknown long-term costs;
g) fear of reciprocities unanticipated by recipient, introduced by provider.

For the care provider, the insecurities or fears may also be significant, and will vary according to the type of provider and relationship with the recipient:

a) fear of personal incompetence, with consequences for both parties;
b) fear of criticism for performance inadequacy;
c) fear of displacement, particularly if long-term commitments made;
d) fear of income insecurity, due to non-compensation or non-assurance of reciprocal assistance;
e) self-exploitation.

The last source of insecurity is crucial, and needs further discussion later. But some of the other concerns also involve high costs for the provider. If I am employed to make tea for the boss, the cost of my making bad tea is hardly substantial. But if you are providing care for a child or a frail person the cost of error could be fatal or at least very serious. This aspect of work and compensation is too rarely taken into account.

Figure 1.1 gives a simplified framework of what is or could be involved in the process of care provision. At the centre is the care recipient served by one or more care providers. Only rarely is it a simple matter of you caring for me, or me caring for you. A lot of other characters may be involved. Hovering in the background is the State, which has, or should have, four functions.

Firstly, it should establish an appropriate regulatory framework, consisting of laws and regulations setting standards of acceptable behaviour by individual providers and recipients of care, and standards and rules for institutions and agencies that have direct roles to play. Secondly, the State should decide on what, if any, income transfers and services should be provided.

Thirdly, it should establish a system for monitoring, evaluation and penalization, distinct from the regulatory framework. Indeed, one could argue convincingly that in the sphere of care work very little effective attention has been given to this third function, so that existing regulations and transfers have been even less effective than they should be.

And the fourth State function should be to respond to the socio-economic structure by creating institutions for supplementary care. For instance, in a rural economy the State might encourage village elders to use moral suasion or provide communal facilities. In state socialism, it typically encouraged enterprises to develop complex care facilities on the premises or nearby. In welfare states, either public agencies have been set up directly or subsidies have been provided to private agencies. In the new Third Way and "compassionate conservatism" models, it seems that the State is expected to subsidize "faith-based organizations" or other civil society groups to do care work – to fill the care deficit. This currently popular way of thinking by politicians in many parts of the world raises some major questions for care work.

In any case, each of these four state functions raises familiar sets of governance issues: trade-offs between efficiency and equity; different forms of efficiency; and issues of accountability, transparency, legitimacy and democracy.

Figure 1.1 indicates that part of the social process of care work is the support system. This comprises at least two distinctive functions, neither of which may exist, but which are required for care work security. The standard one is support in the sense of giving the care recipient the assurance of "last resort" assistance, a feeling that if there is market failure or a governance failure, somebody else might be available, albeit at some cost to the support system or to the recipient and albeit possibly offering a lower quality substitute.

What has been less often emphasized is the second part of the support system, that of providing representation security.[2] It is relatively well understood

---

[2] It is worth recalling the philosophical position of the ILO's Socio-Economic Security Programme. This espouses basic security for all as the fundamental principle of distributive justice and a key to "decent work". In this, priority is given to universal income security coupled with Voice Representation Security – the one without the other would be inadequate. Policies and institutional change are perceived as just if and only if they satisfy what we call the "security difference principle" and the "paternalism test principle".

Figure 1.1   The social process of care

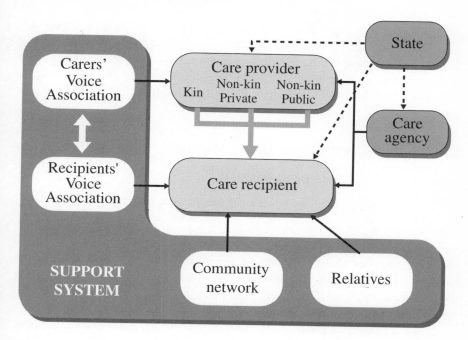

that care recipients need someone or some organization to represent their interests, both individually and collectively, vis-à-vis individual care providers – such as care-providing agencies and the State. Of course, in practice, in most societies the need for collective and individual representation for care recipients has been neglected, and as a consequence there has been either a vacuum or the space has been filled by some well-meaning or opportunistic body subject to governance failure. However, in some countries there are distinguished exceptions, some of which are represented in this volume.

Perhaps even less recognized is the need for a voice for those providing care, particularly those doing so outside a commercial relationship. The long-term caregiver can easily become a sad, oppressed person, easily weighed down by a sense of duty, shuffling through life strangely dependent on the person or persons to whom she (usually a she) is giving care. This form of dependency is embedded in religious, class, sexist, and other cultural structures. Whatever the causes, the high probability that care providers will be led to self-exploitation highlights the fact that those providing care need a voice to guard themselves from themselves as well as from others who take advantage of their devotion, kindness or gentle character.

Whether we call such a voice a trade union, a citizenship association, or something else, a collective body of some type is required for care work security. It must have bargaining capacities as well as lobbying functions, and should be protected or promoted as much as any trade union. In short, there is a need for balance, so that collective associations are give representation security for those providing care, those receiving care, and the surrogates for each side. Without such associations, the vulnerabilities of all parties will be a persistent reality.

Compensation: From gift to market

Let us pose two fundamental questions:

a) Should those needing care have a right to income security?
b) Should those providing care have a right to income security?

These questions are complex, even if we put aside the issue of whether we mean a right in an absolute sense or in the sense of a goal to be realized in the course of economic development, in terms of a society's ability to provide income security. A good case could be made for answering both questions in the affirmative.

Before considering the types of income, and then the types of State support, it is important to acknowledge the position of those who argue that care work should not be compensated. The claim goes something like as follows. Care work is "a gift" to another human being. The motive is not to make money, and bringing in the "cash nexus" belittles or distorts the nature of care. The motive may be religious, a sense of duty, or a desire to contribute to family life or society in some way; or it may be a means of obtaining personal recognition or more extensive social connections. Keeping questions of money out of the relationship can prevent tensions and petty corruption, as well as opportunistic behaviour.

This is a respectable position. Unfortunately, it is one-sided. It leaves open all the dangers of oppression, vulnerability and self-exploitation that a very large number of care providers experience in reality. It smacks of middle-class smugness, even if the motivation is to emphasize the sublime nature of the gift of care. For these reasons, we may conclude that it would be a poor guide for policy-making.

Put simply, there are five main forms of compensation for care work. The first is the one we have just been discussing, the pure gift relationship, care being done for love, charity, duty or societal recognition. Most of us would be disinclined to probe into the motives of individuals, but one needs to recognize that pure altruism is probably rarely the reality. There is more likely to be a mix of oppressive pressures and self-exploitation involved in such a relationship.

Secondly, there is the situation where the person provides care on the expectation that it will be reciprocated later, either by the person being cared for or by another family or community member. In most societies, this anticipated reciprocity has been the main "incentive" to do care work, except where religious or other cultural pressures have been formidable. The reciprocity relationship has some similarities, in terms of the dangers, to the gift relationship. And if the gift relationship is put under intense strain in modern, commercial society, so too is the reciprocity relationship, compounded by increased mobility in industrialized and urbanized society, and the increased tendency for households and families to go through a series of dissolution and restructuring.

In a third form of compensation, the person requiring care, or their surrogate, may hire private care services for a cash payment, which is the standard commercial relationship. The purchaser of care in this case can require a standard of service and in principle could receive compensation or other forms of redress if the service is subsequently found to be poor or erratically supplied. The commercial relationship undoubtedly has been spreading, and it is this that may explain part of the increased attention being given to care by policy-makers.

Libertarians support the marketization of care because purchased services widen individual choice and encourage efficient delivery. Others welcome the trends because they see them as empowering (Morris, 1993). However, the concerns are considerable. One is that the paid carer will act opportunistically, and could withdraw a service at short notice, with potentially severe consequences. The paid care provider is also in a vulnerable position, since the "cost" of error could be very high, or an error perceived as such by the purchaser of care could be a simple mishap with drastic consequences, leading to acrimonious charges of misconduct or negligence. Such situations have given rise to some celebrated and sad court cases in the United States in recent times.

In the fourth example, the care recipient or his or her surrogate could hire the care worker from the State or some quasi-public agency, subsidized by the State. This public service relationship may have been what many social commentators expected to be the main form of compensating care in the long-term development of welfare states. However, political, economic and, above all, ideological developments in the past quarter of a century have changed that perception. For the care recipient, the public service provision may offer a greater sense of trust than the commercial relationship, due to the more limited commercial motive behind the care service being supplied, and because it is somehow presumed that the technical and social skills of the carers would have been established, and that standards of care would be more assured. It is probably correct to state that these arguments are less accepted today than was the case a few years ago.

Fifthly, and finally, the care recipient or his or her surrogate could turn to what might be called the civil society relationship. In this, the person turns to a "non-governmental organization" (NGO), or is steered to such a body, which in turn provides the care. The motives of many of these are surely impeccable. However, one should be wary about romanticizing civil society or NGOs. Questions of quality of service, accountability, transparency and representativeness must be asked.

Recent political developments lend them a renewed significance. In both Third Wayism, which is a name given for recent "social democratic" thinking, and Compassionate Conservatism, which has recently triumphed in the United States, a substantial restructuring of the State is envisaged in which social services, including many forms of care work, should be delegated to civil society groups, and in particular to "faith-based organizations". Proselytizing is almost inevitable in such cases, and even non-religious care-giving bodies are likely to be subject to commercial and other pressures. While the civil society relationship offers many attractions, the existing trends deserve more critical scrutiny than they have received thus far.

Income security: The role of the State

The labourist bias of the twentieth century has much to answer for. Dominating the development of social protection policy were those who, perhaps citing the "reciprocity principle", argued that there should be assured entitlement to income security only if social insurance contributions had been paid, leaving the rest to state or private charity. Very largely, this meant that, except for the incapacitated, only labour counted, so that one could only "earn" entitlement if one paid contributions, in the past (for pensions), recently (for unemployment benefits, etc.) or in the near future (for youth labour force entrants). Non-contributing work did not count. And this was the main reason why care work done by relatives, or by volunteers, typically did not count.

Opposed to this view are those who believe that it is unjust to give income security only to those in jobs, and that income security should be attached to all forms of work besides paid labour. Most of those doing labour could not survive without the unpaid work of carers, most of whom are women. The economic value of such work is enormous.[3] Yet traditional social insurance

---

[3] The United Nations Development Programme's (UNDP) *Human Development Report 1995* guesstimated that globally women's housework was worth US$17 billion. In the United Kingdom, the Office for National Statistics (ONS) estimated that in 1997 housework would have cost the equivalent of US$550 billion had it been paid at market wages, nearly as much as the workforce received from wage labour. Women did about 60 per cent of the unpaid work.

rests on the premise that such work is worthless and undeserving of income entitlement. Not only housework is excluded from the labourist calculus. There is also the vast amount of benevolent social, political and community service work done in all societies.

In short, the State has had three main approaches to enhancing income security for those providing or receiving care, each of which has evolved, particularly in industrialized countries. These may be described as the social insurance approach, the social assistance approach and the citizenship rights approach. It is probably correct to suggest that the social assistance approach has grown in significance in recent years, reflecting the political popularity of selectivity, conditionality and targeting. Governments have been increasingly enthusiastic in encouraging people to undertake more of the total care work to be done because they are eager to cut back social spending.

The twentieth century saw the social insurance approach pushed to its limit in welfare states. In the general social insurance model, one could envisage contributions being paid by an employee or by his or her employer, insuring the worker against the risk of needing care, and one could even envisage similar insurance against the risk of needing to provide care to specified family dependants. In the latter case, the worker would take a period of leave in order to provide care.[4]

The advantages of both are that they give some income security to the person, while for the State they could help finance a social need that might otherwise require more direct public spending. The main drawback is the familiar one of moral hazard, in that because social insurance would pay the person who needs care (if costs were fully met) or who provides it, there could be an incentive to exaggerate or invent a need. This opens up the road to social monitoring and auditing, the public scrutiny that raises administrative costs and creates an atmosphere of distrust and stigma. But there is also another major drawback, because as with other forms of social insurance, the trend towards more flexible labour markets and economic informalization means that the coverage of such a system would be limited; it typically leads to more privileged groups qualifying for such income support, leaving the poor and flexiworkers – mostly women – vulnerable without it.

The second approach to provision is social assistance, which is intended to reach only those in lower-income groups. The popularity of social assistance in recent years owes more to the dominance of neo-classical economics and

---

[4] This practice or variants of it has been introduced in a number of large corporations on an enterprise rather than state basis. Similar advantages and disadvantages arise. This is sometimes seen as part of the development of "family friendly policies" of socially responsible firms.

libertarianism than to common sense. Essentially, in this case, a person needing care or a person providing care can obtain financial assistance if they satisfy some set of tests of eligibility. One might find relatively little to worry about in tests of physical need, as in something like an invalidity allowance. Even here, there are reasons for concern. However, it is the means-testing that gives most cause for concern. For the moment, we may merely note that means tests produce well-known poverty traps. They are particularly saddening when applied to elderly people through savings tests or assets tests, so that they can only obtain financial assistance if they have no savings or only a small amount, leading to their running down that modest source of old-age income security. The application of all these tests produces the well-known syndrome of stigma and low take-up of benefits.

The third approach to conceiving the State's role in income security is the extension of universal human rights. In thinking of how this could develop, as part of a citizenship rights agenda, it is worth reflecting on the main story of the last century, which can be described as the century of labouring man.

Although care work became topical towards the end of the twentieth century, in the early part of it there had been a political struggle, led by feminists, to enable women to undertake caring work, through "breadwinner" or family wages, pensions for widows and lone mothers, maternity leave and protection for women. The biggest drawback to this was that the care regime made women dependent on husbands. But if initial reforms mainly meant some selective "liberation" from labour, by mid-century there was a two-track system, with family compensation, benefits paid to husbands and a professional care system, as part of the "service state". Care was an integral part of socio-economic security, in different ways in different welfare states.

Then, in the era of market regulation (mid-1970s to mid-1990s), in many countries state-based entitlements to care were cut, leading to more reliance on social assistance for lone mothers, on maternity leave for women with jobs, and on residential and home care for the elderly (Jamieson, 1991). But by the end of the century new forms of care were being legitimized, through parental leave and subsidized privatized care.

So far, citizenship rights have omitted the need for care and the need to give care. Traditionally, because it was domestic work, it was not recognized socially or economically. But as more women have become regular labour force participants, loss of "citizenship status" while caring outside the traditional labour force has become more transparently peculiar. To put the matter bluntly, to overcome gender bias in systems of social protection, care must become a dimension of citizenship with rights equal to those received from employment (Knijn and Kremer, 1997).

One middle way between social insurance, social assistance and universalism is vouchers. Vouchers are attractive to governments as a means of formalizing the grey labour market, thereby raising tax revenue, but they retain a paternalistic danger. One imagines a future in which each citizen has a voucher card, with so many points for care, so many for education, so many for basic health, so many for training, and so on.[5]

Feminists see care as leading in two directions One direction leads towards what Nancy Fraser has called the "universal breadwinner model", where State services are provided for day care for children so that women can go to jobs. The other leads towards a "caregiver parity model", legitimizing and rewarding informal care work through caregiver allowances (Fraser,1993). One might say that the first is the labour line, the second the work line.

One strong point of an allowances-based approach that brings care work into the market economy, is that it boosts small-scale local activities and organizations, including charities and other voluntary NGOs, thereby strengthening community and trust (Evers, 1994). The "new volunteering" can be a means of social integration of both carers and recipients of care. The danger of most approaches taken so far is that they give insufficient attention to the issue of control. Several classic failings of labour must be overcome – segmentation, de-skilling and exploitation.

The caregiver model could lead to carers being confined to private care roles, isolated from the public sphere. Ruth Lister, in a brilliant flash, captured the problem by describing it as "the modern variant of Wollstonecraft's dilemma" (Lister, 1994). If commodifying care merely strengthened the sexual division of labour, with women doing most of the care, it would be a form of inequality. The loneliness of the long-distance caregiver is an image of female dependency associated with social hierarchies of the worst kind.

An individualized system could also lead to the Taylorization of care[6], with individuals having to obtain licences to perform care of certain types, and restrictions based on demarcation and procedural rules. This would prevent occupational security, and induce moral hazard. And it could intensify self-exploitation, in the Chayanovian[7] sense whereby the carer gives more time and effort than justified by the allowance because the "gift" relationship dominates the "market" relationship. Or it could intensify exploitation through the care

---

[5] The ILO's InFocus Programme on Socio-Economic Security is undertaking work on the desirability and feasibility of Citizenship Credit Cards, in which care work entitlements inter alia, would be provided.

[6] American engineer F. W. Taylor was an early twentieth-century economist who pioneered fast-paced assembly line methods of work. Taylor's theory was that "To get the most value for the least time wasted, all work should be organized according to principles of scientific management."

[7] A.V. Chayanov, early twentieth-century Russian socio-agronomist advocated equipping the peasantry with scientific knowledge.

recipient taking advantage of the other's labour. These dangers suggest that the care market could remain sexually and ethnically segregating.

The way to avoid these dangers must be through a mix of citizenship rights and strong "voice regulation". Unless there are associations to give collective voice to carers and care recipients, the goal of balanced reciprocity will not be obtained. Intermediary associations have been springing up all over the world to fill these representation spaces, and are an exciting development. But they must give representation and other forms of security, notably work security. The dangers of stress and burnout are extreme in care work.

There are essentially three types of care relationship (Waerness, 1984). There are personal services given by a dependent person to someone in a position of financial, social or labour control. There is care work given to those who are frail or otherwise dependent on help. And there is spontaneous care, where each person is equal in the eyes of the other and in their own eyes, and where there is balanced reciprocity. It is this that should be sought through policies and institutions.

In this regard, the notion of dependence has been pernicious. Only a fool believes in full independence. In society, individuals are interdependent. The attack on "dependency" has been a cry of the privileged throughout history. For the future, we need institutions that enhance self-control in a context of mutual dependency, which some call fraternity and others conviviality. The atomization of consumer-based individualism is a pathological prescription, creating a Wild West independence. When politicians and libertarians criticize "dependency", they should be reminded that they too are dependent – we all are. We cannot work and develop occupation without others' support, and we cannot predict what support they might give, how indirect that might be, or even when we will need it. Recognition of these eternal verities is what defines the human community we call society. This is why the right to live as a human being with dignity – the right to self-respect – overrides the paternalistic reciprocity principle. What right or superior quality do I possess that I should deny you basic security in which to pursue your sense of occupation? This question should be addressed to paternalists and labourists everywhere.

The ways in which policy-makers treat labour market services and care work will determine the character of society and work in the future. The issue of care raises one of the great dilemmas of the movement from a labour-based society to a work-based society. How can it be compensated in a way that does not merely provide income security while confining women, in most cases, to a lower-status, socially-excluding role? This is Ruth Lister's Wollstonecraft dilemma.

Part of this dilemma is still how to pay for care. If payment were indirect, through tax credits or family-based benefits, it would be gender-segregating, and so not give citizenship rights, since it would be a family-unit entitlement, not an individual right. If care were provided directly by the State, paternalism and bureaucratic control of access, cost and inclusion would come into play, with discretionary judgements occurring all over the place. If a payment were given to the caregiver, it would strengthen individual rights, but it could produce moral hazard and monitoring problems. For instance, the carer could make the recipient dependent on the need for care, or not provide the care for which compensation is paid. The recipient would be unlikely to be in a position to "voice regulate". Finally, if a payment were made to the care recipient, analogous problems would arise. Often the person would not know what is required or even provided, perhaps being young, elderly or frail. So, each of the options – paying the carer, paying the cared-for, family-based benefits or tax credits, and direct public or private provision – raise distinct problems.

The trend towards cash payments represents a reduction in bureaucratic control and promotes "welfare citizenship", by giving contractual rights (contractual justice) rather than merely procedural rights. Payment for care, although commodification, represents legitimization of work that is not labour. The payment allows more self-control in principle and reduces the drawbacks of the paternalism of social workers and professionals. It also erodes the distinction between the gift and the market economy. The trouble is that individuals are not equal in their bargaining position, or with respect to the information needed to make optimal decisions.

Conclusion

That care work has emerged from the shadows into the public domain, not only by having a public face but also by being legitimized socially in a context of a labourist welfare state under strain is powerfully subversive (see Folbre, 1999; Chapter 3). Caring for a disabled relative, a sick child or an infirm elderly person is no less valuable than pouring the tea for the boss or standing on a production line à la Charlie Chaplin. Neoclassical economics, orthodox labour statistics, welfare state designers fuelled by their zeal for labour and generations of politicians all ruled otherwise. Only late in the twentieth century, as a result of two forces that made uneasy bedfellows – a desire by mainstream politicians and orthodox economists to cut back on the public welfare state and pressure from the feminist movement to recognize such work – did care work start to become legitimized.

For instance, it is now more widely recognized that care work should be covered by social protection policy. Perhaps the most striking development was the introduction of care insurance in Germany in the 1990s, the first new form of social insurance for many decades. But still the work of caring has not been adequately recognized as part of a total person as a working being. That will happen only when the social division of labour is profoundly changed.

Everybody fortunate enough to have good health and the capacity to do so could probably benefit from spending part of their time working in caring for others, just as one day – any day – we will need to rely on the care given to us. Yet labour force statistics and national income calculations ignore such work, except when it is paid labour. In most cases, making it into paid labour is likely to make it less valuable and less valued by the giver of care because it involves a reduction in the gift relationship.

A fundamental question remains whether the commodification of care can defy the Wollstonecraft dilemma, the difficulty of reconciling the desire to see the activity move into the public sphere (potentially involving commodification) while avoiding the prospect of women remaining predominantly in low-status activity.

At the outset of the twenty-first century, there is something approaching a unity of purpose among policy-makers, feminists and egalitarians in general about the need to legitimize care work. There is a pragmatic, even cynical element in this. Many of the former see carers as reducing the need for extensive social services and state transfers, with "private", personal and low-cost suppliers replacing "public" support. Nevertheless, more analysts are joining feminists in demanding that such work should be recognized and compensated properly. There is no prospect of gender equality unless or until all forms of work are treated equally in social policy. One key question is whether or not the payment system that emerges will lead to more paternalism or to greater self-control.

Other forms of work also tend to be excluded from labour. Civil society or NGOs are perhaps the most dynamic part of social participation. Much of this activity is real work, contrary to the claims of old-style labourism. We need to measure it, to guarantee that those involved can have basic security and to ensure that the more vulnerable who are drawn to a cause are enabled to retain their sense of self-control and pursue their sense of occupation along with everybody else.

CARE POLICIES IN WESTERN EUROPE   2

Mary Daly

This chapter locates care in the social policy landscape in Western Europe. Adopting a comparative perspective, it draws out the complexity of care as a social good and in the light of this scrutinizes various policy approaches. The quality of care is a key theme. One of the main arguments is that care has to be considered as a sociological as well as a social policy phenomenon. This means viewing care in much larger terms than, say, a need of particular individuals or a component of interpersonal relationships. Care is part of the fabric of society and is integral to social development.

The chapter begins by identifying the key features of care. An overview of the relevant literature and a consideration of the policy parameters of care provide the substance here. The chapter then goes on to outline the main policy responses to care and caregiving in Western European welfare states.[1] The main reason for limiting the analysis to the countries of Western Europe is because they have been at the forefront in treating care as an exigency for social policy.[2] In this comparative part of the chapter the goal is to identify the underlying policy models, paying special attention to the combination of different measures and to how European welfare states cluster together on their treatment of care. Finally the chapter considers the pros and cons of alternative ways of compensating for care. For this purpose, a number of parameters of quality are elaborated and subsequently used to reflect upon the strengths and weaknesses of a range of policy approaches.

---

[1] It should be pointed out that, in this kind of overview of so many countries, the context and detail of provisions have been greatly summarized.

[2] Along with the 15 Member States of the European Union (EU), provisions in Norway and Iceland are also included in the empirical work which informs this chapter.

Conceptualizations and definitions of care

Care is conventionally defined as the activities and relations involved in caring for the ill, elderly, handicapped and dependent young. Having taken some time to mature, care is today an established field of study, at least in European countries. Running the risk of over-simplification, one could say that care has had two currents in the literature: as a concept utilized to account for the life experiences of women; and as a tool for the analysis of social policy. While related, they have tended to give rise to two different sets of literature.

The evolution of care as a concept

Care began life as a woman-specific concept. Although one of the original feminist concepts, care initially had strong sociological leanings.[3] In the endeavour to conceptualize the defining features of women's life situation, the nature of labour involved in caring was key. Care was conceived in the context of unpaid domestic labour as part of kinship and marriage relations. The material processes constituting care were emphasized in an effort to theorize why women did this work and why it was unpaid (Finch and Groves, 1983; Waerness, 1984). Over time, research has taken in paid care (Graham, 1991). One of the richer veins of scholarship has been the elaboration of the non-material basis of care. Affective ties are drawn to the fore. To frame this sociologically, care tends to be situated in a logic of gift and/or responsibility inside the sphere of kin or friendship (Joel and Martin, 1994, p.166). But socio-emotional bonds are key features of care in other respects as well. Some scholars draw attention to caring as a disposition, an orientation or attitude (Fisher and Tronto, 1990; Tronto, 1993). Caring about is, therefore, as integral as taking care of or being cared for. Caring is both an expression of the connectedness of social beings and a means of achieving such connectedness. As an ethical practice it requires attentiveness, responsibility, competence and responsiveness (Tronto, 1993).

Care as a social policy analysis tool

The second current of care in the literature concerns its treatment in policy. With strong links to the discipline of social policy, the bulk of this literature focuses on provision of cash benefits and services for care-related needs in the context of the developed welfare state. Much of this has a British, and to a

---

[3] Although it must be said that feminist work was multidisciplinary in spirit and orientation.

lesser extent Scandinavian, focus. A significant slice of the scholarship is, though, comparative, focusing on care as a source of variation among European welfare states.[4] Leira (1992) has drawn attention to how care is situated at the interface of public authorities, especially the welfare state, and private agents. The development of care-related provisions represents the bringing into the public sphere of an activity and set of relations normally treated as private. The differentiation between the provider, usually considered a non-professional, and recipient of care is one of the most important landmarks in this literature. Gender pervades the scholarship as well, for the vast majority of carers, whether paid or unpaid, are women. In general, the particularity of care as a domain of social policy is emphasized. Not only does it criss-cross a broad range of policy domains – social policy, health policy, education policy, labour market policy and incomes policy – but care may also call forth a service and/or cash response. A further layer of complexity is added by the differentiation between care for children and that for adults. The identity of the carer as well as the location and content of care vary, depending on whether the focus is on care for children or for (elderly or ill) adults.[5] This and other features of care have given rise to a tendency to treat the concept dichotomously. For example, a differentiation is commonly made between care in formal and informal settings, between care as provided in the market and the state sector, and between paid and unpaid care.

A newer strand of literature emphasizes the need to go beyond dichotomous conceptualizations. Two general types of response have prevailed: scholars have either concentrated on fashioning a more rounded conceptualization of care or they have sought to improve how the relationship between care and public policy is framed.

In the first *genre*, Abel and Nelson suggest that care needs to be set within its historical and social context (1990, p.7). They distinguish three dimensions in this regard: the relationship of the caregiver to the recipient, the payment, and the location of the activity. While this is helpful, Abel and Nelson do not actually combine the different attributes in any systematic way and provide little guide as to how they vary empirically. Fisher and Tronto (1990) follow a different route. Putting forward an over-arching concept of care, they speak of a "mode of caring". Although not developed conceptually, they identify three such modes empirically: the household/community, exchange (to be found in the marketplace) and bureaucratic modes. This work is certainly attuned to

---

[4] For example, Kraan et al., 1991; Evers and Svetlik, 1993; Alber, 1995, p.2; Anttonen and Sipilä, 1996.

[5] However, Scandinavian writers have endeavoured to consider both together under the heading of "social care" (see the contributions in Ungerson, 1990).

variation and, in this author's view, the concept of "mode of caring" has analytic potential. However, it is unfortunate that Fisher and Tronto sometimes elide setting and process. Thomas (1993) opts for a different strategy. Seeing no need to replace care with an alternative concept, she works on elaborating the component dimensions of care. She considers them to be: the identities of provider and recipient of care, the relationship between them, the social content of care, the economic character of the relationship and of the labour involved, and the social domain and institutional setting within which care is provided. While this is helpful, it provides little leverage for the present endeavour, which is to identify the role of public policy in developed welfare states in mediating care as a social good.

A second type of response addresses this task more directly. Knijn and Kremer (1997), for example, believe that the concept of citizenship provides a valuable way of framing the relationship between care and public policy. They demonstrate how the inferior treatment of care is the mirror image of a citizenship constructed on the basis of typically male activities. Daly and Lewis (1998) are more concerned about how to conceptualize care in such a way as to capture the social and political economy within which it is embedded. They point out that, to employ the concept of care for the analysis of welfare states, one must find a way of retaining its capacity to reveal important dimensions of women's lives while capturing properties of societal arrangements around personal needs and welfare. Treating care as a multidimensional concept, they elaborate it as a form of labour, as located within a normative framework of obligation and responsibility and as an activity with financial and emotional costs which extend across public/private boundaries. Their three-dimensional approach leads to a most comprehensive definition of care. They define care as the activities and relations involved in meeting the physical and emotional requirements of dependent adults and children together with the normative, economic and social frameworks within which these are assigned and carried out.

For the purposes of the present chapter, Daly and Lewis's work is helpful, especially in the way it tries to integrate the woman/gender and the wider sociological aspects of the concept. In a sense though, the relationship between public policy on care and the wider societal settlements around family and "private" relations remains unexplored. At issue is the essence of care as a policy good.

Policy parameters of care

The discussion to date has emphasized the complexity of care as an issue for public policy.[6] Such complexity derives from both the specificity of care and its uniqueness as a concern for policy. Four main forms of complexity are involved. Firstly, although care is typically conceived at a micro level, it is also a macro-level phenomenon in that it affects relations and balances among institutional domains. When welfare states respond to the needs embodied in care, they are, whether they intend to or not, altering the division of labour, cost and responsibility among the state, market, voluntary or non-profit sector and family. In addition, in making provision for care, welfare states are recasting what were, in almost all national settings, previously private forms of solidarity and exchange. In the process, relations of gender and generation are especially altered. A second dimension of complexity arises from the fact that making provision for care may entail the satisfaction of three needs: a need for services, for time and for financial support. The underlying point is that, although welfare states may choose to respond in a unidimensional manner, there are at least three aspects to care as an exigency for public policy. A third complicating aspect of care is that, as a policy good, it has two arms: the person experiencing the set of needs that comprise care and the actor who seeks or is assigned to satisfy that need. Finally, and related to the last point, the provision of care can be done formally or informally. Even in the most advanced welfare states, caring is never completely provided in formal (professional) settings. This distinction between formal and informal care connotes another set of distinctions: the identity of the carer and the location of care. As Almqvist and Boje (1999) demonstrate, there is a relationship between whether care is unpaid or paid and by whom it is carried out. When care is unpaid it tends to be carried out at home by either the mother, in the case of children, or other relatives in the case of both children and the elderly. When care is paid, the location sometimes switches to an institutional setting (either in the public or private sectors) and the identity of the carer is usually a professional of some kind.

All of this may be taken as evidence that making provision for care involves welfare states in one of their most precarious exercises. The issues involved may be viewed by public policy-makers as dilemmas or opportunities. To do justice to the complexity means that welfare states must adopt a multidimensional approach. The policy landscape surrounding care is therefore potentially very crowded. The possible policy interventions range through cash payments, taxation allowances, different types of paid and unpaid leave, social security credits, and services. Table 2.1 is an attempt to map this universe as it is to be found empirically across the range of Western European welfare states today.

---

[6] This is a complexity which is reflected in the difficulty of finding an appropriate term within and across languages. The English term "care" has tended to be imported by other languages because of the difficulty of finding an indigenous term. However, the use of the term "care" in English is not uncontroversial either.

Table 2.1   Universe of provision for care

| Type of measure | Policy domain | | | | |
	Social[1]	Labour market	Education	Health[2]	Income
Cash payments	Means-tested or social insurance benefits paid to carer or care receiver; child-care vouchers	Severance pay for withdrawal for reasons of parent-motherhood		Subsidies/subventions for residential care	
Credits for social security	Credits to carers for pension and other social security benefits				
Taxation					Allowances for care-related expenses
Leave	Paid and unpaid parental, paternity and care leave	Career breaks, time savings accounts, employment rights during leave	Educational/training leave for caring		
Services	Public child care, home helps, meals on wheels	Workplace child care	Crèches, day care, schools, kindergarten	Residential services	
Incentives towards employment creation	Vouchers for domestic employment, exemptions from social security contributions for people employed as carers	Reduction of working time, part-time work			Tax reductions for the costs of employing domestic helpers
Incentives for market services	Subsidies towards costs of care in private provision				Tax allowances for the cost of care in market-run services

[1] Services that fall under this heading may actually be offered by the local authorities/communes.

[2] Provisions by the housing authorities may also be pertinent here.

Source: Daly.

Obviously the diversity of policy responses is enormous, arguably greater than that found for contingencies such as unemployment or illness. No welfare state applies the whole palette of measures although, as we shall see, the Scandinavian states tend to opt for diversity as a care-related policy good. Such a high degree of variation has to be rendered manageable for analytic purposes. This will be done in two ways. The first is to combine them into more general types of measures and the second is to search for the patterns in how states across Europe have dealt with care.

Provision for care in European welfare states

General outline of trends in provision

Following the logic of table 2.1, one can differentiate among welfare state policy responses in terms of a fourfold model:

a) provisions relating to monetary and social security benefits such as cash payments, credits for benefit purposes, tax allowances;
b) provisions relating to employment-related measures such as paid and unpaid leave, career breaks, severance pay, flexitime, reduction of working time;
c) services or benefits provided in kind such as home helps and other community-based support services, child-care places, residential places for adults and children;
d) incentives towards employment creation or towards provision in the market such as vouchers which arrange for the payment of social security con-tributions, exemptions from social security contributions and tax reductions for employing a domestic helper, re-arranged working hours, subsidies for private care.

None of these is in itself unfamiliar. However, in an emerging field of policy, otherwise familiar policy measures may assume particular features and objectives.

The first of the welfare state policy models concerns monetary benefits. Paying benefits for caring is unusual in social policy because, in so doing, welfare states are commissioning certain amounts and types of labour. They may do this in a direct and/or indirect fashion. Welfare states directly commission labour when they pay benefits to someone to care for another person. In this case, they are commodifying rather than decommodifying, the now more widely recognized welfare state activity (Ungerson, 1995). They indirectly commission labour when they pay a benefit to adult care receivers, who can then decide how to expend the benefit. Payments for care involve a second type of departure from conventional cash payments in that they have a quasi-wage character – they could be regarded as a wage for familial activities. They are certainly a long way from the "reimbursement of expenses" orientation of classical family policy. The underlying point is not the obvious one – that cash payments for care may be oriented to different ends – but that ends are often complex, not clearly thought out and may even be inseparable from one another. Cash benefits may aim to offset expenses incurred, to enable people to purchase outside help, to compensate carers for the services they provide or to affect labour demand and supply.

The second type of general measure in relation to care are employment-related provisions. These also have specific features in the context of care. Given that they most often take the form of leave from work or flexibility in working time, the main good which is being proffered in this regard is time. Sometimes this is paid time, and in fact the overriding trend in Europe as we shall see is towards financially covered leave (especially for the care of children). Employment protection rights comprise another possible good here. Regardless of whether time or employment-related rights are the substance of provision, the direct beneficiary is usually the provider of care (rather than the person requiring care).

Services, the third policy measure, are traditionally the most widespread means of meeting the need for care. Services are unusual in this context in that they can work in two ways: either they precipitate a removal of care to a professional, formal setting or they facilitate its provision at home. In the latter case, the services may be sufficient of themselves to constitute the sole form of care but in many cases they act to supplement private care. Another remarkable factor about care-related services is that they span a broad range of policy spheres (as table 2.1 shows).

The fourth and last welfare state response – incentives in relation to employment creation – are unusual in that they appear to be explicit policy goals in some countries (Finland, France). We know that most policies contain hidden or implicit incentives but it is not so common for social policies to seek explicitly to affect employment creation in the domestic sphere. This kind of policy is at its most developed in France. Those who employ a carer at home, whether for children or an elderly person, are entitled to reductions in social security contributions for the employee as well as in some instances to reductions in tax. They may also use a voucher scheme designed to simplify administrative procedures when employing a domestic assistant (including duties in relation to care) working up to eight hours per week. The service voucher, which consists of a chequebook containing 20 duplicated cheques, relieves the employer of the obligation to draw up a contract of employment or to calculate the social security contributions. The amount due in social contributions is calculated by a national service voucher centre according to the duplicates sent by the employer and then directly debited from his or her account.

These "pure" policy measures are never put into practice in isolation. The next section tries to identify the main trends and experience in policy-making on care in Europe.

Public policies on care in European welfare states

The purpose of this section is to draw out general lessons about care as an exigency for public policy from a comparative perspective and to move on from that to identify national policy profiles (Ungerson, 1995; Anttonen and Sipilä, 1996; and Bettio and Prechal, 1998).

The differentiation between care for children and that for adults is crucial. With children, it seems as if care has always been on the public agenda. However, for all European social security systems, apart perhaps from the Scandinavian states which have favoured collectivization, the care of children is relatively new as a contingency for income support. While benefits like child or family allowances have involved welfare states in a long-standing commitment, such benefits were actually never intended for paying for care. Rather, they sought to assist families with some of the material costs of children, in the process redistributing resources horizontally and to a period of the life cycle when families are most likely to be hard pressed financially (Bradshaw et al. 1993, p.1). It is only relatively recently that caring for children has come to be seen as a "cost" in terms of opportunity income forgone. Child care as a concern of public policy has also undergone something of a metamorphosis. Public provision of services for the care of young children owes its origins in most countries to educational goals, such services being intended as a good for children (rather than parents). With child-care services increasingly viewed as an incentive or support for maternal employment, there is, then, something qualitatively new about care as a public exigency in relation to families with children. Parental, as distinct from maternity, leave, has taken on a new light. It is one of the first welfare state measures oriented to compensating for costs (and time) involved in caring for children. How have welfare states responded to the redefinition of child care? Parental leave, together with public child-care facilities, are the two measures which form the heart of European welfare states' responses to care for children.

In recent years most Western European countries have seen developments around parental leave (Daly, 1997). Indeed, there is a strong trend in Europe towards parental leave, so much so that Ireland and the United Kingdom are unique in not having paid parental leave. Elsewhere, both paid and unpaid varieties are to be found and while they are, as their name implies, intended for both parents, the fact that they are taken up almost exclusively by mothers has led to the introduction of some father-specific provisions in recent years. Countries with relatively generous parental-leave schemes (in terms of either the duration or level of payment) include Austria, Denmark, Finland, Germany, Italy, Luxembourg, Norway and Sweden (Bettio and Prechal, 1998, pp. 20–22). Looked at overall, the growing use of paid leave indicates a trend towards greater subsidization of parental caring of young children. It seems to be the case that, apart from perhaps Finland, expansion of cash benefits is not designed as a direct substitute for child-care services. But there is a policy switch involved in the current trend, in that countries are choosing to expend money on making payments directly to parents rather than investing in child-care facilities. To the extent that one can speak of cross-national convergence, it is a convergence around a double trend. On the one hand, there is a movement towards a low-level, conditional payment to parents; on the other, the quality of social rights attaching to caring is being improved through ancillary protection measures for care providers, such as labour market and (often basic) pension recognition. However, exceptions are frequent and child-care-related cash benefits tend to be introduced as add-ons to social security systems.

European welfare states have assumed a responsibility for care for elderly, ill and handicapped adults for a longer time than is the case with children. This tends to take the form of public provision of residential care with some community support services rather than, say, cash payments. Provision tends to be supplemented, to varying degrees, by local social services. In regard to services for the elderly, the Scandinavian countries, along with the Netherlands and the United Kingdom, have the highest levels of provision. The current trend in Europe, however, is towards home-based care, driven especially by the decrease in residential provision in the Nordic countries. The exigency of caring for the elderly and the disabled has been lent a new complexion. European welfare states are increasingly willing to make a payment specifically for the activity of home-based care for the disabled and the elderly. The United Kingdom was the first to pay for private care for ill and elderly adults with the introduction, in 1976, of a social security payment for the person providing the care. Finland, Iceland, Ireland and Luxembourg followed the United Kingdom's lead. However, other countries have chosen a different route – Austria, France and Germany also pay for this activity, but they make the payment to the care receiver. The developments in Germany are of profound significance, the need for care having been elevated to the status of a social insurance risk. This has led to the introduction of the first new branch of social insurance in Germany since unemployment was made a social risk in 1927.

Thus, when it comes to care for the elderly, European countries appear to be undecided about which arm of the relationship to support. The choice has potentially deep ramifications. In the first instance – making the payment to the person requiring care – welfare states are distancing themselves from how care needs are satisfied, whereas making the payment to the carer is a trend in the opposite direction, drawing more people within the direct embrace of the welfare state. In comparison to the approach taken to the care of children, time off work for the purpose of caring for elderly persons is underdeveloped in Western Europe. While many countries have provision for a short period of leave to care for ill adult relatives, Denmark, Norway and Sweden provide the most generous leave. Overall, while there is variation in how countries have managed care for the elderly, the use of cash benefits for the purpose of private caregiving is growing in popularity in Europe. In recent years, only Greece, the Netherlands and Spain have seen no major developments towards this end. Evers (1994, p.19) captures the cross-national trends with his remark: "Attendance allowances are no longer an unspecified add-on for people in need, but rather are specific tools for creating rights and appropriate steering mechanisms in a service and welfare society".

Overall, even though the range of measures at the disposal of welfare states in respect of caring is relatively large, they can basically be thought of as measures oriented to the supply of either public or private services. Until recently, if European countries had a policy on care, the public supply of caring-related services was the focus but, in the last decade or so, policy attention in Europe has turned more to the private, non-market supply of services.

Models of managing care in European welfare states

For the purpose of classifying European welfare states, it is helpful to retain the distinction between care for children and that for adults.

Judged by the duration and generosity of parental-leave provision and the extent of child-care provision (table 2.2), European countries can be categorized into three groups.[7] In the first, consisting of Greece, Ireland, Italy, the Netherlands, Portugal, Spain and the United Kingdom, the care of children

---

[7] The limitations of this exercise must again be emphasized. Local, as against national, dimensions fundamental to care provision have to be ignored here along with the linkages across service areas (e.g. whether receipt of cash affects one's right to receive services). Furthermore, not all countries are unequivocally classifiable. Austria tends to fall between the medium and high groupings and Italian provision varies widely across indicators.

Table 2.2   Clustering of European countries on the basis of their provision for children

Country	Equivalent of leave weeks paid in full[1]	Publicly financed services for children	
		0–3 years old	3–6 years old
Group 1: "Care is a family matter"			
Greece	Low/Medium	Low	High
Ireland	Low	Low	Medium
Italy	Medium	Low	High
Netherlands	Low	Low	High
Portugal	Low	Low	Medium
Spain	Low/Medium	Low	High
United Kingdom	Low	Low	Medium
Group 2: "Do it yourself but with help"			
Austria	High	Low	High
Finland	Medium	Medium	Medium
France	Low	Medium	High
Germany	Medium	Low	High
Iceland	Low/Medium	High	Medium
Luxembourg	Medium	Low	High
Group 3: "Multiple options"			
Belgium	Low/Medium	High	High
Denmark	Medium	High	High
Norway	High	High	High
Sweden	High	High	High

[1] Pertains to both maternity and parental leave.

Source: adapted from Bettio and Prechal (1998, p.47).

tends to be a family matter, with states providing few services and making little or no national provision for paid parental leave. In these countries families are largely left to their own devices in organizing their child-care arrangements. Some of these countries have no clear strategy and appear ambivalent about how the care of children should be managed. The countries in the next group, which could be labelled "do it yourself but with help", tend to favour a mix of provisions. Austria, Finland, France, Germany, Iceland and Luxembourg are included here. They offer quite generous parental-leave provisions and good public child-care facilities.[8] However these countries put limits on their provision, thereby ensuring that young children are cared for by their parents (effectively mothers). Finally there is the group of countries that offer parents the greatest variety of options. Belgium, Denmark, Norway and Sweden opt for diversity, providing moderate to high levels of all care resources and generally allowing parents a choice about how they organize the care of their children (Bettio and Prechal, 1998, p.48).

When welfare states are compared on their provision for care of the elderly, the clustering is not all that different (see table 2.3). The southern and Nordic countries still form the opposite poles, although the composition of the three groups of countries varies. Greece, Italy, Portugal and Spain all score low on public provision for care of the elderly whether this is conceived as institutional or home-care services, or as a financial payment towards the cost of securing care personally. The continental European countries (including Austria, Belgium, France, Germany, the Netherlands) along with Ireland form the core of the middle band. These tend to give priority to cash payments for elder care. Finally, the multiple-option countries once again comprise the Nordic countries but are in this instance joined by the United Kingdom.

While there is no unidimensional relationship between the way they provide for the care of children and that of ill and elderly adults, most European countries have what could be called a "coherent care policy". It is important to note, though, that in most countries provision for care involves a mix of financial, leave and service measures. It is more accurate to speak therefore of "a care mix". When provision for the care of children and that of the elderly are combined, the 17 states considered here can be grouped into four categories. The reason we have four groups rather than three (as we have had up to now) is because Ireland, Italy and the United Kingdom approach provision for children in a very different way to how they treat provision for the care of the elderly. They therefore form a separate category. The groups of countries are as follows:

Caring states:	Denmark, Finland, Iceland, Norway, Sweden
Pro-family caring states:	Austria, Belgium, Germany, France, Luxembourg*, Netherlands
Hot and cold states:	Ireland, Italy, United Kingdom
Non-caring states:	Greece, Portugal, Spain

* Rated on child care only.

---

[8] These are countries that tend to make a distinction between the care of very young children and those aged three and over. Social policy provisions indicate that these countries favour parental care for the very young, whereas for the older age groups out-of-home child care is considered appropriate.

Table 2.3   Clustering of European countries on the basis of their provision for the elderly

Country	Payment for care[1]	Share of elderly in institutional care	Share of elderly receiving home services
Group 1: "Low public provision of elder care"			
Greece	Low	Low	Low
Italy	Low	Low	Low
Portugal	Low	Low	Low
Spain	Low	Low	Low
Group 2: "Cash payments for elder care"			
Austria	High	Low	Medium/High
Belgium	Low	Low	High
France	Medium	Low	Medium
Germany	High	Low	Medium/High
Ireland	Medium/High	Medium	Medium
Group 3: "Multiple options"[2]			
Denmark	Medium	Medium	High
Finland	High	High	High
Iceland	Medium	High	High
Netherlands	Low	High	Medium
Norway	Medium	High	Medium
Sweden	High	High	Medium
United Kingdom	High	Medium	High

[1] This is operationalized in terms of whether a designated payment exists for care to or of the elderly and the relative generosity of this payment.

[2] Luxembourg is excluded because of insufficient information.

Source: adapted from Bettio and Prechal (1998, p.52).

In the "caring states", consisting of the Scandinavian countries, the guarantee of social security embraces not only monetary security but also high-quality care for the very dependent (Leira, 1993). Care, conceived mainly as the right to receive it, is a constituent of social citizenship. These countries have been forced in recent years to consider the matter of who provides care, because of escalating costs of public provision or because people are seeking the right to provide care personally for young, and to a lesser extent elderly, relatives. In the second group, consisting of the continental European countries, there is also a clear position: it should in the first instance be provided by the family. These countries, labelled "pro-family caring states", have always placed limits on their readiness to utilize public resources to make financial and other arrangements for a good which they view as most appropriately located in civil society. They have, though, been forced in recent years to rethink that position, in the light of the increasingly costly trade-off between caring and other aspects of life, especially for women. The third group, the "hot and cold states" of Ireland, Italy and the United Kingdom, are characterized by inaction on some fronts but considerable public provision on others. They tend, with the exception of Italy, to be poor on public services for children but to have quite a developed network of provision for elderly care. Finally, there are what we call the "non-caring states": Greece, Portugal and Spain. These have more or less left care to the family by policy inaction rather than action. Moreover, there are few if any policy developments around care in these countries – care is not an exigency for public policy. When one looks across the countries, it is notable that care emerges as an issue under a particular rubric, intimately related to the prevailing ideology surrounding the family. Hence it is not a great surprise that care as an activity to be paid for from public funds should have first emerged in the United Kingdom where the ideology of family solidarity, especially as it pertains to intergenerational relations among adults, is relatively weak.

Evaluating alternative ways of compensating for care

Looking at developments in social policy through the lens of care, one could say that whereas in the past European societies constructed institutions on a large scale, contemporary developments are turning the emphasis towards the more small-scale solidarities of family and community. As Evers (1993, p.26) points out, problems of social integration and quality of life require more than taxpayer solidarity: they are dependent on interpersonal relations and the readiness to help and support at the everyday level. The great irony is that to cope with care, European societies are now required to call forth a form of solidarity which has been diminished by the individualizing effects of their own social rights and benefits (ibid.).

The different features of care as a policy good

Given the complexity of the issues involved, one has to be specific about what is the "good" for policy purposes in relation to care. This, I suggest, may be thought of as "good quality care".[9] Of course, it is not by any means self-

---

[9] Tronto (1993, p.109) would probably define this as an "integrated well-accomplished act of care". Neither the meaning nor desirability of integration is obvious. It is her fear about fragmentation in the caring process (in which she separates caring about, taking care of, caregiving and care receiving) that leads her to emphasize integration. However, setting the integration of care up as an ideal may have the effect of adding further to the responsibility of the caregiver.

evident what constitutes good quality care. The perspective and interests of the care receiver constitute one starting point. Quality of care from this viewpoint refers to the calibre of the forthcoming service and/or income compensation (the latter to compensate for expenses incurred in meeting the costs associated with care). At issue here is the matter of standards. The right to receive care becomes an empty right if provision is sub-standard (Bettio and Prechal, 1998, p.54). However, comparative research has found that European countries have shown little explicit concern with the quality of life achieved by people with long-term care needs in private households (Glendinning and McLaughlin, 1993, p.149). Quality also connotes a matter of choice (of carer and of care locus, especially to allow people to remain in their own homes or to move to residential facilities). Finally, there is the matter of the quality of the relationship within which care is received. Power relations may be important here for, as Abel and Nelson point out, caring can so easily shade into social control (1990, p.16).

The needs of the care provider are another integral part of the quality of care scenario. One could postulate that the good in this instance is the opportunity to provide high-quality care. If one retains the understanding of quality used in relation to the care receiver – as having material, choice and emotional components – then security for the provider relates not just to emotional or financial security but also to a choice about whether one proffers care at all. With care so often set within a culture of social obligation, it may involve little or no choice for the provider. Another aspect of quality pertains to what one might term "the conditions of work", matters of job security, payment levels, hours, supports and so forth. Thanks to feminist research we know that emotional fulfilment, what one might term "the intrinsic reward", is hugely important for the well-being of the carer as well. Feder Kittay usefully reminds us that we need to think in terms of resources whereby the carer can care for her/himself as well (1999, p.143).

A further complexity relates to a more macro level: care policies in welfare states can be said to affect a number of broad societal balances. One such balance pertains to gender equity. It has been said that gender actually overrides kin ties in determining who assumes the caring role (Hooyman and Gonyea, 1995, p.120). The reason is that care is built into the fabric of unequal gender (and other) relations. Whereas men are viewed as choosing to care, there is an obligation on women in many societies to be the caregivers, even when this interferes with their own income security and other needs. Hence, public policy on care has huge import for individual women and men and, writ large, serves to either alleviate or intensify gender inequalities. The matter is not exhausted by whether the work is paid or not: even if it is organized as employment, care work is often low paid and undertaken with little choice in poor conditions. In the context of gender equity, good quality care implies a free choice for both women and men.

Public policy on care also serves functions in relation to the societal value placed on care. This is a contentious issue and one that has ignited much feminist fire. Because the line between (under)valuing care and confirming it as a woman's domain is a fine one, feminists divide in opinion both about the desired goals of the activity and the effects of public policies (Fisher and Tronto, 1990, pp. 36–37). It is clear that recognition is not enough, if only for the reason that recognition does not necessarily imply valorization. The appropriate good in this instance is, we suggest, the legitimization of care work. This includes both recognition and valorization, whereby care work is not just regarded as a good for society but policies are put in place to value it.

An important balance affected by care policy is that of a welfare mix in society.[10] In this regard at least part of the objective may be to influence the economics of care. Social objectives may also be present, however, such as mobilizing a wider range of actors, especially voluntary or civic organizations and private firms. While a welfare mix *per se* was not a widespread goal of social policy in the past, it is becoming increasingly important. There is a growing feeling today that one form of provision is (almost *per se*) insufficient. This is especially the case in countries where the State has traditionally been a strong service provider. State-dominated provision is said not only to curtail choice but to be inferior to the market which is portrayed as efficient, competitive, profit maximizing and rational. This kind of thinking opens the way to market provision as well as portraying family provision as a form of "freedom and choice". Thus, recent European debate does not take issue with the desirability of a pluralistic welfare mix but rather, taking this for granted, concentrates on the respective roles of state, market, voluntary/non-profit and informal (family) sectors within this mix (Evers, 1993, p.4). The underlying rationale varies among the different domains. Universalistic orientations predominate at the state level, where the market values of instrumentalism and choice are uppermost, whereas in the family and community norms and traditions of personal obligation and linkage are prevalent (ibid., p.15). Moreover, care policies do not just affect intra-sectoral though, but are fundamentally about the distribution of costs and responsibilities across sectors.

Another balance relates specifically to costs. In developed welfare states, care policies (for either the provider or recipient) may have the intent of reducing the costs of care services to the public budget. It is conventional

---

[10] For an elaboration of this concept, see Evers and Wintersberger (1990).

wisdom that institutional care is more costly to the public purse than care in the community. The moves towards paying for care at home, which as we have seen have recently been prevalent in Western Europe, are likely to be motivated as much by expenditure considerations as by the quality of care.

An additional parameter relevant to care policies is the demand for, or supply of, labour. Other things being equal, if services are created for care, then demand for labour increases. Utilizing care policy as an instrument to affect the demand for labour has taken a new turn in recent years with the increasing use of incentives for domestic employment. This strategy of using care as a feature of labour market policy, pursued especially in Belgium, Finland and France, treats care or the increasing need for it as an opportunity for particular types of job creation. Making provision for care constitutes, therefore, a form of labour and employment policy, seen in some countries as an inexpensive way of alleviating unemployment levels, for example.

How then do some of the main policy measures to be found in European welfare states appear from the viewpoint of these parameters?

Considering the likely effects of different policy measures

What follows should be regarded as a thought experiment, an attempt to draw attention to possible trade-offs and effects of different policy approaches rather than an evaluation based on definitive results. It is speculative, not least because the policy approaches are compared in a very general manner and, for the purpose of comparison, have to be removed from the national context. Table 2.4 compares the different policy measures in terms of the parameters set out in the last section for care as a goal for policy.

A cash payment to the carer appears positive in relation to most table 2.4 parameters except those of choice/quality for the carer, gender equity and the creation of a welfare mix. In the last regard, it is predicted to have a negative effect since it constitutes no change in the status quo of the welfare mix. The most likely effect of a cash payment to the carer is to strengthen informal, private care, thereby either crowding out other sectors or exonerating them of responsibility. As regards choice/quality for the carer, the danger in this kind of payment is that it is usually at a low level and brings with it few social security or employment rights. To the extent that it runs the risk of being symbolic, it tends to reinforce relations of subordination (Ungerson, 1995, p.48). This tendency, effectively a weakness, gives it negative features from a gender-equity perspective. Although making a payment for the work which women have usually done may valorize that work, it also tends to confirm the woman as the care provider. Overall cash payments to carers bear the danger of

Table 2.4   How policy provisions rate in relation to different objectives

	Choice/ quality for care receiver	Choice/ quality for caregiver	Gender equity	Legitimization of care	Creation of a welfare mix	Alteration of labour supply/demand	Reduction of public costs
Cash payment to carer	+	?	–	+	–	+	+
Cash payment to cared-for person	+	?	?	?	+/–	+/–	+
Public services	+	+	+	+	?	+	–
Leave	+/–	?	?	+	?	+	+
Incentives towards employment creation	–	–	?	?	?	+	+
Incentives towards market-based care	?	?	+	?	+/?	+	?

+ = positive effect – = negative effect +/– = neutral ? = effect could go either way +/? = effect either positive or unknown.

fostering exclusivity and privatism rather than a sense of collective responsibility (Abel and Nelson, 1990, p.7).

The implications of the strategy of making a payment to the person requiring care are even less positive. Such payments are likely to be positive only for choice/quality for the care receiver (by empowering that person to choose their preferred form of care) and for the reduction of costs to the public purse. It is not clear that they improve choice/quality for the care provider because they may tie the carer in a relationship of dependence with the care receiver (who is given financial control). This possible negative implication may also undermine gender equity and contribute little to legitimizing care work as a valuable social activity. The effects of this type of measure on the welfare mix and labour supply are thought to be neutral since the level of the payment is unlikely to be such as to bring about major shifts either way.

Public services for care-related needs have a number of advantages. They are, in theory anyway, likely to improve choice and quality on the part of both the care receiver and the care provider, to be good for gender equity, to help to legitimize care work and to bring about a change in the demand for, and supply of, labour. These hypothesized effects are associated with the tendency for care work to be (better) paid when it is located in the public sector than when undertaken privately by individuals. This is a matter of degree though, since experience suggests that locating care work in the public sector is not, in itself, a panacea for the inferior conditions that plague it. A clear downside is that public services are expensive and therefore add significantly to the public budget. Their effect on the welfare mix is somewhat unknown for they may act to stifle the emergence of a broader welfare mix by, for example, crowding out the market and voluntary, non-profit sectors.

The strategy of leave from employment for the purposes of caring for adults and children is, as noted above, increasingly popular in Western Europe. Leave is conjectured to have a positive effect in legitimizing care work, in altering the demand for and supply of labour and in reducing public costs (because it saves on institutional costs). There are, however, many question marks about the implications of leave. Its effect on quality is predicted to be either neutral (for the care receiver) or unknown (in the case of the care provider). The latter is in fact the case because while leave confers time to care, it is in many countries remunerated at a low level, if at all. To the extent that leave provides incentives to exit the labour market, its implications for gender equity could go either way. These provisions vary quite a lot across countries in how they construct incentives and disincentives for female employment. They are therefore rarely neutral as regards gender equity. However, there is some potential in this type of measure to improve gender equity if it is targeted to men as well as to women and if it contains incentives for a return to the labour market. The effects of leave provisions on the welfare mix are also difficult to predict because these will vary depending on the conditions attaching to the leave.

Another policy approach is to grant incentives towards domestic employment creation. This is a policy with few positive effects – its advantages are confined to affecting the demand for and supply of labour and its relatively low cost to public funds. Because the incentives are such that they make for temporary, insecure employment, it is suggested here that they lower the level of choice and quality available to both care receiver and care provider. In addition, the generally poor conditions of the jobs created render questionable the effects of leave on gender equity, the legitimization of care work and the creation of a welfare mix.

Lastly, incentives towards market-based care are also becoming popular, especially in Ireland and the United Kingdom where widespread state provision of services sits uncomfortably with contemporary political discourse and deeply-rooted ideologies. Their effects are hypothesized to be quite mixed, with a number of negative or unknown consequences. Incentives towards market-based care may be positive for gender equity because they represent a shift from the norm of home-based unpaid care, which tends to be care by women. They are also likely to have a positive effect in increasing the demand for labour (and presumably also the supply, because if caring is shifted to the market then more women are available for employment). Nevertheless, there are questions about the extent to which they improve quality and choice for both care receiver and care provider. We are not yet in a position to make definitive statements about whether market-based care is superior to care provided privately in the family or through public services. Too little research has been carried out on quality aspects of this provision. As long as information is lacking, predictions about the effects of increasing incentives towards market-based care cannot be made. The cost to the public purse is also an unanswered question since in some countries – such as the United Kingdom – subsidies have had to be set at a high level and end up being quite costly.

Overview

Care is as much a feature of societies as it is of an individual's situation. It is, in other words, embedded in a set of social relations which are integral to well-being. As an issue for public policy care is complex. The literature on social policy and sociology has examined care in informal settings, most often treating it as a private, family-based activity. Care is for the most part provided by women and is remunerated only when European countries decide, usually reluctantly, that it requires to be supported by public funds. For the purposes of the present exercise, a broad definition of care has been used: the activities and relations involved in meeting the physical and emotional requirements of dependent adults and children, together with the normative, economic and social frameworks within which these are assigned and carried out.

European welfare states are under a lot of pressure in relation to care. Not only has longevity increased but families, women in particular, are insistent that the care of children can no longer be an entirely private or an entirely public good. The situation could be summarized by saying that the demand for care is increasing at a time when its supply, both in the public and private non-market sectors, is decreasing. Whether conceived of in relation to caring for children or for adults, this is one of the most dynamic and innovative areas of social policy in Western Europe. The measures introduced include payments (to either the care receiver or the care provider), leave from employment, public services, incentives towards domestic employment and subsidies for market-based care. The trend in Europe is for countries to be increasingly willing to make a financial contribution to private/family care, a good formerly provided free by the family. Such willingness must be placed in the context of rising costs of public services and shifting public opinion about the appropriate form and conditions of care. In any case, they are not necessarily generous provisions because payments tend to be low and, in those countries where it has been created, domestic employment remains insecure and largely unregulated.

One of the main arguments of this chapter is that making provision for care involves welfare states in one of their most precarious exercises. This is because the issue of quality pertains not just to material and physical welfare but also to emotional well-being and choice. Moreover, the needs which have to be met are not just those of the person requiring care. Security for the potential care provider is even more demanding since quality must also include the choice not to care. The conditions under which the care work is carried out are also pertinent to matters of quality. In addition to the well-being of those directly involved, the policy analyst must have an eye to a larger set of balances in society when examining the implications of care-related policies. Such considerations include the gender balance, the extent to which care work is itself legitimized, the appropriate welfare mix in society, the demand for, and supply of, labour and the balancing of public finances. They together constitute a set of parameters whereby the effects of different policy options for care can be considered.

When existing provisions are viewed in the light of these parameters, it becomes clear that different measures have particular strengths and weaknesses. Referring again to table 2.4, making a cash payment to the carer is likely to improve choice/quality for the care receiver and to affect positively both the demand for labour and public finances (the latter in that it saves on institutional care). Payments to the person requiring care are conjectured to be beneficial mainly in bestowing greater choice/quality for her or him (by empowering the person to choose the preferred form of care) and reducing costs to the public purse. It is suggested that public services have the largest range of positive effects. They should ideally serve to improve choice and quality on the part of both the care receiver and the care provider, be good for gender equity and for the valorization of care work and be likely to bring about a change in the demand for, and supply of, labour. Leave from employment can also have a number of positive effects (especially in legitimizing care work, altering the demand for, and supply of, labour and reducing public costs). It is, however, either neutral or unknown in its effects on quality/choice for the care recipient and provider and on gender equity. The penultimate measure in table 2.4 – incentives towards domestic employment creation – is thought to have few positive effects. Its advantages are confined to affecting the demand for, and supply of, labour and its relative economy of public funds. The final measure, incentives towards market-based care, has mixed effects, although much about them remains unknown, since they are a relatively new development.

This chapter has emphasized the complexities involved in care itself and also in how Western European welfare states have responded to this growing need. Care-related policies have ramifications which reach deep into the social fabric. They affect and potentially alter a series of balances in society, balances as fundamental as the boundaries between the family and the State, the obligations attaching to kinship and the rights and duties of citizenship. When it comes to providing for care, there is a series of hard choices to be made. Such choices are not confined to individuals and families. Societies too are involved in such fundamental decisions.

LEGITIMIZING CARE WORK AND THE ISSUE OF GENDER EQUALITY 3

Jane Lewis

The crisis in care

Any dependent person, young or old, requires care. Care has historically been carried out mainly on an "informal" basis, usually by the family and sometimes by neighbours and the wider community (Horden and Smith, 1998). Western countries also usually made some kind of formal provision, often through a deterrent poor law system. But care for adults and for children only became a major issue in the late twentieth century, driven by major and rapid social changes in population ageing, women's paid employment and increasing rates of family breakdown and lone motherhood. There are therefore major issues of how provision is to be made, who is to benefit and who is to pay, just as there are in respect of all the major programmes of modern welfare states. However, the existing arrangements for social care provision are often messy because of the way in which policy has developed and because care raises particularly difficult questions regarding values, how we treat each other, and the way in which we order our societies. Care work is intimate and is subject to deep anxieties.

Across societies it has tended to be assumed that the vast majority of the care needed by dependent people will be provided informally by the family, and in particular by women in the family. The male breadwinner model family, in which men earn and women take responsibility for housework and care work, described, with varying degrees of accuracy in different countries at different historical moments, the pattern of economic activity in the family. In Western countries it also exercised considerable prescriptive power for much of the twentieth century. This meant that governments tended to assume that care would be provided by women in families and legislated accordingly. The basic programmes of social protection in Western countries were in large measure built around the labour market and the male worker's relationship to paid work.

Social insurance in particular operates via the labour market and has always privileged the full-time, usually white, male worker (Gordon, 1990). The post-war welfare settlements in Western European countries were based firmly on the twin principles of full-time male employment and stable families. The growing labour market participation of women, together with their increasing labour force attachment, as well as higher levels of family breakdown, have posed major challenges to the whole welfare settlement. How care is to be provided is a part of that.

In the main then, the issue of care remained relatively invisible on the policy agenda until the late twentieth century. The development of social care services in the public sector lagged far behind the other major services of the welfare state: health and education. Indeed, outside Scandinavia, the formal provision of care has tended to be part of the "mixed economy", involving the non-profit sector and the market as well as the state, to a greater extent than have health care systems (Anheier and Salamon, 1997), and in some countries the boundaries between public and private formal provision have become increasingly blurred (Burchardt et al., 1999; Lewis, 1998). At the level of policy and provision, care is complicated: it is both formal and informal and may therefore involve paid and unpaid work; formal provision may be in the public or independent sector and may be made in the form of cash or services. With welfare state restructuring in the 1990s the balance between all these elements has become more of an issue. Thus the major policy questions are first, whether it can be assumed that women will continue to provide care, and if so on an unpaid or paid basis? Wrapped up in this question are the twin issues of what should constitute a proper recompense for care and how to secure time to care. Second, there is the question of whether care should be collectively provided by the State, privately provided by the family, or left to the market and the voluntary sector?

There is a strong case for arguing that the family has always been the largest provider of welfare (Oakley, 1986). Yet paradoxically in the debate about welfare states, family care has tended to figure rather insignificantly. In large measure this is because of the invisibility of so much care work. But it is also a product of strongly held views about the rightful separation of private (in the sense of the family) and public, and that care belongs primarily in the former. The issue of care is therefore entangled in the politics of the family, as well as the politics of labour markets and the welfare state. The suggestion that the amount and quality of informal care may no longer be adequate is part and parcel of anxieties about the growth of selfish individualism, the erosion of trust, and the decline of family and community.

This chapter will argue that for all these reasons it is appropriate to talk of a "crisis in care" (Hochschild, 1995), certainly in the liberal, English-speaking welfare regimes, whose model of social protection is in the ascendant. The first part of the chapter shows how the issue of care is linked to the erosion of the male breadwinner model and also how there is a degree of convergence in western countries towards a dual-earner family model, not just at the level of behaviour, but also at the level of the normative assumptions made by policy-makers. In face of these shifts, two rather different discourses have raised the alarm regarding care. The first discourse – conservative and communitarian - fears the growth of individualism and the erosion of the kind of family arrangements that made informal care possible on such a wide scale. Its policy proposals have a tendency to hark back to the male breadwinner model. The second – feminist – discourse begins by making a greater effort to understand the nature of care and then to construct a care ethic based on relationship and connection (rather than individualism), which, if taken seriously, would trans-form the whole approach to work and social provision. Whether it is politically possible to adopt such a care-centred approach in the face of such a strong trend towards an individualized adult worker-citizen model is doubtful. Nevertheless, this care-centred lens is crucial to an understanding of how care must be con-sidered as a policy issue in its own right.

I will suggest that the political reality of convergence towards a dual earner model, together with an understanding of care as relational, means that care must be valued, which also means that it must be treated as work. But in addition, policies must promote the capacities of both men and women to engage in it, in other words, to share care.

Care and the erosion of the male breadwinner model

The early 1980s literature on care emphasized the extent to which it was unpaid work performed by women. Ann Oakley's (1974) pioneering research in the 1970s conceptualized housework as unpaid work; the research of the early 1980s differentiated care work from other forms of household labour. Falling fertility rates and the advent of birth control technology making it possible to choose how to space children have meant that a much smaller proportion of women's lives are spent in caring for children. Titmuss (1976) calculated that the average working-class British woman marrying in her teens or early twenties during the 1890s experienced ten pregnancies and spent 15 years in pregnancy and nursing compared with four years so spent by her counterpart in the years following the Second World War. With the decline in the years spent in childbearing and the improvement in women's health came concomitant possibilities for greater labour market attachment. On the other hand, ageing populations mean that increasing numbers of elderly people require informal care. Given the demographic trends in Western countries and in Japan, it is increasingly likely that "women in the middle" (Brody, 1981) will find themselves caring for both children and elderly relatives at the same time. Since early Northern European research on the numbers of female carers, representative sample surveys have revealed that the largest category of carers are spouses and that as many as half of these are husbands (Arber and Ginn, 1992). Nevertheless, women are the largest group of unpaid carers and there is substantial evidence to suggest that they do much more by way of intimate, personal care tasks. When there is a female carer on hand, there is less likelihood of formal, public care being provided (Lewis, 1998).

There is no evidence that the informal care work performed chiefly by women has diminished. At the same time, women's employment has increased and consists largely of service-sector, care-related jobs. The comparative data on women's post-war labour market participation for Western countries all show an upward trend (table 3.1).

It is no longer only the Scandinavian countries that have virtually equal proportions of men and women in the labour market. The British General Household Survey showed that in 1975, 81 per cent of men aged 16–64 were economically active and only 62 per cent of women. But by 1996 this figure was 70 per cent for both men and women (ONS, 1998, tables 5.8 and 5.9). Married women are as likely to be employed as non-married women and the contribution by men to family income has fallen from nearly 73 per cent in 1979–81 to 61 per cent in 1989–91 (Harkness, Machin and Waldfogel, 1996). In the United States, the deteriorating economic position of manual male workers, particularly black men, has made these men poor marriage prospects and has been linked to the growth of lone mother families (Wilson, 1987).

However, the nature of women's participation in the labour market varies considerably between countries. Table 3.2 shows the extent of women's part-time work; men are still predominantly full-time workers. But the meaning of part-time work varies considerably. In the United Kingdom, short part-time working is very common. Almost a quarter of women with children under ten worked 15 or fewer hours per week in the late 1990s (Thair and Risdon, 1999), and 24 per cent of all female employees worked under 20 hours a week (Rubery et al., 1998). In the Scandinavian countries, where female part-time work is also common, women usually work relatively long hours, often exercising their right to work part time while they have young children. This part-time work attracts proportionate benefits and is not the precarious employment that is so common in the United Kingdom.

Thus the precise nature of the erosion of the male breadwinner model is complicated. There has been no simple move from a male breadwinner to a dual

Table 3.1   Labour force participation as a percentage of population from age 15–64

	1960		1994	
	Male	Female	Male	Female
Sweden	98.5	50.1	78.1	74.4
Finland	91.4	65.6	77.1	69.9
Denmark	99.5	43.5	84.2	73.8
United States	90.5	42.6	85.3	70.5
France	94.6	46.6	75.9	59.1
United Kingdom	99.1	46.1	83.3	65.6
Austria	92.0	52.1	81.0	62.1
Germany	94.4	49.2	80.8	61.8
Australia	97.2	34.1	85.5	63.8
Belgium	85.5	36.4	72.5	51.6
Netherlands	97.8	26.2	79.1	57.4
Italy	95.3	39.6	76.9	43.4
Ireland	99.0	34.8	81.8	43.9

Source: Organisation for Economic Co-operation and Development (OECD) annual Labour Force Survey.

Table 3.2   Part-time employment in 13 OECD countries ranked by part-time employment as a proportion of female employment (1979 and 1995, percentages)[1]

	Total		Female	
	1979	1995	1979	1995
Netherlands	16.6	37.4	44.0	67.2
Australia	15.9	24.8	35.2	42.7
Sweden	23.6	24.3	46.0	40.3
United Kingdom	16.4	24.1	39.0	44.3
Denmark	22.7	21.6	46.3	35.5
United States	16.4	18.6	26.7	27.4
Germany	11.4	16.3	27.6	33.8
France	8.2	15.6	16.9	28.9
Austria	7.6	13.9	18.0	26.9
Belgium	6.0	13.6	16.5	29.8
Ireland	5.1	11.3	13.1	21.7
Finland	6.7	8.4	10.6	11.3
Italy	5.3	6.4	10.6	12.7

[1] Based on country definitions of part-time work. Data for Belgium, Denmark, Germany, Ireland, Italy and the United Kingdom are from the annual European Labour Force Survey. Data for all other countries are from national labour force surveys.

Source: OECD,1996b, table E.

career model. Rather, in most Western countries some kind of dual breadwinner model has become the norm. Often, given women's lower earnings, this amounts to a one-and-a-half earner model. Furthermore, the different patterns of paid employment in families and households are paralleled by different patterns of provision for care. We lack research on the precise nature of these patterns for different countries and what it is that has given rise to particular configurations. It is not just the pattern of paid work that determines the arrangements for care. In the first place, care may not be the dependent variable. Hakim (1996) has argued strongly that the female labour market is divided into women who are committed to careers and women who see their paid work as secondary, in other words, the pattern of paid labour is a matter of choice. However, the availability of affordable and acceptable alternatives to unpaid care is also crucial. Figure 3.1 suggests some of the possible patterns of male and female paid work and the arrangements for care. In practice, most countries are far from achieving a fully individualized adult worker model, and this has major implications for social provision more generally. Joshi and Davies (1992) have shown that Swedish and French women do much better than British and German women when it comes to the material costs of caring for children.[1]

The erosion of the male breadwinner model has been significant and has had a major impact on the nature of the mixed economy of care, but it is doubtful as to whether it amounts to a revolution in terms of women's employment. Women are still taking responsibility for large amounts of informal care and paying a family penalty that varies between countries. This is important in view of the major shift in thinking at government level about the behaviour of men and women in families. In both the United States and the United Kingdom the new view of work and welfare in the 1980s and 1990s has stressed the obligation of all able citizens to undertake paid work. In the mid-1980s, Mead (1986) made the case in the United States for the State to assert its moral authority in order to insist that welfare recipients fulfill their obligations as citizens by engaging in paid labour. He presented this solution in terms of a model of equal citizenship and something that would bring about greater social integration. Welfare-to-work, implemented first in the United States, embodied these ideas and was applied to all able-bodied adults, lone mothers included. The 1996 Work Responsibility and Personal Opportunities Act in the United States went somewhat further down the yet more radical route charted by Murray (1985), whereby welfare benefits were seen as the root of welfare dependency and forcing recipients into work as the only desirable alternative. But the idea of an adult worker-citizen model has also taken root in social

---

[1] Such a "family penalty" has substantial knock-on effects in terms of the feminization of poverty in old age.

Figure 3.1 Patterns of male and female paid work and arrangements for care

Earning model	Care supplier
1. Male Breadwinner Male full-time earner	Female sole carer
2. Dual Breadwinner (a) Male full-time earner, Female short part-time earner	Mainly female earner and kin
3. Dual Breadwinner (b) Male full-time earner, Female part-time earner	Mainly kin, and state/voluntary/market
4. Dual Breadwinner (c) Male part-time earner, Female part-time earner	Male and female earners
5. Dual Career Male full-time earner, Female full-time earner	Mainly the market, and kin/state/voluntary sector.

democratic European states. It has long had purchase in Sweden, but alongside extensive supports for care, and it has also become central to "Third Way" politics. In the United Kingdom, as Deacon (1998) has suggested, the welfare-to-work programme represents a combination of welfare conceptualized as self-interest, as authority and as moral regeneration.

What appears to have happened is that the increase in women's labour market participation has effected a shift in the male breadwinner model at the level of behaviour, but also at the level of normative expectations. The whole fabric of gender roles, which has been widely assumed – by policy-makers and people – to flow from the model have been thrown into question. The norm now seems to be that women will engage in paid work, but to what extent, is far from clear. Nevertheless, assumptions regarding the male breadwinner model, which clearly informed mid-century policy-making in many Western countries (Lewis, 1992), regardless of the fact that a "pure" male breadwinner model was never achieved by many families even in the 1950s and 1960s, have been replaced by equally firm assumptions regarding the existence of an adult worker model. But again, the model is much simpler than the social reality. Indeed, in making the shift, the assumptions of policy-makers have run considerably ahead of the social reality.

Most of the increase in women's paid work in Western Europe in the post-war period has been in service of the welfare state (in the United States the private service sector has been more important). Much of this employment has been relatively badly paid. The fact that care work is assumed to carry with it emotional rewards is often cited as a reason for the low pay that is also associated with it (Folbre, 1995). James (1989) argued additionally that the more common the type of emotional labour involved, the lower the pay. The stress inherent in emotional labour is conveniently disregarded in these arguments. Graham (1991) has drawn attention to the fact that a dispro-portionate amount of low-paid care work is often carried out by black women, and Walker (1983, p.111) remarked on the "close coincidence of status and interest between elderly dependants and the women they depend on". In other words, carers, whether paid or unpaid, share a dependent status as a result of their restricted access to the labour market and the implications this carries for earnings and pensions.

Indeed, particular kinds of care work have moved between the family, the non-profit sector, the state and the market. Lunches for schoolchildren are a good example. In the period of the expansion of the "classic welfare state" (Lowe, 1993), care work tended to move out of the family and into the public sector. The vast increase of women's employment in Western European countries was largely accounted for by the expansion of human services. In Scandinavia, the initial response was to see such work in terms of "public patriarchy" (e.g. Siim, 1987),[2] the idea being that women were being drawn into the labour market to do the same tasks as they had performed in the home. During periods of public-service retrenchment, it has been possible for governments to "repatriate" care work. For women, movement between the formal and informal care sectors, for whatever reason, exacts a heavy price in terms of lack of career advancement and income and pension contributions foregone (Joshi and Davies, 1992; Harkness and Waldfogel, 1999).

With welfare state restructuring in the 1990s, the conditions of work of many paid carers deteriorated. Research in the United Kingdom has found that two distinct social care labour markets have developed, one employing women on very low wages, with poor working conditions to do routine tasks, usually on a contracted-out basis, and the other employing better qualified women to deliver more specialist services, usually still in the public and voluntary sectors (Ford et al., 1998; Ungerson, 1999). Nor has significant deterioration in the working conditions of paid carers been confined to the United Kingdom (Lewis, 1998). These developments raise further issues about the extent to

---

[2] See also Walby (1997).

which a fully individualized adult worker model may emerge. This underlines the problems of policies that increasingly assume a fully individualized adult worker model, which tends to be optimistic in terms of expectations regarding self-provisioning (especially in terms of pensions).

Anxieties about growing individualism and the implications for care

Alongside this strong emphasis on the obligation to engage in paid work, equally strong arguments have been put forward stressing the importance of the obligation to care. Anxieties about care are part of a much wider set of concerns expressed by academics and policy-makers about what is perceived as growing selfish individualism. Expressed most powerfully in the United States, this has turned into an effort to revive community, neighbourhood, network and connection. Although the term "care" does not figure largely in this broader debate, one of the major fears is that people are no longer prepared to help or make sacrifices for each other. The anxieties are deepest at the level of the family, where it is suggested by much (but not all) of the research that adults are more concerned to pursue their own happiness at the expense of their children.[3] Family breakdown, with the concomitant problems it poses of care for dependants, is attributed to individualism, and the increase in women's employment in particular is seen by a broad spectrum of commentators as the most significant manifestation of growing individualism and a cause, direct or indirect, of breakdown.

Ideas about care have been central to a set of fundamental assumptions about the division of labour and the stability of the family. The rise of the male breadwinner model family as an ideal has long encapsulated the notion of a separation between public and private spheres. Herbert Spencer (1876) argued that the more highly developed the society, the greater would be the differentiation in the roles of men and women (and the more able women would be to produce superior offspring). The public sphere of employment and politics was one of ruthless male competition. The weak were to be cared for by women in the private sphere of the family. In terms of the social reality, this picture described only late nineteenth-century middle-class families. However, as an aspiration it appealed to working men and women as well, not least because of the material conditions in the first half of the twentieth century, when frequent pregnancies, large numbers of surviving children and hard housework carried out without labour-saving devices meant that women who also had to "go out to work" were to be pitied.

---

[3] See Rogers and Pryor (1998) for a review of the evidence on the effects of divorce.

The new "home economics" of the late twentieth century also suggested that men and women make complementary investments in marriage. Becker's (1981) model argued that women (naturally) desired children and looked for a good male breadwinner, while men looked for a good housekeeper and carer. The complementary investments were held to result in higher joint gains. Becker relied on a notion of male altruism in order to argue that the gains made from the gendered division of labour in terms of paid and unpaid work were equally shared. Research on the household division of resources (e.g. Pahl, 1989) showed that in fact this was often not the case and later neo-classical models dropped this assumption, relying instead more heavily on ideas of marital bargaining and exchange (Lundberg and Pollak, 1996). But in all these models, the increase in women's earning power has been held both to disrupt the balance in the gendered division of labour and to threaten the stability of the family.

The point about these kinds of analysis is that they rely on the idea of individuals making rational choices to maximize their rewards and minimize their costs (Cheal, 1991). However, more complicated ideas involving love and duty, desert and reputation may be involved. Finch and Mason's (1993) study of family obligations stressed that while Becker was right in perceiving the essence of commitment to reside in the fact that at some point it becomes too expensive to withdraw, the nature of the expense is not necessarily material.

Sociologists have focused rather more on mentalities and the search for personal growth and development, stressing the growth of an individualism that is inherently selfish. Bellah et al. (1985) opened their influential account of middle American life with a statement as to their concern that "individualism may have grown cancerous" (p. vii). They identified two forms of individualism: first the utilitarian, which amounted to the traditional American desire to "get ahead" and to be self-reliant, and second, the expressive, which emphasized self-expression and the sharing of feelings rather than material acquisition. In respect of the first, they argued that the values of the public sphere – for example, "the coolly manipulative style" (p. 48) that is required to "get-ahead" – were invading the private world of the family. In Bellah et al.'s view, the contractual nature of commercial and bureaucratic life threatened to become an ideology for personal life. Such an anxiety has a long history. The notion of the home as a necessary, caring haven from the rigours of the market-place was central to the ideology of separate spheres.

In respect of expressive individualism, the "therapeutic attitude" threatened to replace notions of obligation and commitment by an ideology of full, open and honest communication between "self-actualizing individuals". Inglehart's (1997) comparative data for economically prosperous countries showed a clear shift from "materialist" values, emphasizing economic and physical security above all, to "post-materialist" priorities, especially self-expression and the quality of life. Yankelovich's (1981) work on survey data from the United States confirmed the shift to more "me-centred" concerns. From this evidence, it seemed that the "duty to self" was becoming primary.

However, not all academic sociologists subscribing to the importance of growing individualism are pessimistic about the effects on other-regarding relations. Giddens (1992) also argued that late twentieth-century relationships amount to "pure relationships", that is, they are "entered into for [their] own sake, for what can be derived by each person from a sustained association with another; and which is continued only in so far as it thought by both parties to deliver enough satisfactions for each individual to stay within it" (p. 35). However, unlike Bellah et al., Giddens does not consider such relationships to be inherently selfish, indeed, he believes that they have served to democratize the family. Nevertheless, they are "contingent" and if a particular relationship does not provide one of the partners with what they seek, then they will move on. Giddens' analysis is different from the pessimists who see growing individualism as primarily selfish, but it is also far from those who seek to construct a care-centred analysis.

The underlying anxiety about increasing individualism, whether expressed in the value-neutral language of the neo-classical economist, the value-conscious language of the sociologist, or in terms of the practical concerns of the politician and the polemicist, centres on its implications for the sources of moral commitments. The atomized individual is unlikely to engage fully with either family or community, which results in an "emptying out" of these fundamental building blocks of society.

Bellah et al. suggested that the therapeutic attitude begins with the self rather than an external set of obligations and that love between "therapeutically self-actualized persons" is incompatible with self-sacrifice. The strong belief in the freedom to choose by what is assumed to be the rational individual actor, unfettered by the regulation that characterized the long period of conservative government in the United Kingdom and the United States in the closing decades of the twentieth century, also played a major part in this process of "emptying out".

Reflecting on the politics of the New Right in the 1980s, Marilyn Strathern (1992) identified the emergence of a "hyper-individualism". Morality, like everything else, became a matter of individual choice and preference; it was to come from within, "but the interior has itself no structure" (p. 159). As Sandel (1996) had already suggested, a person without constitutive attachments is a person wholly without character. Strathern severely questioned the effect of fetishizing individual choice on the person, arguing that individuality becomes fragmented in the face of such a consumerist ideology (see also Gergen, 1991).

Similarly, from a critical feminist perspective Estin (1995) commented on the nature of reforms to family law, which she suggested had been directly influenced by the priority accorded by economists to exchange and bargaining models, to the detriment of social relations. Thus the implementation of no-fault divorce treated men and women as self-interested actors, which, she argued, ignored the extent to which marriage was rooted in love and obligation, sharing and sacrifice, and thus served to contribute to selfish behaviour. Treating people as if they are indeed self-interested may indeed encourage self-interested behaviour (Le Grand, 1997).

The difficulty of exercising choice in a moral and social vacuum has become an increasingly dominant theme in the literature and, as a social problem, unites commentators from very different points on the political spectrum. This compelling and frightening picture of a world in which there is no vision of the common good and in which rampant individualism is in the process of destroying the very foundations – the family and the community – on which the market and modern liberal democracies depend has been widely echoed. Etzioni (1993), for example, talked of a "parenting deficit" and cited data to show that the total time parents spend with their children has dropped 40 per cent in one generation.

The most frequently cited manifestation of the growth of selfish individualism is the increase in women's employment. Feminists have been as likely to endorse a theory that stresses the importance of women's economic independence as right-wing polemicists, but they have stressed women's right and/or need to work. From a rather different political perspective, George Gilder (1987) in the United States and Geoff Dench (1994) in the United Kingdom have seen the increase in women's labour force participation and attachment as something that has stripped men of their traditional breadwinning role with the family, and they blame women for pursuing self-fulfilment in the form of a career at the expense of the welfare of their families. Dench (1994, pp. 16–17) argued strongly that family responsibilities are an indispensable civilizing influence on men: "If women go too far in pressing for symmetry, and in trying to change the rules of the game, men will simply decide not to play... The family may be a myth, but it is a myth that works to make men tolerably useful." In this interpretation, as much blame is attributed to women for undermining the traditional male role of breadwinner as to men themselves. More recently, Fukuyama (1999) has argued that the change in women's employment behaviour has allowed men to behave irresponsibly and opportunistically, leaving their families usually for younger women.

While polemicists railed against what they perceived as selfish behaviour, academics began to try and find ways to talk about the importance of "social glue". Thus Coleman (1988) used the concept of social capital as a way of challenging the rational individual action paradigm. Social capital as a set of informal values and norms permits cooperation and fosters trust (Coleman, 1988; Fukuyama, 1999). Trust and cooperation are held to be learned in the private sphere of the family[4], and pass from there into the public sphere of politics and the market. This is not dissimilar to the long-standing insistence of feminists on the importance of connection and the relational self to women's moral sense (Gilligan, 1982; Held, 1993; Griffiths, 1998). The new-found attention to social capital represents a wider appreciation of the extent to which no one is an "unencumbered self" (Sandel, 1996), and stresses interdependence and hence the obligations people have towards one another.[5] For example, Wolfe (1989) and Anderson (1993) argue that the market and the family are structured by norms that express different ways of valuing people and things and must therefore be kept separate, but this encourages the dichotomous treatment of public and private spheres, which is problematic in respect of the care.

The tenor of this kind of commentary is logically directed towards reversing the increase in women's employment. But most writers do not go so far as to advocate direct curbs on women's work. Fukuyama (1999) relies on a "spontaneous re-norming of society", which he hopes will involve women recognizing the importance of staying at home with young children. Similarly, in the United States, Popenoe (1993) has expressed the hope that women will see fit to stay at home with children under three (no recompense or supports to enable this to happen are mentioned). Galston (1991, p. 281) has gone further and argued that the liberal state has to take action to protect and promote its distinctive conception of the human good: "[r]easonable public arguments for traditionalism" in respect of the family have been, in his view, overlooked. Such arguments in favour of women undertaking more care work are tied to a strong desire to resuscitate the male breadwinner model family. But, as Iris Marion Young (1995) observed in her comments on Galston's proposals, this is effectively to argue that women be prepared to make themselves dependent on men for the sake of their children and others who may be in need of care.

The nature of care work and an ethic of care

In 1981 Parker made an attempt to define care work as "tending" and suggested that it could be divided into four component parts: duration, intensity,

---

[4] Putnam (1993) also stresses the importance of civil society in this respect.

[5] But the solutions favoured by this school tend to be backward-looking, with a strong hankering after the male breadwinner model, and certainly eschew any collective role for the State.

complexity and prognosis. The argument was appealing not least because it meant that care could then be measured and costed. Furthermore, the precise nature of the tasks of tending require careful differentiation. For instance, caring for the physically ill presents different problems from caring for the mentally ill (Levin et al., 1983). Furthermore, caring has its own sequence and biography. The task changes over time and often in response to particular triggers, whether social or physical (Lewis and Meredith, 1988). However, the problem is, as Graham (1999) observed, that it is not possible to divorce the labour of tending from the feelings of love and commitment and the ties of obligation that are usually part and parcel of care in the private sphere of the family. Caring becomes both labour and love because of the way in which the capacity to care for and care about someone else have collapsed. Informal care has been conceptualized most convincingly as a process of "loving, thinking and doing" (Leira, 1993, p.27). As Dalley (1988) noted, "the concentration of multiple functions in the role of mother seems to be at the root of the caring issue". It is therefore not surprising that different family members feel very different levels of obligation to care (Finch and Mason, 1993).

Concern for others is not necessarily some kind of happy altruism. This is not surprising when much of care remains invisible and care work is at best an add-on to the policy agenda. As Gilligan (1982) pointed out, women may also judge themselves by their capacity to care. Thus failure to do so, for whatever reason, commonly induces guilt. On the other hand, given women's often restricted opportunities in respect of paid work, caring – combining as it does labour and love – might appear to be especially worthwhile to many. The injunction to undertake unpaid care is therefore complex and powerful. To treat it as non-market work that women voluntarily choose for its intrinsic satisfaction is inadequate. Land and Rose (1985) have suggested that it is hard to know where the love involved in unpaid caring ends and the "compulsory altruism" begins. The division of work, paid and unpaid, is profoundly unequal between men and women, and while paid work has become more equally shared, unpaid work has not. Given the injunction to care that women experience, they often feel guilt if they do not, but overload as a result of the "double day" if they do.

Informal care is widely believed to be "natural". The models of neo-classical economists assume that women will choose to care (e.g. Becker, 1981). Beginning with children, it is assumed that because women bear them they will also rear them, whereas a man can be a biological parent and not be expected to care for his child on a daily basis. His duty is assumed to be that of provider. Feminist economists have stressed the constraints that bear upon women's decision to care (e.g. Folbre, 1994). Lack of accessible and/or affordable child care will affect women's labour market participation. But the decision to care is more complicated than the presence or absence of affordable substitutes of an acceptable quality. Women in particular may want to care and may also feel obliged to care, for children and for elderly relatives.

Given that family-based care combines labour and love, neo-classical economic explanatory models run into difficulties. Market rationality assumes the existence of independent, competitive individuals who make choices. The rationality of care, on the other hand, assumes connection, relationship and interdependence. In Gilligan's (1982) influential analysis, the feminine personality comes to define itself in relation to and in connection with others more than does the masculine personality, which is defined primarily through separation. In this construction, concern for others rather than self – an "ethic of care" – becomes central to understanding femininity. Gilligan comes close to a biological essentialism that is in turn not dissimilar to the assumptions on the part of neo-classical economists that caring comes "naturally" to women. Other feminist theorists have also depicted women's willingness to care positively, seeing it as part of an intrinsically female culture and value system that is sometimes represented as being of a higher moral order than that of the public sphere (e.g. Elshtain, 1981; Noddings, 1984). These arguments end up in virtually the same place as the communitarians, who are concerned about the growth of individualism, but who are also anxious to maintain a strict division between the State and civil society.

However, the development of an ethic of care does not have to depend on an elaboration of gender difference. Almost 20 years ago Coote (1981) asked how we should care and provide for our children, pointing out that if this, rather than questions about, say, how to achieve economic growth, was allowed to take centre stage, then the whole approach to economic and social policy would shift profoundly. Some of the more recent work on the ethics of care has endeavoured to develop a care-centred approach that goes beyond care as activity and care as love and obligation to see care as a central social process, a human activity and a moral orientation and to propose policies that enable people to develop their capacity to care (Tronto, 1993; Svenhuijsen, 1998; 1999).[6] Tronto (1993) proposed four ethical elements of care:

a) "care about", which establishes the need for care and may be summarized as "attentiveness" to care;
b) "care for", meaning the taking of responsibility for care;
c) "care of", which amounts to the daily tasks of tending; and
d) "care receiving", which is interpreted as responsiveness to care.

---

[6] See also Nussbaum and Glover, 1995.

The perspective underlying this formulation of care amounts to a different world-view, which starts from connection and relationship rather than from the individual. Such attempts to theorize care draw the conclusion that the caring ethic should become the property of men as well as women.

Policy implications

Whether care is paid or unpaid it cannot be understood simply in terms of activity, tasks or tending. The love and duty that are involved are powerful elements of care work. The injunction to care is felt more powerfully by most women than by most men and explains why women have tended to add their increasing hours of paid work onto unpaid care work. However, it is the understanding of care as a process of human activity and moral orientation that makes it possible to challenge the policy-making discourse and to seek "equal billing" for care in the policy debate. The literature that develops an ethic of care proposes an alternative model of relationship and connection and makes a strong case for enabling all human beings to care. While the arguments for and against full individualization, together with the policy trend towards assuming an adult worker model, signal the importance of treating care as work in order to securely value it, the arguments that take a care-centred perspective highlight the importance of time to care and the sharing out of care work. Unpaid care work is unequally shared between men and women, which has substantial implications for women's position in the labour market. Given the lack of good quality affordable care in the formal sector, many women have little option but to continue to provide it informally,[7] and to depend to some extent on a male wage. Nevertheless, a significant number of female carers want to prioritize care, or feel that it is right to do so. Men currently do not have the opportunity to do the same.

Anything to do with care tends to be poorly valued. Wages in the formal sector are low and benefits and allowances for carers in the informal sector are also low. This means both that in a world in which individualization and the capacity for self-provisioning is increasingly being assumed by policy-makers, carers are profoundly disadvantaged. It also means that care continues to be associated with women rather than with both the sexes (Leira, 1998). For example, the German social care insurance scheme for adult dependants offers elderly people services or a cash payment. Most claimants choose the latter and then route the money through to the female carers who have hitherto been providing care on an unpaid basis (Evers et al., 1997). It is difficult to know

---

[7] Land and Rose (1985) referred to this as "compulsory altruism".

whether this outcome should be seen positively as a step towards recognizing unpaid care work, or as a policy that reinforces women's traditional role.

Policies based on an ethic of care that stresses the desirability of men and women being able to care must be attentive to the issue of how care is shared. It is important that both men and women have the possibility of genuine choice, and that women can also choose employment, especially given that their welfare increasingly depends on their own efforts. Care policies may promote the traditional division of labour associated with the male breadwinner model or they may promote a more equal division of labour. Conservative and communitarian commentators tend to favour cash allowances as a means of recognizing care (Morgan, 1995). Thus Coleman (1993, 1995) has advocated "bounties" that would both compensate parents[8] for the costs of child care and reward good childrearing outcomes. Cash benefits and allowances are often promoted as a means of permitting women greater choice as to whether to care at home or to hire a carer and work outside the home. In practice, the choice is usually a figment, because the costs of choosing one option over another are not equal.

The provision of care services in the formal sector tends to work in the reverse direction, providing paid employment for women and allowing female carers to enter the labour market. Bradshaw et al.'s (1996) cross-national study of lone mothers' employment showed affordable child care to be the key variable explaining the differences in employment rates between the countries. But accessibility and quality are also key. In fact, genuine choice between caring work and employment requires the provision of both cash and services. A carer with children under school age, requires good child-care services to carry on working, which even in EU countries are available only in the Scandinavian countries, Italy, France and Belgium. To have a genuine option of taking parental leave, the carer must be able to return to her job and to receive cash compensation at a high replacement level. Furthermore, if care is to be shared and capacities for caring work are to be developed for all human beings, then men must be allowed to take leave and be recompensed. In Norway and Sweden, part of parental leave is reserved for the father and is lost if he does not take it. A policy such as parental leave can be implemented such that it promotes female labour market exit (as in Germany) or as a way of promoting greater gender equality in respect of paid and unpaid work.

In a world where dignity as well as welfare in the broadest sense derives mainly from wages, it is crucial that care is valued. Some fear that commodification will undermine the motivation that inspires care (Himmelweit, 1995). But if care is not valued, it is degraded and exploitative. The argument that

---

[8] Strangely, Coleman (1995) has denied that his scheme carries any gender implications.

73

gender justice requires care to be properly valued is strong (Bubeck, 1995; Nelson, 1999). Given the convergence towards an adult worker model it is necessary to think more closely about how a balance between paid and unpaid work is to be achieved. It is useful to look at the Scandinavian and American models in this regard as well. Both have a fully individualized, adult-worker model. However, in the case of the United States, the obligation to enter the labour market is embedded in a residual welfare system that often borders on the punitive, whereas in Denmark and Sweden it is supported by an extensive range of care entitlements in respect of children and older people. The position of lone mothers – always a border case for the study of social policy – is particularly instructive in this respect because of the problem of combining unpaid care work and employment. The United States has gone much more wholeheartedly than the United Kingdom down the road of treating these women as available for work, imposing time-limited benefits. Employment rates of lone mothers are high in the United States; the push factor is strong. But employment rates are higher still in Denmark and Sweden and lone mothers' poverty rates are much lower than in the United Kingdom or the United States. Indeed, Sweden comes closest to having achieved Mead's ideal in that all adult citizens are obliged to engage in paid work in order to qualify for a wide range of benefits, which then permit them to leave the labour market. However, Swedish lone mothers get almost as much income from the State as they do from earnings (Lewis, 1998). The system is based on a commitment to universal citizenship entitlements, rather than, as in the United States, grafting equal citizenship obligations on to a residual welfare model.

Put simply, the Scandinavian model recognizes care. All able-bodied adults are treated as citizen-workers, but after that permission to exit the labour market in order to care with wage replacement is granted, and formal care services are provided. In effect, Denmark and Sweden operate a similar sex equality model to the United States, but their systems have the capacity to graft on respect for difference that manifests itself in the form of an unequal division of care work (Lewis and Astrom, 1992). The family penalty experienced by female carers is less than in most other countries, although there is still a penalty to be paid for moving between the models outlined in figure 3.1. For Sweden has one of the most sexually segregated labour markets in the Western world, which brings us back to the issue of sharing care. In any case, until men do more care work, in all probability it will not be valued any more highly. Creighton (1999) has concluded that policies to address this aspect of care are vital. At the supra-national level, the OECD (1991) promoted the idea of combining work and care for men and women almost a decade ago, a policy also promoted by some EU countries (for example, in the Netherlands with its

"Combination Scenario" produced by the Committee for Future Scenarios set up by the Minister of Social Affairs).

It needs to be recognized that care work has to be done. While birth rates are falling in most European countries, the proportion of frail elderly people is increasing; those aged 85 and over are projected to grow threefold by 2050 in the United Kingdom, where the dependency ratio is not now so unfavourable, (Royal Commission, 1999). An adult worker model ignores the provision of care at its peril. Without access to affordable, good quality support for care, women may resist the injunction to full individualization so far as they are able, or a substantial lack of welfare may be visited on dependants, young and old.

PART II

CARE IN DEVELOPING COUNTRIES

DEVELOPMENT, FREEDOM AND CARE: THE CASE OF INDIA

4

Umadevi Sambasivan

Introduction

A New Delhi newspaper recently reported that a father and mother "in their 70s" were thrown out of their house by their three sons and daughters-in-law and had been on the street for more than a week. This was because the sons wanted the property to be divided and given to them immediately. Luckily the house was in the name of the father and, as someone from the neighbourhood got hold of a news reporter who flashed this in the newspaper, the Human Rights Commissioner appeared on the scene and promised legal help. As a result, the children realized that they could be sued for their action and apologized to their parents and took them back home.

Ammal, living with her daughter in Kerala state, received the widow's pension from the state government. Her son-in-law pressured her to part with her life's savings of 11,000 Rupees, earned by working as a cook in rich households – to buy a colour TV. As a result she was forced to leave her daughter's house to go back to working as a cook for someone else.

Meenakshi, a single woman and university professor, left Delhi in search of her roots in the small town of Trivandrum. Unable to look after her mother back in Delhi, who had suffered a stroke, a sense of guilt had her care for another lady unrelated to her. Meanwhile, five childless relatives over 70 with the financial means to support themselves also relocated to Trivandrum. The arrangement with Meenakshi was that they would have their own separate establishments but be under her overall care; if any of them became ill, they would move to Meenakshi's house where there was a paid helper to take care of the household. If any became bedridden, a trained home nurse would also be employed. But Meenakshi's professional career required her to go abroad for two years. She could neither leave the old people alone nor with the paid helper so each had to move to other relatives in other towns, a painful upheaval at their age. One aunt went to live with her sister, herself 75 years old and her 80-year-old husband suffering from Parkinson's disease. Another aunt went to her niece of 60 who was looking after both her own 80-year-old mother and her eight-year-old grandson because her daughter-in-law, an engineer, had been transferred far away.

These three cases reveal the plight of the elderly in India. Each points to the way individualism has found its way into Indian society, irrespective of class, region or caste. The case of Ammal shows how consumerism is redefining the relationship of the old and the young. The younger generation would like to spend the savings of the earlier generation on the purchase of consumer goods. The third case draws our attention to the fact that even those who want to take care of the elderly are constrained by the nature of their work and career (and in many cases due to the need to migrate), which makes it difficult to provide care for the elderly, the sick and children. The first case shows how in a metropolis like Delhi, civil society came to the rescue of an elderly couple.

Development policies, modernization and industrialization are turning the non-modern societies of the Third World, which are based on a different system of knowledge and a different concept of the self, into a more individualistic society. The biggest onslaught of the pursuit of competitive individualism is on the provision of care, in particular the care of the elderly and children. The aim of this chapter is to discuss the implications of development policies promoting individualism in Third World countries, and in particular India, for the provision of care for children and the elderly.

Individualism and care in industrialized countries

It is important to note that, while India is by virtue of development policies moving towards an individualistic society, sociologists, psychotherapists, economists and feminists in the advanced industrialized societies are expressing concern about the consequences faced by their own societies from the pursuit of external freedom and competitive individualism to the neglect of a communal life. The so-called advanced societies are faced with the problem of combining the pursuit of individual freedom with the preservation of a communal life. What should be the nature of the family? How can care be provided without jeopardizing the freedom gained by women? How can people have plenty and yet not be trapped by consumerism and overwork?

The marketization of non-economic functions is placing greater pressures on the individual. Freedom is turning out to be a mechanism of coercion. Freedom based on disembodied reason alone has led to the depletion of all institutions that formerly protected the life-world. Thus some suggest that the way of life has to be transformed to restore the organic relationship between human beings and the biosphere (Bellah, 2000). If individuality is extolled and each person rings himself with a fence of rights, then he also faces isolation. As Bergmann (1977, p. 10) says, "alienation may be a completely inevitable by-product of 'freedom' and discussions of the modern 'loss of community' will be mawkish as long as they do not acknowledge that individuality and community do tend to exclude each other, that the space occupied by one will be taken from the other".

How has this form of individualism impacted on care? With individual fulfilment ranking higher than ever before, the family as an institution has suffered the most. The nuclear family, which provided space for "emotional intimacy of the heterosexual couple, their sexual life, and socialization of the children", is unable to keep itself intact (Bellah, 2000). But alternative arrangements for the care of children have not been worked out. Recourse to paid care is beset with new sets of problems, particularly if the caregiver is recruited from certain ethnic groups or from the Third World (developed countries passing on care work to women from the developing countries). "It is factually wrong and morally insensitive to blame these changes in the family on 'women's liberation' – returning women to a situation where they lack legal rights – so as to 'save the family' would be not only repugnant to women but wholly incompatible with the current understanding of the dignity befitting any human being." (Bellah, 1991, p. 46).

Although no one is able to say that the modern nuclear family is the only possibility for raising children, many are trying to understand the changes in society that are making such a family unattainable and whether they can be altered. Family is under pressure from the state as well as the economy (Bellah, 2000).

Much rethinking of the "family" is being undertaken by sociologists as well as by feminist scholars. One such attempt is by Barrie Thorne (1982), a sociologist and feminist, showing that feminist positions on the family that devalue its importance have been easily enlisted to serve the interests of the State. Another feminist scholar voices her concern by pointing out the difference between "a theory of individuality that recognizes the importance of the individual within the social collectivity" and "the ideology of individualism that assumes a competitive view of the individual". According to this view, the feminist theory of liberation must take account of this difference and not fall prey to the latter view (Eisenstein, 1981, p. 5). Bell Hooks (1984), a feminist who is very critical of the feminist theory emanating from "privileged women at the center", argues that:

The ideology of "competitive, atomistic liberal individualism" has permeated feminist thought to such an extent that it undermines the potential radicalism of feminist struggle. Feminist activists need to affirm the importance of family as a kinship structure that can sustain and nourish people; to graphically address links between sexist oppression and family disintegration, and to give examples, both actual and visionary, of the way family life is and can be when unjust authoritarian rule is replaced with an ethic of communalism, shared responsibility, and mutuality. The movement to end sexist oppression is the only social change movement that will strengthen and sustain family life in households (p. 8).

The problem is that the family, of whatever type, has been the location of power and oppression as well as of love, care, and nurture. The challenge is to see how this institution can cater to the latter without becoming a tool of oppression. Pursuit of competitive individualism is not the answer because the ultimate aim of ending power and oppression is to move towards an ethic of love and caring.

The development of freedom philosophy (Sen, 1999), with its emphasis on competitive individualism, has also led to an extreme form of consumerism, greed and materialism. As a result, in some quarters, there is growing dissatisfaction with "the work-and-spend culture". A study by Juliet Schor (1998) shows that nearly one-fifth of all adult Americans have made a voluntary life-style change by "downshifting". Another 12 per cent were involuntarily downshifted by losing a job or getting a pay cut. People have started looking for happiness "inside" and have been adopting a simpler way of life. This clearly shows that development linked to individualism and freedom should not necessarily be equated with progress. There are more collective, self-transcending, care-oriented human "outcomes" (ways of being, ways of raising children) that have strengths but are being undermined by economic development of this type.

These issues are very relevant for Third World countries in general and for India in particular, since their model of development is the same as that of the advanced industrialized countries. This path of development places a premium on individualism. However, the consequences of the pursuit of individualism in Indian society are more severe because culturally the concept of self in India is different from that in the West. There is, therefore, a case for building a different path of development for India, one which takes account of the familial self as opposed to the individualistic self, to promote the growth of a care-oriented society. It is worthwhile comparing and contrasting the concept of self in the East with that in the West. It is also interesting to see how the concept of the familial self is instilled from childhood, through child-care practices in India, and how the cultivation of such a self in itself becomes a resource for care of the elderly.

The familial self in India

Indian thought interprets human relations in terms of the debt which individuals owe one another. This conception postulates a social structure and relationship in terms of human obligation as prior to human rights and as arising out of them. The idea of community expresses the basic truth of human relations. Community is a more inclusive conception than the State. The consciousness of freedom therefore unites the right means with the right ends in action (Nikam, 1959).

Culture theorists like Geertz (1975), Johnson (1985), Roland (1988) and several others have recognized the differences in the construction of the self in the West and East. According to Geertz (1975, p. 48), "Westerners see themselves as individuals who are 'bounded unique' with a more or less integrated motivational and cognitive universe organized into a distinctive whole set contrastively both against other such wholes and against a social and natural background." Indians, on the other hand, see themselves as parts of a whole, hierarchically determined, collective social order, inseparable from their social context and their relationships. They are interdependent rather than independent, and much of their motivation and cognition arises in the context of their relationships and obligations (Dumont, 1980).

If self is comprised of both self and object, with self as subject being the internal state and self as object being the externally related self, Westerners see self and object as divided but Easterners see themselves as unitary beings, simultaneously subject and object (Johnson, 1985). The implications are that Easterners tend to identify with phenomena (Shearer, 1993) and Westerners tend to see divisions between themselves and phenomena.

Roland (1988) contrasts the characteristics of Eastern, predominantly familial self and Western, predominantly individual self. According to him, the inner representations of self are different for Indians and Westerners. The latter have a strong differentiation of self-other but for the former the self-other images are "interconnected and suffused with affect" (Roland, 1988, p. 225). Goodman (1996), quoting Roland, contrasts the monistic imagery of the inner "we" or relational "I" with the Western dualistic "I-you" imagery:

Indian we-self images are multifaceted and organized hierarchically in the context of the extended family, the group and the *jati*. Westerners tend to strive for the development of strong ego boundaries in order to form relationships which are characterized by separation, privacy and autonomy. In contrast, permeable ego boundaries are suitable for relationships in the more symbiotic mode, characterized by "giving and asking, of caring for and depending on, of influencing and being influenced, of close, warm, emotional connectedness and interdependence. The centrality of relationships completely transcends any other considerations of separate or individualized self" (1988, p. 226).

In India, individuation is not relevant in the social realm (Roland, 1988). According to Goodman (1996, p. 80), it is manifest in the inner life of the private self, where fantasy or spiritual life are activated in retreat from the world. The individual self of the inner life is subordinated to and kept in check by the familial self. Fulfilment of personal wishes is renounced in deference to the needs of others and the group. On the spiritual level, individuation increases later in life after social obligations of the householder stage have been fulfilled.

Furthermore, "the permeability of the boundaries of the Hindu self", as pointed out by Goodman (1996, p. 72) heightens the influence of interpersonal interactions on the "transactional self". For example, the concept of *samskara*, which refers to the imprint of actions and experiences that effect the inner transformation, is the result of the influence and interactions with others upon the self. Contact with gross substance is to be avoided. A transformation of the self from the gross to the subtle and the divine state of the *atman* leads to the ultimate goal of liberation or *moksha*. Thus culturally, human development for Indians is not merely literacy and an increase in life expectancy and income but the transformation of the self from the gross to the subtle. Prime place is accorded to spirituality (not to be equated with religion and mere rituals) or the inner contemplative side of life, which in development policies is belittled, derided, and understood as underdevelopment.

In fact, in India child-care practices are based on the goal of inner freedom. Children are brought up to understand interdependence and are not encouraged to work for individual freedom in the social realm. Some of these practices are very similar to ones being worked out by some thinkers in the West, those who are disenchanted with the extreme competitive individualism of their society as promoted by education and other child-rearing practices.

The self and child-care practices in India

Based on an understanding of the self in Hindu philosophy, Goodman (1996) presents the findings of her field data collected through observation and interviews conducted in Mysore (India). She shows how each of the ceremonies performed during the first year after a baby's birth, such as the first visit to the temple, the cradle ceremony, the naming ceremony and the first year ceremony, leads to the formation of the familial self. For example:

The first time the Hindu baby leaves the house after birth is to go to the temple where offerings are given and the baby is prostrated before the god. This act of prostration serves to inculcate humility and teach a gesture of self-abnegation and deference to others in a more exalted position starting in the first days of life and continuing lifelong. Learning this attitude starts with a physical act of holding the baby's body and in time becomes a stance carried intrapsychically (Goodman, 1996, p.93).

Similarly, Goodman highlights the fact that a child has no name until the naming ceremony takes place. This, according to her, is an interesting comment on the "non-individuality of the infant":

It is religious authority that confers the status of personhood that a name grants. This is in keeping with Hindu ideas of self and *karma* wherein spiritual forces determine destiny and rebirth. Powers of agency or initiative lie in *karmic* forces and the collective group rather than the individual. Similarly, the religious or astronomical names are given before the individual name. The religious precepts have profound consequences for the formation of the collective self. Messages about collective values emphasizing the predominance of the group over the individual and encouraging a sense of interrelatedness and interdependence permeate physical acts of care taking from the first days of life. Collectivist beliefs permeate acts of socialization and affect the process of self-other differentiation (Goodman, 1996, p. 99).

Among the beliefs in the acts of socialization, Goodman (pp. 99–101) lists the following:

a) from an early age in basic acts of daily life the child is shown that nothing can be accomplished alone. For example, more than one woman is required for bathing the baby, more than one person feeds the baby. Only breast-feeding is left totally to the mother;

b) women caregivers are largely interchangeable in their child-rearing functions. Female relatives contribute as a team to provide such basic care as feeding, bathing, and holding the infant. This interchangeability tends to de-emphasize the individual's importance. Not even the primary emotional ties with the mother are allowed to interfere with the smooth functioning of the joint family as a unit. Goodman (1996, p. 100) argues that, "the whole object of socialization in India is to encourage the child to renounce infantile pleasures and special ties with the mother in order to be accepted into full membership in the larger family group";

c) caregivers act as extensions of the child, providing vital support by holding, feeding, and cleaning up after the baby without complaint until the baby is fully ready to accomplish that function. There is no pressure toward or even encouragement of independent functioning. Thus a sense of interpersonal boundaries between the baby and the caregiver is blurred during the first and second years of life;

d) there is an active discouragement of physical autonomy or separate functioning;

e) young babies are gratified as much as possible because they are considered to be gods and treated as such. Another reason for providing gratification as the baby turns into a toddler is in order to avert the development of assertion or wilfulness, which would tend to increase a sense of separateness or I-awareness, *ahamkara*;

f) breast-feeding of the child sometimes continues for four to seven years. When children start eating solid food, mothers feed them by putting the morsel of food directly into the child's mouth. This act is again seen by

Goodman (1996, p. 111) as de-emphasizing even "somatic self-other differentiation, blurring physical boundaries". Sleeping arrangements are also communal. Children most often sleep in the same bed as their parents. At least until the age of eight the children are never allowed to sleep alone. In the West, learning to sleep alone is part of becoming an independent person and children are expected to sleep separately from their parents and alone from birth. Indians teach their children to walk while supporting them. Here again "the child perceives that learning to walk does not depend on individual effort, but is a cooperative effort which depends on the help of their parents. Thus the achievement of the child is under-played while the interdependence of the child and the family group is reinforced."(ibid.).

From the very beginning, therefore, a hierarchical relationship is developed between the young and the old. Besides, as Stephen Marglin points out, a non-modern society like India is based on a system of knowledge which he terms *techne*, as opposed to *episteme*, on which modern societies are based. Contrasting the societies based on these two systems of knowledge, he shows that in the societies based on *techne* there is a hierarchical power relationship within, while this is reversed in the case of the societies based on *episteme* (Marglin and Marglin, 1996). While there is an egalitarian relationship between people within the *episteme* knowledge system, it claims superiority over those falling outside its system. The way knowledge is transmitted and modified in the two systems also differs. In societies based on *techne*, the master passes on the knowledge to the apprentice. It is not a purely verbal and cerebral exercise as in the case of modern societies based on *episteme*. Similarly, in the case of the former, modifications to knowledge are made through a commentary on earlier texts and not by way of criticism as in the case of the latter. Thus in craft-based societies like that of India based on *techne*, a special place is accorded to the elderly and their experience. The son would respect the father as much as the apprentice would the master. Thus the old were made to feel needed, and just as the infants were taken care of by all other women rather than by their mother alone, so the elderly were cared for by the extended family and the community as a whole. Today in India, *episteme* as a system of knowledge has come to dominate *techne*. How did this happen?

The relationship of self and freedom with society and community in India was first assailed under colonial rule, and now the concept of economic development, by promoting competition and greed and the development of a consumerist society, is rapidly eroding this conception of self and freedom. This is not to suggest that there was no oppression in the family and society in India before colonialism. But resorting to development as freedom (of the purely external variety) will not end oppression. In modern Indian society, for example in child care, considerable authority is given to the paediatrician, whose "advice can supersede not only that of the priest, but also that of the grandmother when it comes to prescribing correct diet and care of the infant" (Goodman, 1996, p. 114). Who is to assess that the paediatrician's knowledge is superior to that of the grandmother? If it is not, how does one guard against the danger of the modern system of medicine becoming oppressive? With women and men taking paid employment outside the home other questions arise: would it be possible to continue the child-care practices described by Goodman? If not, what is the way out?

In an alternative type of development, the paediatrician, grandmother and the priest would have to enter into a dialogue. The paediatrician, instead of being arrogant about his knowledge-system, would have to lend an ear to the "other system" and then prescribe judiciously. Paediatricians should not be done away with but they should get acquainted with local practices. For example, several local practices for immunization are not only cost-effective but are also without side-effects. Similarly, post-natal care of the mother and child and the baby's food vary not only from region to region in India, depending on the climatic conditions and availability of resources, but also across caste and community, based on dietary habits.

The elderly in Indian society

Similarly, in this system of philosophy, the elderly are supposed to withdraw from the world in what is termed the *vanaprastha ashram*, the fourth stage of one's life – the other three being: *brahmacharya* (student), *grahasta* (house-holder) and *sanyas* (recluse) (Ramanujam, 1989). In this stage of life, a person has to learn not to interfere in the affairs of their children but at the same time they are expected to be available for advice when called upon. In the description of child-rearing practices given above, we saw that elderly women in the household participated in bathing the child. In this and numerous other ways the elderly members of the household are given roles and status in every social and religious practice, so that they do not feel that they are not useful to others. Life is thus meaningful for the elderly, which is not the case in many retirement homes. It is not enough to give money or other facilities for senior citizens; it is equally important to make them feel that they are needed.

In India, culturally and philosophically, the elderly are respected and continue to be useful members of society but, given the way work and production are organized in modern society, it is becoming difficult to maintain this tradition. Even today in India the non-modern sector exists alongside the modern. The former is poor but continues to have a community life and the elderly are taken care of by their family and community. But the growth of the modern sector is continually eroding the community in the non-modern sector. In the modern sector the rich can resort to paid care, but in the non-modern sector once the community is destroyed, provision of care, particularly for the elderly, suffers badly. Any public policy providing care and security for the elderly in India would have to take into account the needs of these two sectors separately – modern and non-modern. Their needs are different. A large part of the non-modern sector can be found in rural areas and in the informal, unorganized sector of the economy.

The non-modern sector is still based on *techne* and is craft centred. It is also home based. As a result not only are both men and women productively employed, having scope for creative work, but both are able to manage care of the elderly and children. But when the young migrate to the modern sector in search of jobs, care of the elderly becomes a problem. Greater commercialization and growth of individualism is posing a threat to this community. The aim of public policy for the care of the elderly in this sector should be to see how the community can be kept alive and protected from the onslaught of modernization and individualism. All support should be extended to the community to enable it to continue to extend support to the elderly. However, one would have to also ensure that the powerful in the community do not take advantage, and for that, institutions would have to be created to keep a check on them.

Problems faced by the elderly in the modern sector in India are similar to those of their counterparts in advanced industrialized countries. A philosophy of competitive individualism is taking hold of the young in this sector. Moreover, care of the elderly in the modern sector is also likely to be affected owing to the migration of young software professionals to the United States, Europe and Australia as a result of globalization. The elderly in this sector are likely to make recourse to paid care. Some may migrate to the country in which their children live. Migration policies at the international level should, therefore, take into account the needs of the elderly left behind or taken along by the young migrants.

In the Indian state of Kerala, where life expectancy at birth is high, the fertility rate is low and there is a high level of migration to the Middle East, many homes for the elderly have sprung up. Many NGOs are also training women as home nurses. In those upper middle-class households, where women go out to paid work, home nurses are employed to look after the sick and the elderly. However, in this arrangement the elderly are made to feel that they are a burden on their children and do not get the status they enjoyed in the traditional system described above.

Conclusion

The pursuit of inner freedom and a society that values care are not possible in an economic system that produces on a large scale, with its urge for constantly increasing productivity guided mainly by the profit motive, irrespective of its adverse impact on the environment. Such a system of production turns human beings into robots. The focus of the development debate would thus have to shift from culture to the system of production. Is the system of production that has come to exist since the industrial revolution human? Custom and tradition in Eastern society may be oppressive but a switch to the system of production emanating from the industrial revolution brings with it newer forms of exercising power that sometimes reinforce rather than eliminate the older ones,

Therefore, the alternative model of development would have to work for a different system of production and consumption, where wants and activities or consumption and production are organically connected – not artificially through advertisement and other marketing strategies. In this type of development, "work" would not be so demeaning that the self becomes empty, only to be filled by the compulsive urge to buy more and more, irrespective of the need. A care-rich society can be built only around a system of production in which work and life are not separated, where labour is not merely a painful exertion but a joyful experience. Labour in such a society should be oriented towards the production of life and not merely the production of things and wealth as the goal of work. Such a concept of labour also has a different conception of time, in which time spent on burdensome labour and that spent on leisure are not separated; rather, times of work and of rest and enjoyment are to be alternated and interspersed. It stresses maintenance of work as a direct and sensual interaction with nature, organic matter and living organisms. The most important characteristic of work should be its purposefulness and usefulness (Mies, 1986; Schumacher, 1997). Care and relationships are built into such a system – care for the young, the old, the sick and for everything animate and inanimate. Love, not competition, is the basis of such a society. The "ideal worker" should also be provided with time for caring activities.

In such an attempt the developing countries are not alone. Frithjof Bergmann initiated the movement for "new work" in the United States. This movement attempts to minimize "job-work" and provide the possibility of spending part of the time pursuing a "paid calling". The members of this group are expected to train themselves in the gestation of ideas, and the presumption is that they live in a society in which valuable ideas are encouraged and supported in a colourful variety of ways; so any number of people might say that they will seek support for one of their "callings" and, in exchange for that, relinquish their claim to one of the currently endangered part-time jobs. "The indispensable condition for any Economic Freedom is the freedom to say No to a new technology, No to new line of products, No to a yet more concocted line of 'services', No to Goliath-corporations. Even when they dangle the promise of jobs" (Bergmann, 2000, pp. 501–502).

This comes close to the craft-based society in India where "work" and "caring" could take place simultaneously.

EARLY CHILDHOOD CARE AND DEVELOPMENT IN INDIA: SOME POLICY ISSUES

5

Rekha Wazir

Introduction

The Indian child has not figured prominently in government policies and programmes, nor in societal debates over developmental rights, entitlements and practices. In general, the care and education of children has reflected the capabilities and orientations of the parents. In this way, parental poverty and disadvantage have affected the early life experiences of children, damaging their growth and development, affecting their sense of well-being, compromising their future and, in extreme cases, leading to early death. However, there is mounting evidence of an ever-widening space for potential interventions benefiting children, and an increasing recognition that such interventions matter and can transform the life chances of children, and indeed also of their families. This paper focuses on the care needs of children in India with a view to highlighting ongoing debates in this subject and raising key policy issues.[1]

The case for ECCD

The inclusive concept of ECCD which refers to the whole range of activities that promote the care, socialization and education of children – be they in the home, in the community, in centres or in school – is used in preference to the narrower term child care. The latter is generally used to describe services for pre-school-age children that take place in group settings outside the home, such as in a crèche, kindergarten, day-care centre or nursery. But not all child care takes place in institutional settings outside the home. Many children are looked

---

[1] This paper draws on an earlier version (co-authored with Nico van Oudenhoven): "Early childhood care and development in India: Policy perspectives", presented to the workshop on "Women workers: An agenda for the future", 19–20 Mar. 2001, organized by the Study Group on Women Workers and Child Labour, National Commission on Labour, New Delhi.

after at home by mothers, older relatives and siblings, and many others are taken care of in informal arrangements outside the home. From a policy perspective, it is useful to use this wide interpretation as it gives due recognition to the needs of all carers – professional and family. It also acknowledges the relationship of ECCD to larger social issues such as child rights, parental health and education, women's employment, poverty alleviation and community development.

Early childhood, as defined by ECCD, covers the period from birth until the age of 6–8, depending on the age at which the child enters school. Children under 8 are usually divided into three age groups: 0–3, 3–5, and 5–6/8-year-olds. Each period calls for its own specific set of interventions and responses and each context sets its own conditions. The perinatal period, which starts at conception and ends with the birth of the child, is also included in this comprehensive definition of ECCD. This is justified by the fact that the society, culture and economy into which the child is born will determine to some extent the future of the child. For instance, the prevalence of gender bias in a society will influence attitudes and values towards girl children within the family and determine not only their well-being but also their very survival. The likelihood of girl children falling prey to sex selective foeticide, infanticide and neglect is high in these systems.

The health, nutrition, education and status of the mother will also have a bearing on the future of the child, as will the family's access to health services, safe water, housing and employment. A malnourished mother is likely to give birth to a low birth weight child. With a literate mother, children will be better nourished, more likely to go to school and attain higher levels, and live in families with fewer siblings, who are also better spaced. It is obvious, then, that quality of care, interaction and education provided during this period – whether by parents or outside the home – will have an impact on the healthy growth, development and school readiness of the child. Early intervention programmes are also associated with longer-term benefits to children in the form of higher employment, higher earnings, lower criminal behaviour, reduced delinquency and higher literacy levels.[2] The case for ECCD has been made quite systematically and it is now widely acknowledged that the early months and years are crucial for the future of the individual.

The child's family and community also benefit from ECCD. The availability of day care can facilitate the entry of mothers into employment. Women's

---

[2] The High/Scope Perry Preschool Study is the most frequently quoted study on the benefits of ECCD programmes. It has followed two groups of randomly divided African-American children living in the same neighbourhood since the 1960s. One group attended a good quality pre-school programme while the other received no pre-school services. These two groups were assessed annually from ages 3–11, at age 14–15 and then again at 19 and 27. At age 19, the programme group had significantly higher general literacy levels than the control group (Schweinhart et al., 1993).

participation in the labour force is on the increase, as is their entry into informal-sector employment, which is typically low paying and exploitative.[3] Other social trends, such as the breakdown of traditional extended family support systems, and growing urbanization and migration, also make the provision of affordable, convenient and safe childcare services a priority area for working women and sometimes a crucial factor in their ability to participate in income-generating activities.

In developing countries early childhood programmes can make an important contribution to releasing siblings from childcare responsibilities and allowing them to attend school. Where suitable arrangements for child care are not available, infants may be left in the care of older siblings – generally girls – who are frequently little more than children themselves. The quality of care provided in such arrangements is at best inadequate, and likely to have a detrimental effect on the healthy development of both sets of children. It has the added disadvantage of depriving the older children of educational opportunities.

ECCD is increasingly being viewed as a force for reducing poverty and creating equality in society. The latest statement from the United Nations Children's Fund (UNICEF) (2001, p.43) on this subject claims that "To break [the] cycles of poverty, violence, and disease, interventions must come early in life, the earlier the better. ECCD is the key to a full and productive life for a child and to progress for a nation." There is also a growing trend, spearheaded by organizations like the World Bank, to justify investments in ECCD especially in terms of cost-benefit calculations, cost savings and economic outcomes. It is argued that ECCD leads to increased employment and economic productivity in later life.

These claims need to be duly qualified. International research confirms that children from disadvantaged groups benefit more from early intervention programmes than those from advantaged backgrounds. However, these studies also reveal that these early gains taper off after some time (Boocock, 1995). It is obvious, then, that while ECCD programmes can help to narrow the educational gap for children from low-income families, they cannot compensate for the poverty of the parents, nor for the deficits of the school system and the environment in which they live.

The claim that ECCD programmes can be a force for creating equity in society should also be treated with caution. If the provision of early childhood care and education is not universal nor of equal effectiveness, children may be set on a track early in life which leads them away rather than towards equality. In India, as in most countries, early education facilities reflect the inequalities

---

[3] Women's labour force participation is not only increasing but forms the bulk of labour force growth in many countries. Women's labour force growth has been substantially higher than men's labour force growth since 1980 in all regions except Africa (ILO, 1998).

inherent in society in terms of the stereotypes and biases against girls, specific socio-economic, ethnic, religious or language groups, or the physically and mentally handicapped.

This leads to the related issue of quality, which is a recurring debate in the discussion on ECCD interventions. The proponents claim that only high-quality care will succeed in promoting the healthy development of children. But if quality is defined as the use of highly trained and motivated teachers or care-givers, a scientifically tested curriculum, a rich variety of educational and other stimulation materials, and a stress on staffing ratios and good physical structures, then what does this imply for poor countries? Counter claims from developing countries suggest that it is possible to develop a variety of initiatives aimed at normalizing conditions for children at risk without necess-arily meeting the standards of "high quality". Clearly, this is an area that needs further clarification and discussion.

Finally, although the search for long-term effects of early childhood education is legitimate, it carries with it the inherent danger of looking at children only as future adults and, in particular, as economic performers. The well-being, needs and aspirations of children in their own right, regardless of their future status or of the economic returns to investing in their welfare, can be easily over-looked. Children have the right to receive care, even when it cannot be proved that this care will be translated into positive outcomes later on in their lives.

ECCD in the Indian context

The Indian Constitution does not make any references to early childhood care and development. Consequently, there are no constitutional or legal directives making provision for this age group the total responsibility of the State. The main policy pronouncement of the government in this direction is the National Policy for Children (1974).[4] This is considered to be a landmark document as it spells out the importance of children as valuable human resources and puts the responsibility for their well-being with the State. ECCD issues have been referred to in policy statements regarding other related areas such as education and women's development, but the National Policy remains the major statement on children. India is also a signatory to the Convention on the Rights of the Child (CRC) and has agreed, in principle, to taking a rights-based approach to ECCD. However, the commitment of the government has remained largely at the level of rhetoric and has not yet been reflected in adequate budgetary provision, policies or programmes.

---

[4] For a concise mapping of childcare policies and programmes, see Kaul (1992) and Prasad (1998).

The low priority that the government gives to ECCD is evident from the meagre resources that are allocated to this sector. In the absence of constitutional directives in this regard, lack of resources has become a convenient excuse for the State abnegating its responsibilities to the young child. The fact that successive governments have not yet been able to deliver the constitutional guarantee of "free and compulsory education for all children until they complete the age of fourteen years" is given as further justification for the State's inability to take on the additional burden of providing for pre-school children. The result is that, as in the formal education system, a two-track system operates, with the commercial private sector catering to the needs of the upper classes while inadequate and limited provision is available for the rest.

These developments have to be seen in the context of actual childcare needs in the country. These needs have changed dramatically from what they were even a generation ago. There is an increase in the absolute, as well as relative, number of children requiring some form of non-parental child care. The assumption that young children will be taken care of in traditional family arrangements no longer holds true, at least not for the poor, who form the majority of the population. These arrangements have broken down because of changes in family structure, the disappearance of the traditional three-generation family, increasing income insecurity, growing migration and urbanization, and the need to travel further afield in search of work.

The number of women seeking employment outside the home has also increased. In 1997, 28.9 per cent of women were employed in the formal work-force, representing a decrease from 30.5 per cent in 1980 (ILO, 1998). Structural adjustment programmes and the ensuing recession and unemployment within the organized sector have led to an increase in self-employment and informal-sector activities. In fact, this sector accounts for 92 per cent of total employment in India (Unni, 1998). Unfortunately, national data on women in the informal sector are not available but female participation in these activities is likely to be high.

Given the high levels of poverty in the country and the lack of affordable child care, it is reasonable to assume that the children of working women are taken care of in tenuous informal arrangements or left in the care of siblings. In the context of the United States, these makeshift arrangements have been succinctly referred to as the "childcare underground". Some working mothers are forced to take their infant children with them to the workplace and in extreme circumstances to leave them unattended. In the absence of alternative childcare arrangements, they may resort to drastic measures to keep their children quiet while they are at work. For example, it is reported that women working in the sandstone mines in Rajasthan frequently give opium to their babies so that they can work undisturbed.[5]

Despite the obvious need for childcare facilities – particularly among poor working women – this has not yet been articulated into a concerted demand. Nor has this felt need been converted into a national (or for that matter local) movement demanding ECCD provision as the young child's right. Concerned individuals, professionals, researchers and voluntary organizations have highlighted attention to the urgent need for ECCD provision. The efforts of the Forum for Crèche and Child Care Services (FORCES) – a nationwide network of 47 organizations – are especially notable in this regard. FORCES has made policy recommendations focusing on specific aspects such as maternity benefits, regulations about breastfeeding, and the needs of women in the unorganized sector. However, these efforts are still small scale and have not resulted in any significant policy changes.

ECCD indicators[6]

All available indicators show that the early years continue to be a hazardous period for the Indian child. Although improvements have been made on all fronts, these are limited in relation to the performance of neighbouring countries like China and Sri Lanka. They are also limited in relation to the scale of the problem and the gains that have been made only serve to mask the increase in the absolute numbers of children experiencing human misery.

Table 5.1 provides data on the three crucial components that make up a child's development – health, nutrition and psychosocial development. According to the latest estimates, India has an under-five mortality rate (U5MR) of 98, ranking it 49 in descending order out of 187 countries. Many other Asian countries, such as Maldives, China, Thailand, and Sri Lanka all rank better than India. The infant mortality rate (IMR) shows a similar picture – 70 out of a thousand children born live, die within the first year of life. The percentage of one-year-olds fully immunized against tuberculosis is 72 per cent, against polio 69 per cent and against measles only 55 per cent.

A third of Indian infants are born with low birth weight and a staggering 53 per cent of children under 5 are malnourished, while 18 per cent suffer from wasting and 52 per cent from stunting. In terms of absolute numbers, 73 million (or 40 per cent) of the world's total of 190 million malnourished children live in India (Gupta et al., 2000). Even sub-Saharan Africa performs better as a region, with corresponding figures for malnutrition at 31 per cent, wasting at 10 per cent, and stunting at 37 per cent. The nutrition figures alone should give cause for

---

[5] Author's field notes from Jodhpur District, Rajasthan, March 2001.

[6] Unless otherwise stated, the statistics in this section have been compiled from UNICEF (2001).

Table 5.1   Child survival and development

Indicator	India	South Asia	World
Infant mortality rate (per thousand)	70	74	57
U5MR (per thousand)	98	104	82
Infants with low birth weight (%)	33	31	16
Under-fives suffering from moderate and severe underweight (%)	53	49	28
Under-fives suffering from wasting (%)	18	17	10
Under-fives suffering from stunting (%)	52	48	32
Net primary school enrolment ratio (female)	64	64	79
Net primary school enrolment ratio (male)	78	78	85
Primary school entrants reaching grade 5 (%)	52	54	75

Source: UNICEF (2001).

alarm as they clearly show that a sizeable proportion of the child population starts life on a weak foundation. UNICEF calls this the "silent emergency".

It is estimated that nearly 35 million children in the 6–10 age group are still out of school and this figure rises to 75 million (33.5 million boys and 41.9 million girls) if one extends the age group to 14 (Sudarshan, 2000). Dropout rates are also high. Only 52 per cent of primary school entrants make it to class 5. Reference should also be made to the children – a large majority of them girls – who are involved in sibling care. These children are often categorized under the inaccurate label of "nowhere children" in the literature, i.e. those children who are not enrolled in school and not registered as child labour. The so-called "nowhere children" make up approximately 35 per cent of all children in their age group and the representation of girls is high. Far from being "nowhere", these children are engaged in a wide variety of tasks, including child care, that release adult labour. The non-availability of alternative child-care arrangements takes away the basic rights of two groups of children, with negative consequences for the healthy growth, development and education of both.

To the extent that maternal health and parents' education, particularly maternal education, have an impact on early childhood indicators, the data reveal a grim picture. The proportion of pregnant women suffering from anaemia in India is 88 per cent (Haq and Haq, 1998) and every year 410 out of 100,000 women die of pregnancy-related causes. Here again, a comparison with other Asian countries is telling. The corresponding figures for maternal mortality for China, Sri Lanka and Thailand are 55, 60, and 44 per hundred thousand. Adult literacy also leaves much to be desired: only 44 per cent of Indian women as against 71 per cent of men are literate. Corresponding male and female adult literacy rates for China are 91 and 77, for Sri Lanka 92 and 88, and Thailand 92 and 83. The higher literacy rates in these countries account partly for their better performance on all ECCD indicators.

The importance of maternal education for children's health and survival is clearly demonstrated by data from within the country as well (Shariff, 1990). The general trend is for states with low female literacy levels to have a high IMR. Not surprisingly, Kerala, which has the highest female literacy rate (70.8 per cent), also has the lowest IMR, at 39. The all-India IMR for the corresponding year is 126. Conversely, the low female literacy rates of 12 and 14 per cent in Rajasthan and Uttar Pradesh are reflected in the above-average IMRs of 129 and 167.

With respect to the environment into which the Indian child is born, 35 per cent of the population lives in poverty. This is exacerbated by the fact that 15 per cent of the population does not have access to health services, 37 per cent to safe water and 71 per cent to adequate sanitation. Only 34 per cent of births are attended by a trained midwife (Haq and Haq, 1998).

Finally, it is important to point out the sharp differentials that mark the situation of young children in the country. Gender bias is one aspect of this disadvantage; it pervades all aspects of life and colours the life chances of the girl child. The cycle of disadvantage starts at birth and continues through childhood to motherhood and its eventual perpetuation in the next generation. It is reflected in the inferior health and educational status of women, the high maternal mortality rate, the neglect of the girl child, the declining sex ratio, lower enrolment in school and subsequent higher participation in the child labour force. But this is not the only aspect of differentials. Sharp disparities in ECCD indicators are also visible between different socio-economic groups and between urban and rural areas.

ECCD programmes

The Integrated Child Development Services (ICDS) is the government's main intervention effort for pre-school children and pregnant and lactating mothers from disadvantaged communities. This programme was launched in 1975 as a direct response to the needs and priorities set out in the National Policy for Children (1974). Since then, it has grown to become one of the largest programmes of its kind, reaching out to 4.8 million expectant mothers and 22.9 million children under the age of six (UNICEF, 2001). The programme aims to deliver an integrated package of services consisting of supplementary nutrition, health services, immunization, vitamin supplements and pre-school education for children aged 3–6. These services are delivered through a network of *Anganwadi* or courtyard centres, each run by an *Anganwadi* worker and a helper.

Evaluations of the ICDS programme consistently reveal a positive impact on the health and nutritional status of the child population covered. However, serious concerns have been expressed about other aspects of the programme. Some weaknesses arise from the indiscriminate expansion of the programme and the minimal quality levels under which it operates. Other problems are more inherent in the design of the programme. A major disadvantage is that ICDS is not geared to cater to the needs of working women who need full day care for their children. Pre-school services are available for just a few hours during the day for the 3–6 age group, leaving the younger and more vulnerable 0–3 group largely unserved. The *Anganwadi* centres are also open at a time when most women are at work and cannot access the other services provided.

The emphasis on volunteerism is also out of proportion to the services that the *Anganwadi* workers are expected to provide. Poorly trained and poorly paid, they are exposed to a constant barrage of rules and directives, with the supervisory support staff largely concerned with control, inspection and meeting targets. Nationwide agitation has led to a slight increase in the remuneration of these workers but they continue to be regarded as volunteers and their wages are still not commensurate to the tasks they perform.

A more recent pilot study, aimed as a prelude to a national census of the ICDS programme, has highlighted several shortcomings responsible for the poor utilization and delivery of services. These range from the poor physical infrastructure of *Anganwadi* centres to irregular supplies of the supplementary meals and vitamins, and limited immunization coverage of the target population. The low levels of skills and training of workers compound these problems further – as many as 40 per cent of *Anganwadi* workers were not literate, and the same percentage again had not received any training, leading to difficulties in dealing with the burden of paperwork and in maintaining the growth monitoring charts.

The drawbacks of the ICDS, programme have to be seen against the fact that it absorbs the bulk of the budget allocated by the government for mother and child services. There are a few other smaller initiatives, but some of these are being phased out or merged with ICDS, which remains the showcase programme of the government. The voluntary sector in India also provides a range of child-care services, but these are too small in scale to have any significant impact.

Despite the impressive size of the ICDS programme, its coverage is extremely limited and it does not reach even a fraction of the children in this age group. Kaul (1992) estimates that only 12 per cent of children in the age group 0–6 take part in some form of early childcare programme – state-sponsored or voluntary. Although this amounts to approximately 6,224,000 children, it is only the tip of the Indian iceberg. In addition, such provision as exists caters largely to the 3–6 age group. It is not just the coverage of crèches and day-care programmes that is limited. The poor performance of the country on several early childhood and maternal indicators points to the failure of a wide range of programmes aimed at health, nutrition and welfare to reach poor families and those most in need.

Key policy issues

India's children continue to be marginalized and denied access to their basic right to survival, health, nutrition, safety and education. The sheer dimensions of the problem make this an urgent situation requiring immediate attention. And yet, this sense of urgency is not reflected in government programmes and policies. In the words of S. Anandalakshmy (1997, p.34), "The State does not assume responsibility for all children born; the children of the very poor can be described as the orphans of the State, though voluntary organizations do sometimes adopt them or provide for certain aspects of their development." However, the scale of the problem is such that voluntary efforts alone will not result in tangible outcomes for the country's children. This section will raise some key policy issues that emerge from a review of the ECCD scenario in India.

The first and most obvious point is that there is no comprehensive policy on ECCD. The rhetoric about children being valuable human resources and the responsibility of the State for their well-being in policy documents has not yet been reflected in budgetary provision, policies or programmes. So far, policy development in the area of ECCD has been piecemeal and has not dealt with children's issues in a holistic manner. What is more damaging is that there is no coherence between the various policies and programmes of the government, with the result that some interventions that are supposedly aimed at improving the situation of children may actually end up harming them. A few examples follow.

The Non-Formal Education programme is a key element in the government's strategy for reaching literacy targets. Rather than making a sizeable proportion of the child population literate, this programme has in fact served to perpetuate the problems associated with non-enrolment. It has kept children away from formal schools and has legitimized child labour. To the extent that many of these working children are employed in full-time sibling care, it has also jeopardized the healthy development of the children who are left in their care. These contradictions are even more apparent in the Child-to-Child programme, which is aimed at strengthening the skills of children to look after their younger siblings.[7] One could say that by implementing such a programme

---

[7] The intention is not to devalue the many merits of the innovative child-to-child approach in delivering health and nutrition messages through the medium of children. The contention is more with the uncritical acceptance of the institution of sibling care.

the government actually confers its blessings on sibling care, without assessing whether this is in the best interests of the children involved.

Similarly, the government promotes breastfeeding but has changed maternity benefit laws in a way that it is impossible for working mothers to breast-feed their children. Maternity benefits are also seen as an instrument of population control and there is a proposal to restrict such benefits to the first two children (Chhachi, 1998). Such a move is bound to have negative consequences for the welfare of poor women and their children. Obviously, there is a need to spell out the intersecting needs of women and children in order to make a distinction between areas where there is an overlap of interests and those where there is a conflict. For example, breastfeeding is one area that benefits both mother and child. So does the mother's access to employment, but there could be a potential conflict here: if sibling care is used to release the mother for work, it takes away the carer's right to be in school. A clear policy statement on these matters would help to remove some of the contradictions that currently exist at the policy level.

Secondly, at present there is an undue focus on the ICDS programme, at the cost of other initiatives. Given the diversity of needs in India, it is not possible for any one unitary, centrally controlled childcare programme to provide a solution for all these varied scenarios. A variety of approaches will be required to meet the ECCD requirements of the entire population. For example, the needs of mothers selling vegetables in a market will not be the same as those of factory or construction workers. In the same way, families living in remote rural communities will need to be supported in different ways from those living in urban slums. The needs of caregivers will also vary. Mothers looking after their children at home need information about pregnancy, breastfeeding, healthy nutritional practices, and the value of early stimulation while community workers running a day-care centre require training in child development and growth monitoring. An altogether different approach is required when the carers are themselves children. Their right to education and to healthy development should take priority.

Thirdly, a policy statement on children can be meaningful only when it is backed up with adequate resources. This has not happened so far. The fact that ECCD is not a priority area for the government is evident from the meagre resources that are allocated to this scheme. However, it is important to bear in mind that the investments in ECCD benefit not just the children and families concerned, but all of society. The returns are also more than economic: they help to lay the foundation for the subsequent development of citizenship and enhancement of human capabilities.

Fourthly, the present emphasis on volunteerism in the delivery of government-sponsored ECCD programmes needs to be questioned. The *Anganwadi* workers are expected to volunteer their services in return for an honorarium that is at best inadequate for the tasks they are expected to perform. Questions about wages, conditions of work, training and accreditation of ECCD care workers need to be given due consideration at the policy level.

A range of workers – health-care personnel, pre-school teachers, crèche attendants, parent educators, trainers – are involved in the delivery of ECCD programmes run by the government and by NGOs. Given their pivotal role in making these programmes successful, responding to their needs should become the cornerstone of the government's social policy. The essential needs are adequate compensation, improved working conditions, access to training and accreditation, and finally an appreciation of their inputs into ECCD. Pleas for better working conditions run into the familiar argument that financial means are not available. However, a closer examination of budgets shows that lack of interest, rather than a total lack of resources, is the root cause for under-funding and the poor attention given to the needs of ECCD care workers.

Fifthly, the low quality of services is frequently cited as one of the major drawbacks of ICDS and other government-sponsored programmes. While it is necessary to list the obvious weaknesses of these programmes, it is equally important to supplement this critique with an identification of the dimensions in terms of which "quality" has to be defined in relation to scale. This is particularly relevant in India, given the vast numbers of children at risk and the obvious resource constraints of the parents and, to a more questionable extent, of the government. However, this discussion is complicated by the fact that there is no global consensus on what constitutes quality nor is there any agreement on the indicators that should be used to assess it. Expectations of what ECCD should achieve also vary dramatically. These range from viewing it merely as a compensatory intervention designed to reduce inequalities in society to seeing it in a rights-based framework.

While the emphasis on high quality may be appropriate, the problems involved with delivering a nationwide programme of this kind make it unrealistic. When quality interventions are introduced, as for example by NGOs, they soon become white elephants, depleting all available resources, and unable to sustain themselves without external support and funding. In addition, NGOs have not been very successful in replicating their success in micro situations on a larger scale. Another issue is the imposition of minimum standards. Enforcing minimum standards is tenable only when it is accompanied by the means to attain them. Without such provision, it leads to facilities closing down or going underground.

A more effective approach might be to shift the discussion to identifying "thresholds of quality" or levels below which children's development is compromised and above which developmental gains occur.[8] In other words, it could be better to shift the debate from "more is better" to "how much is good enough". The issue of quality might also be resolved to some extent by exploring the creative responses developed by families that live outside the ambit of government services. There is evidence to show that exposure to some form of ECCD provision – provided it is not of poor quality – matters more than the particular curriculum or approach that is followed (Boocock, 1995). Experience from developing countries also clearly shows that low-cost, community-based initiatives can have a positive impact on child development indicators. These need to be analysed in terms of their impact on the overall development of children and validated accordingly.

And finally, any policy directed at children should first address the way society treats its children in general. For example, what are the socio-cultural norms regarding children? What value does society put on children? How does it protect their rights? Are boys and girls treated equally? What obligations do parents, families and communities have? How and where does the responsibility of the State come in? And, most importantly, to what extent are individuals inclined to accept that what their own children deserve applies to other children as well. Are they motivated to apply the same principles to children who are not part of the same social group or who live far away? Do they feel that children of other ethnic groups, from poorer families, or from "lower" social backgrounds should have more modest needs and fewer entitlements?

The concept of childhood and the need to protect children from cruelty and harm is a twentieth-century construct. Before that, beating, child labour, confinement, and food deprivation were considered to be acceptable ways by which families could discipline and train their children. These views still prevail in large parts of the developing world and India is no exception. Children continue to be treated as possessions of parents and not as individuals with rights. The situation of girl children in India deserves special attention, as they seem to suffer more from the child unfriendliness of society. Gender bias is prevalent in all aspects of life and is expressed in terms of differential treatment of male and female children with regard to food, health care, education and, in extreme cases, female infanticide. Little wonder then that there is poor recognition of the rights of children, particularly of girls.

Tackling societal attitudes to children and women would have to be an essential component of any ECCD policy framework. Achieving meaningful

---

[8] This suggestion was made by a participant at a workshop to discuss child care for low-income families in the United States (Bridgman and Phillips (eds.), 1996), but it has wider relevance to the discussion on quality, particularly in developing countries.

child friendliness is inextricably tied, in the first and last analysis, to overcoming gender biases at all levels. Thus, social movements against dowry, child marriage, special pension schemes for parents of girl children, or opening up new professions to women could all be regarded as legitimate child-friendly interventions operating through indirect causal chains.

Conclusion: The need for dialogue

Discussions on ECCD have traditionally taken place within the restricted group of persons or organizations that are professionally involved with the care and education of children. These are educators, child-oriented NGOs and government departments of health, welfare and education. Within the United Nations family, it is the United Nations Educational, Scientific and Cultural Organization (UNESCO) and UNICEF that are customarily concerned with the young child. The level of debate has not changed much in this group over the last two decades: the same rationale, policies and programme directives are repeated and rehashed with hardly any new thinking entering the discussion. In the last decade, other major donor agencies such as the World Bank, the Asian Development Bank and the Inter-American Development Bank have added a new dimension to the thinking on ECCD by focusing on the economic benefits of investing in young children.

Moving the debate on ECCD to an ever-wider audience could enhance this process even further. Prime candidates here would be professionals and groups concerned with issues such as women's employment, globalization, macroeconomic policies, urban development and pollution, to name a few. In short, the very process of social change could be looked at through its impact on children. This interaction would be a two-way process leading no doubt to new insights and innovations in both fields.

Another way of elevating the debate to a higher order would be to explore social issues that have been largely ignored in the discussion on ECCD. Illustrations of these are child abuse – particularly sexual abuse, domestic violence, gender selection, child prostitution and the transmission of HIV/AIDS to the new-born. ECCD policies and practice in India have largely managed to skirt around these unpleasant but important issues. It is evident that children who are sexually and physically abused, who witness domestic violence, who are not welcome because they are girls, who are traded into prostitution, or who start working at the age of 5, will not grow into healthy and mature adults. Yet, most of these forms of violence against children take place during the early years and are widespread. No discussion on ECCD can be complete without incorporating a full exploration of all the problems children face.

CHILD CARE AS PUBLIC POLICY IN BRAZIL

6

Bila Sorj

Introduction

Care policies are still quite modest in Brazil: children, the aged, and the sick are basically looked after by women in a private capacity. Some changes, however, are occurring, particularly at the level of public discourse and legislation, which increasingly demand that these forms of care be undertaken on the basis of social investments.

Brazil is going through a period of abrupt demographic transition. The decline in fertility rates in the second half of the 1960s, which has continued up to the present, has introduced important changes in the age structure of the population. As a consequence of this decline, the reduction in the proportion of children from 0–6 years in the total population fell by 0.7 per cent in a period of only three years, between 1995 and 1998 (from 14 per cent to 13.3 per cent).

Simultaneously, the significant increase in the proportion of the aged[1] has led to important changes in the demand for public policies in the sphere of health. It should be borne in mind that in Brazil, the relation between ageing and dependency is quite complex. A number of studies (Camarano, 1999) have shown that intergenerational income transfers have increasingly assumed a bidirectional character. Social security has played an important role in income transfers from the old to the young, since it has ensured an income for life for an important contingent of the aged population, both urban and rural. The income of the aged represents an important proportion of family income particularly at a time when unemployment has hit the younger population with greater intensity.

---

[1] The proportion of the aged (60 years and over) in the total population has increased from 4 per cent in 1940 to 8 per cent in 1996.

This chapter concentrates its analysis on public policies for child care. This choice of focus finds its justification in the importance with which social movements have come out in favour of pre-schools in Brazil during the last three decades and the impact which this has had on the redefinition of the right to education of children from 0–6 years. In addition, the fact that the extension of basic education to all children is now being completed,[2] creates favourable conditions for making pre-schooling too a priority in the country's educational agenda. And finally, the universal extension of pre-schools plays a relevant social role both in the service which they offer to the children and the opportunities which they open up for women.

We will show that the government policies for pre-schools for the general public have consisted of the partial privatization of this service, through the provision of subsidies to NGOs. Consequently, pre-schools have reproduced rather than reversed the situation of deprivation in which these children live.

Public policies directed specifically at children up to age 6 are a recent phenomenon in Brazil, going back three decades at the most. Until the beginning of the 1970s, central and local governments generally limited themselves to subsidizing private bodies who cared for needy children, imagining that they could in this way avoid the risks which poverty might imply for social order. These philanthropic and paternalistic institutions had a social service view of the nursery's function, seeing it as an act of kindness or as a favour for poor families, helping them prevent their children from falling into bad ways.

Given this approach, child care gave exclusive attention to nutrition, health, the development of obedient behaviour, a cooperative spirit and self-sufficiency, while the educational aspects of a child's development were hardly taken into account (Oliveira and Ferreira, 1986).

Since the 1970s, the Government has assumed a more active role. Based on the approach of compensating for the deficiencies of the poor, the federal Government promoted the opening of pre-schools either by directly supporting municipal administrations or by subsidizing the initiatives of needy groups in society. This government initiative was inspired by views fashionable in the United States in the 1960s which attributed the educational failure among racial minorities and the poor to a culture of poverty. Pre-school attendance by these groups would help reverse the high indices of repetition and drop-out among needy children.

As a result, there was a large expansion of pre-schools in the country (Rosemberg, 1999; Kramer, 1992). The pre-school model, aimed at broad sections of the population and which would guide government action in later

---

[2] Basic education is composed of eight years of schooling and is compulsory for children from 7 to 14 years old.

decades, was ironically known as "schools on the cheap for the poor" (Franco, 1984). These services were characterized by their low cost and they were generally based on the voluntary or badly paid labour of mothers, women, communities and NGOs with no professional qualifications for carrying out functions relating to education and care.

In the 1990s, although the changes may not have been so radical as to suggest a new model of social policy, certain alterations were made both in the conception of childcare services and in the political institutional framework. In the 1988 Constitution, pre-schools were recognized as educational services and their responsibility transferred to the municipal level of government.

This chapter will analyse the diversity of conceptual constructions and public discourses on pre-school child care in Brazil together with the responses which public authorities are adopting for the implementation of policies in this sphere. In the first section we will present a general picture of the supply and demand of pre-schools in the country. In the second part we will analyse the emergence of social movements and discourses mobilized around the struggle for crèches for the poor. In the third section we look at child care as a social good and, finally, we will examine the public policy model adopted by the Government and the debates which this provoked.

Profile of the supply and demand for crèches and pre-school nurseries

Brazil is still a long way from ensuring universal coverage of crèches (0–3 years) and nurseries (4–6 years) for its infant population. In 1998, only 27 per cent of children in these age groups were registered in crèches or nurseries (Kappel, 2000). In spite of this low coverage, which corresponds to less than a third of the demand, expansion has been continuous. Between 1995 and 1998 the growth in the proportion of those who attended pre-schools increased from 25.1 to 27 per cent. This evolution was better in the case of children from 0–3 years, where the proportion rose from 7.6 per cent to 8.7 per cent, an increase of more than 10 per cent. For children from 4–6 years, the growth was less significant, advancing from 47.8 per cent to 50.7 per cent, an increase of 6 per cent. It should be noted that the proportion of children in nurseries is much higher than in crèches.

One of the factors which most influences attendance at crèches and nurseries in Brazil is family income (Kramer and Kappel, 2000). In fact, education in early childhood is a social good which is more readily available to higher income families. In 1998, the chances of schooling for children from

0–6 years within the top 20 per cent income group was 3.3 times higher than in the lower income groups (56.5 per cent as against 16.8 per cent). This disparity was more pronounced in the 0–3 age group where the chances of higher-income family children attending crèches was 5.4 times greater than for lower income families. For children in the 4–6 age group the difference persisted but was less notable: higher-income children had 1.8 times more chance of attending a nursery than lower-income children. Gender distribution is similar but white children are more highly represented than black or coloured children, compared with the racial mix of the whole population: 54 per cent white and 45.3 per cent black or coloured.

The participation of women in the labour force is another factor which increases the chances of a child attending educational establishments. Children from 0–3 years whose mothers work have 3.8 times more chance of attending a crèche than those whose mothers do not work (the attendance rate being 14.9 per cent and 3.9 per cent respectively). The children from 4–6 years whose mothers work also have a higher attendance rate than those with non-working mothers (59.8 per cent as against 51.6 per cent).

When the children are not at school the mother is the main person responsible for looking after the children (67.8 per cent),[3] followed by grandparents (7.4 per cent), brothers and sisters under 14 years (6.1 per cent), brothers and sisters over 14 years (5.9 per cent), and domestic employees (3.6 per cent).

While the overall demand for pre-schools in Brazil has declined in line with the demographic transition,[4] the highest rates of fertility are to be found in the poorest sectors of the population. The highest proportion of children within the 0–6 age group is therefore to be found in the lower-income groups. Of all families with children in this age group, 30.5 per cent had an average income of half a minimum wage (defined as poor families).[5] Families with from half to one minimum wage accounted for 25.1 per cent of children in this age group. The educational level of heads of families with children from 0–6 is low, on average, most not having completed the first eight years of schooling.[6]

Sabóia and Sabóia (2000), analysing the living conditions of families with children in the 0–6 age range, drew attention to the high levels of deprivation. Among these families are to be found the worst indices of domestic comfort –

---

[3] These data refer to children under 15.

[4] In Brazil in 1998 there were approximately 21,096,000 children between 0 and 6 years of age (excluding the rural population in the north). Comparing the data of 1998 with the results of 1995, one notes that there was a drop of around 212,000 children. See the National Household Sample Survey (PNAD), and Kappel (2000).

[5] The minimum wage at the time of writing was R$151,00 (US$80 dollars).

[6] The average length of schooling in the country is less than six years, according to the PNAD of the National Census Bureau (IBGE) in 1998.

an average of three members per bedroom, the lowest percentages of adequate water, sewerage, and waste collection, together with the lowest possession of consumer durables.

Types of pre-school

There is, currently, a very varied supply of pre-schools, which prevents any simple distinction between private or public, market or state responsibility being made. A more adequate, although far from perfect, classification points to the existence of at least five types of pre-school from the point of view of their financing:

a) "public pre-schools": those which are entirely under the financial control and direct management of the public authority;
b) "philanthropic pre-schools": run by religious or philanthropic institutions;
c) "employer pre-schools": those provided by firms for their employees in fulfilment of labour legislation;
d) "community pre-schools": those emerging from associations of informal groups which receive support from NGOs and from public authorities;
e) "private pre-schools": those supplied by the market whose services are designed and paid for by higher-income families.

In practice, however, these institutions combine various types of financing simultaneously. The option by public authorities to conclude very varied agreements with society-based initiatives makes classification difficult. Often the same establishment can count on the support both of a philanthropic entity of a religious nature, and on public funding (through agreements at municipal level), and also draw on human resources from the community (mothers who work voluntarily in the pre-schools).

The school census statistics collected by the Ministry of Education in 1998 only include institutions which are officially registered and therefore do not include many initiatives belonging to "community" or "philanthropic" networks. However, the IBGE household surveys recorded children's attendance at both registered and non-registered institutions. The difference registered between these two systems of data collection was 26.3 per cent, with the IBGE identifying more than a million cases of attendance at non-registered institutions.[7]

---

[7] The World Organization for Early Childhood Education (OMEP) calculates that 55 per cent of the country's crèches function without any kind of regulation, and that a large part of these are in the shanty towns and poor districts of Brazil's cities, set up by women from among the poorest populations.

In 1996–97, for the first time the IBGE's Research on Living Standards (PPV)[8] included questions on the ownership of pre-schools attended by children up to 6 years. The alternatives were limited to "public" or "private", which meant that "community" institutions or those linked to any type of NGO would be classified as "private". According to this research, a little more than half the population of children from 0–6 years is accounted for by the public network.

The categories used by the PPV, however, are not easily recognized by the parents who reply to the questionnaires, making the data rather unreliable, also demonstrating the degree to which these categories no longer reflect current practices. It is highly likely that a mother interviewed for the PPV would consider a philanthropic pre-school, for which she did not have to make any financial contribution, "public". In the same way, she would probably consider a "community" pre-school supported by an agreement with the local authority as "private" if she had to pay a "symbolic contribution" for each child matriculated. In fact, it is not clear how one should classify "public" and "private". In one neighbourhood, for instance, we noted that mothers referred to the pre-school attended by their children as the church's pre-school, even though the management was entrusted to the community, while NGOs had some participation and finances were also provided by the local authority.[9]

Another example which highlights the difficulty of defining the frontier between "public" and "private" is provided by the "employer pre-schools". In 1967, labour legislation opened up the possibility of firms establishing agreements with other public or private bodies as an alternative to the legal requirement to maintain pre-schools in firms with more than 30 employees, during the period of breastfeeding.

These agreements, often made with public pre-schools, led to the introduction of private funding of the public system; inversely, this can be seen as public funding of firms in their fulfilment of labour obligations, which should be the latter's exclusive responsibility. In 1986, the Labour Ministry's Decree 3296 authorized firms to adopt the "pre-school payback system" as a substitute for the legal requirement referred to above. With the "payback cheque" an "employee-mother" can opt for the pre-school of her choice whether this be private or one associated with the public authority.[10]

---

[8] This research was carried out only once and was limited to two of the country's regions: the south-east and the north-east where more than two-thirds of the total population live. In spite of being less extensive than the PNAD, it contains a broader set of information on the quality of life for children.

[9] Another interesting observation is that the crèche workers in this case considered it to be a "community crèche".

[10] It is important to note that the implementation of the "pre-school payback" system depends on its previous explicit inclusion in collective agreements with the workers.

Pre-school management

The supply of pre-schools for the population functions, in general, precariously, with buildings, furniture, equipment, didactic materials and staff reproducing the deprivations in living conditions which the children experience in their homes.

The profile of pre-school workers reveals a low level of professionalism in infant care. The workers can be said to be "minders" rather than "educators". With low levels of schooling and low incomes, the "minders" are often heads of family who see this work as an extension of their domestic chores. In the workplace, they experience the same difficulties which they confront on a day-to-day basis, difficulties which also mark the daily experience of those who use these services.

The relations which pre-school and nursery workers establish with these institutions are, in general, informal. Although "volunteers" are gradually disappearing, wages continue to be very low (an average of one minimum wage) and their level of schooling is normally the first eight years of education. Only a few pre-school administrators have reached university level. A recent piece of research showed that pre-school workers do not see themselves as workers (Teixeira, 1997). It is common to find situations in which fund transfers suffer delays. In fact, many of the agreements with the municipal authorities are no more than subsidies for food, for services or for the payment of staff.

The relations which these "subcontracted" pre-schools maintain with the families are fraught with conflict. In the first place, unlike the private establishments maintained by families in higher-income brackets, the mothers or the parents are always called on to assume responsibilities and to provide some form of collaboration. They are asked to make "symbolic" monetary contributions, which may in fact seriously affect their budgets, or to substitute such contributions through the provision of services: cleaning, repairs, caretaking, building repairs, etc. Mothers and families are encouraged to demonstrate that they are active and interested in the maintenance of an establishment, sometimes described as a "charity" or a "favour" for the families concerned.

Sometimes the opposite occurs, with the director of these establishments identifying the mothers and families as the victims of great deprivation and assuming all decision-making on their behalf. In other cases, the families may be so well organized in the management of the pre-schools – as sometimes is the case with the "community" pre-schools – that they come to assume all the decisions without any interaction with the pre-school workers.

The low level of functional differentiation between the different actors who participate in the pre-schools and nursery schools, as for instance between the mothers and the pre-school workers or between the management of the establishment and the community, shows the professionalism and consolidation of these institutions. The frontiers between the values associated with the intensification of community life, or the natural ability of women in caring for children, and educational values are not clearly demarcated. This internal confusion in relation to the identity of establishments dedicated to early childhood is reflected also in the relations which they maintain with the outside world: different sources of financing, responsibilities divided between public authorities, the market and NGOs.

Child care as a social good

The transformation of child care into an activity institutionalized outside the family setting is far from being a reality in Brazil. Some steps in this direction are, however, under way and are the result of a complex process of legitimization in which different actors and conceptions acquire visibility in the public arena, demanding that the State provide collective goods dedicated to the period of early childhood.

Since the end of the 1970s there has been a change in the perception and actions of the poorer classes[11] towards an understanding that childcare should be undertaken outside the exclusive context of the family. However, given the low level of public sensitivity to the provision of this service, it was necessary for the population to organize itself and assume responsibility for the setting-up and maintenance of pre-schools in the districts while at the same time putting pressure on the public authorities for funding.

A variety of factors of a structural nature partially explain the strength of the popular mobilizations for pre-schools in the 1970s and which became even stronger in the 1990s: the growing incorporation of women into the labour market, particularly those with dependent children (Lavinas, 1997; Bruschini, 1998) and changes in the organization of families with a reduction in their size, the increase in separations and divorces, and the growing importance of the female single parent model (Goldani, 1994).

These structural developments, however, account only partially for the change in attitudes to child care. It is important also to identify discourses which are politically stimulated and which provide new meanings for these child-care activities.

---

[11] Middle-class women, even when they could rely on domestic workers, use private crèches and pre-schools for their children on a large scale. Rather than serving as a resource which allows them to participate in the labour market, their resort to crèches and pre-schools reflects the positive values which they attribute to the socialization of their children in collective contexts outside the family.

Social struggles

The political conjuncture in the 1970s, which saw the emergence of diverse forms of expression, mobilization, organization and popular struggles on issues relating to greater access to collective consumption goods, created strong community action. In the face of increasing urban deprivation and the timid response provided by the public authorities, a popular movement emerged for the setting-up and the maintenance of community pre-schools in the outlying neighbourhoods of the country's major cities. Supra-local organizations were rapidly created and became the negotiators with the public authorities.

Although in each neighbourhood and in each city, such initiatives relied on the involvement of different social actors, it is possible to identify the central role played by mothers, neighbourhood networks, feminist groups and housing associations. One of the groups which most influenced the emergence of community action for the creation of pre-schools was the Catholic Church, or at least, a sector of the church, which since the 1960s has given priority to activities aimed at the poor and the promotion of social justice, in accordance with the orientation of the Vatican Council. With an ideology directed to the creation of community districts based on solidarity, participation and self-help, this wing of the Church supported the formation of pre-schools in poor neighbourhoods. Public institutions, particularly town council administrations, also contributed to the strength which the community pre-school movement demonstrated by conceding subsidies to such bodies.

Filgueiras (1994) refers to the struggles for pre-schools in Belo Horizonte, the capital of the State of Minas Gerais, as the result of community and women's group experiences in the years 1978–79. The origin of the movement is located in the first initiatives of "childcaring", supported by neighbours, mothers and parish priests. These initiatives were brought together in the Struggle Movement for Crèches in 1978. Later, left-wing political groups and feminists joined the movement.

The participation of the feminist movement in the struggles for pre-schools occurred only in the early phases. The reasons behind their short-lived involvement in this movement are still not entirely clear. It might be thought that the feminists resisted building their identity on the role of "mothers" and that their social position, principally in the middle classes, allowed them to rely on the private supply of pre-schools or on domestic workers. In addition, the identification of the community pre-school initiative with the Church was a source of great discomfort for the feminists, given the profound divergences which separated them from the church's vision of the woman's condition.[12]

The demands for pre-schools in São Paulo had their origins in the mothers' groups organized in the suburbs.[13] It was the mothers who were the first to put pressure on public authorities, on private firms and on foundations for the creation of pre-schools. In collaboration were the "Youth Pastoral", linked to the Catholic Church; the Societies of Neighbourhood Friends; and the Struggle Movement for Crèches. This latter defended the right to pre-schools and pointed to the need for society, with the support of the State, to assume the responsibility for looking after the sons and daughters of the working population.

In the State of Rio de Janeiro, the initiative for organizing pre-schools was also taken by groups of women from the poor urban districts. In general, these women came together for the parish activities of the Catholic Church. In the Baixada Fluminense, these initiatives were undertaken by the older women of the community, who, with their children already reared and with lives which were "a little more stable", saw the community pre-school as a way of helping working mothers in the first instance, but also as "a possibility for looking after children abandoned by their mothers who are in a situation of social and psychological distress".[14]

In the initial phase of creating community pre-schools, two legitimate arguments can be identified: the idea of the pre-school as a right for the working mother who needs an alternative for the care of her children, and a view of the pre-school as a right for poor families. Even today these discourses remain, implicitly or explicitly, producing tensions between the different actors present in the political sphere and the perceptions of the general population.

The first perspective of the pre-school as a working mother's right was seen by militants as a necessary evil, given the needs of mothers to work either to complement family income or, in the case of heads of families, to earn the only income of the family group. Articulation between the discourse on pre-schools and the liberation of women from chores imposed by the unequal gender division of labour only appeared in the case of militants close to the feminist movement. Relying on strong support from the church, these initiatives were valued as positive demonstrations of the population's capacity for self-organization.

---

[12] One of the militants of the popular movement commented ironically on the precocious abandoning of the struggle for pre-schools by feminists: "I think their children grew up very quickly."

[13] The history of this movement in São Paulo was reconstructed through access to the research carried out by Oliveira and Ferreira (1986). Since this text analyses the situation until 1986, the information was complemented by the accounts of representatives of the movement for pre-schools in Rio de Janeiro.

[14] As related by the leaders of pre-schools, NGOs and social movements.

The trade union struggles which regained momentum at the end of the 1970s and beginning of the 1980s also influenced the discourse on pre-schools as "a right of the working mother". Women workers in industry, especially in the electro-electronics sector, demanded the inclusion of items specific to the conditions of women workers in the negotiations with employers. One of the principal demands, in fact rarely observed, was that firms should obey the labour legislation of 1943, which stipulated that pre-schools be provided for the children of workers.

The second formulation which holds pre-schools to be a right of poor families was based on the perception that the struggle for pre-schools should involve a wider group of demands: food, work, health, etc. As Filgueiras (1994) notes at the First Congress of Community Crèches in 1985 one of the principal demands was for the creation of jobs. This formulation, which incorporates the demand for pre-schools in the broader framework of the improvement in the living conditions of the poor, was influenced primarily by the presence of left-wing political parties in the poor districts. The effort to build political unity out of the diverse social movements provided yet another meaning to the struggle for pre-schools: "a right of the poor".

The 1990s, characterized by the democratization of the political regime, saw the consolidation of a new public discourse on the issue of child care. This discourse now sees pre-schools as "a right of children to education". The symbolic reference for this change is the Constitution of 1988, which in clause VI of Article 208 declares that it is the duty of the State to guarantee "pre-school care for children from 0–6 years". More specifically, the National Education Guidelines Law of 1996 included infant education within the school system, attributing responsibility for its maintenance to the local authority, with technical and financial cooperation provided by the Union and the state governments.

This new conception of the fundamental rights of children from 0–6 years, together with the corresponding policies for their implementation, was also expressed in other pieces of legislation. Law 8069 of 1990, known as the Statute of the Child and the Adolescent (ECA), was created as a result of a social movement which from the end of the 1980s grouped together very diverse civil organizations. These influenced a considerable segment of public authority representatives through symbolic appeals full of social preoccupations, expressed in the idea of the country's responsibility for a project for the future. The ECA confirmed the constitutional obligation to protect the child which is the responsibility of the family, but also of the State and of society as a whole. This law also confirms the need for decentralization and municipalization in the development of policies already recommended by the Constitution of 1988.

The new legislation became a powerful instrument of struggle for putting pressure on public authorities for infant education. It called for the Government to act, based on the notion of rights and no longer simply to improvise in emergencies, to compensate for the cultural, economic and social deficiencies of the under-privileged populations. These legal texts are considered to be an important conquest. Their implementation has been extremely slow and, today, this constitutes one of the principal demands of the sectors involved in the struggle for the universalization of pre-schooling in the country.

Public policies

Up until now the Government's response in terms of public policies has been to respond to demands and pressures in a precarious manner, either by managing pre-schools directly, or by establishing agreements with NGOs, without, however, formulating a consistent public policy which would guarantee standards of quality.

Three aspects of the government response to the issues of early childhood, which have come to predominate over this period, can be highlighted. The first is related to the reproduction within the public domain of the ideology of gender which attributes to women natural abilities for looking after children. Rosemberg (1994) notes that lay teachers, i.e., those with fewer than 11 years of schooling, are responsible for the expansion which has occurred. The absence of a policy for the professional qualification of these workers, the low remuneration offered and the limited investments reveal the lack of importance which the Government attaches to the early education of children.

Secondly, the policy adopted suggests that the Government transformed the precarious solutions which the communities were finding (improvised installations, low levels of training of those in charge of care) to offset the lack of funding into a model of public policy. Thirdly, the character of this public policy which is primarily oriented to offering subsidies for private initiatives, indicates that the Government sees itself as having a limited role in this area. The voluntary organizations (community organizations, NGOs and philanthropic institutions) have come to be seen as the best instruments for carrying out public policy. Considered to be less corrupt, administratively more streamlined, and better informed on the realities of needy populations, their actions should more easily reach the public most in need.

Paradoxically, until recently the adoption of this model by the public authorities met little resistance from the organizations responsible for community pre-schools, except in relation to the paucity of funds which the Government was prepared to invest. In the 1970s, it was thought that the "community pre-schools", as the product of community initiatives and based on the use of local educators, would be working, advantageously, within the framework of its own local culture and structure. Experiences of this type, it was imagined, would lead to the emergence of a strong popular organization with its own project of schooling which would share only technical responsibilities and financial costs with the State. In this way, it was thought, the participation of the community and the democratization of the State would be guaranteed.[15]

Child care as a "right to education"

This low-cost model of public policies for attending to the needs of early childhood has come to be criticized by a variety of interest groups. A new public discourse is emerging which has as its hallmark the importance of offering a quality-based social and educational service.

The work of academics and research centres will have an important role in changing attitudes towards care in early childhood. Their research and evaluations have shown the fragility of the public policies adopted by the Government, based on the universalization of low-cost infant education, directed primarily at the north and north-east, the country's poorest regions (Rosemberg, 1999). These policies had the merit of including new social sectors within the educational system and opening up new job opportunities for women with low levels of schooling, generally from the least-privileged sectors of the population. However the provision of low-quality education served to reproduce rather than mitigate, the social inequalities within the educational system itself.

In a pioneering study, Rosemberg (1991) showed that the educational opportunities offered to black children are the of worst quality provided by the system. The establishments are in improvised surroundings, employ untrained staff, lack teaching materials, and they put an excessive number of children under a single teacher. One indicator of the frustrating educational experience to which these children are submitted is the striking presence of children between 7 and 9 years old attending pre-school, particularly black children in the north-east of the country. The pre-school, rather than increasing the chances of a child's regular progress within the educational system, becomes transformed into an alternative to basic education.

The new discourse on pre-schools incorporates the dimension of quality which was previously neglected and also introduces notions of citizenship

---

[15] For a view of the difficulties in the relations between the State and the "community pre-schools" until the 1980s, see SMDS/RJ (1992).

which question the compensatory, social assistance and emergency-oriented practices which predominated previously. In addition to the demand for an increase in funding, the qualifications and professionalization of workers in the pre-schools have acquired priority status.

Professionals from the education sector are also key actors in the formulation of this new mentality. Public policies promoting the expansion of educational services without quality and based on the use of lay teachers are criticized for devaluing the professional status of the teacher. While this criticism stems from basically corporate interests, it has had the positive effect of introducing quality parameters into the debate on child care.

The 1996 Law on Guidelines and Foundations of National Education demonstrates the power which professionals and specialists in education have had in its formulation. The curriculum guidelines for infant education require teachers to have a diploma of higher education (equivalent to a full undergraduate qualification), allowing as a minimum a teacher training diploma. Given the large number of professionals without the minimum training demanded by law, the transitory clauses advise lay professionals, who are already working, to speed up their training. The law also demands that all pre-schools be registered and that they formalize their activities.

Another important actor responsible for the change in discourse on infant care is the sector of national and international NGOs, particularly those geared to the defence of children's rights. These are legalized civil bodies providing support services for community pre-schools and they are particularly involved in the training of teachers. In general, they depend on public funds, foreign foundations or the private sector and have a formal professional organizational profile.

In the absence of a precise institutional framework for the supply of services, the NGOs function as an intermediary between the State and society. On the one hand, they confer a greater coherence to the demands emerging from society; on the other, they allow the public authorities to tackle these demands more easily. Some agreements exist between public authorities and these NGOs for the transfer of funds to educational establishments.

Acting as mediators between the public authorities and community initiatives, the NGOs focus particularly on:

a) training pre-school workers;
b) reinforcing the value of the professional identity of the educator among pre-school workers;
c) disseminating to a wider public the precarious living standards of the needy by using the social and communication resources available to them;

d) strengthening the autonomy of popular initiatives in the face of political cronyism and the electoral favours in which the organization of pre-school is often caught up;[16]

e) formulating projects for pre-schools and schools by obtaining funding, drawing up agreements with public authorities and contributing to financial and administrative management;

f) supporting entities which struggle for the implementation of public policies for infant education.

In recent years a new type of NGO has been active in the educational field linked to business initiatives which develop a discourse on children's rights. The ideology of the "citizen firm" is gaining increasing attention in the marketing strategies of the large firms and can be associated with a new model in which the State works to transfer part of its responsibilities for social protection to civil society.

The actors engaged in struggles in favour of pre-schools have of late found a common ground for the communication and promotion of public policies in the area of infant education. "Forums on crèches" were organized in a number of states as follow-ups to the First National Symposium on Children's Education, which took place in Brasília in 1994, at the initiative of the Ministry of Education. More recently, in 1999 these forums were organized at national level, identified as the "Interforum Movement for Infant Education in Brazil", which is supported by limited financial contributions for the infrastructure, meetings and the running costs of its activities. A wide range of organizations are involved: public and private universities, foundations in the areas of education and health, NGOs, community and women's movements and associations. The "community pre-school" movements, which are generally organized in each locality, also have an important participation in this arena of representation.[17]

The principal objective of the Interforum Movement for Infant Education is the struggle for the implementation of the basic rights of children from 0–6 years, guaranteed in the law (the Federal Constitution, the ECA and the Law on Guidelines and Foundations). The principal challenges this movement has to confront are quality improvement, financing, integration into the teaching system and the training of professionals. More specifically, it is possible to identify the following proposals it presented to the candidates for the municipal elections of 2000:

---

[16] The interviews showed that pre-schools linked to philanthropic and religious bodies were more susceptible to clientelistic appeals.

[17] The "Forum of Rio de Janeiro crèches" brings together approximately 150 people in monthly meetings.

a) the municipal authorities should fully invest 25 per cent of its budget in education as the law demands. According to the movement, the implementation of this legal equitable requirement and the equitable distribution of the funds between the different segments of teaching would allow for an increase in quality of educational services to children from 0–6 years;

b) the educational councils[18] should confirm themselves as deliberative and regulatory bodies in relation to informal pre-schools;

c) the educational councils, when defining criteria for the regulation of these institutions, should take into account the experience of women living in the shanty towns and poor districts who assumed responsibility for creating pre-schools, given the omission of the public authority. This demand aims to preserve the power of the popular pre-school movement in defining the educational values to be transmitted to the children, as in the management of the pre-schools themselves;

d) the secretaries of education should promote the training of professionals who still have not reached the educational level required by law.

The demands of the Interforum Movements point to important changes in the orientation of the pro-school movements in Brazil: there has been a weakening of the resistance which the popular movements displayed with regard to the State. Until the end of the 1980s the popular movements vigorously defended the autonomy of their initiatives and there was a fear of subordination to the State. Today, not only do the movements consider it appropriate to participate in the spheres of public policy formulation, they also support and demand the fulfilment of the legal provisions for the regulation of the alternative network of pre-schools which the pro-school movement created.

The Interforum Movement's Campaign programme also makes clear that the "statist" argument identified with the left and according to which the pre-schools should be completely run by the State has disappeared from the political agenda. All the signs point to a broad consensus, including within the Interforum Movement, that the fiscal crisis of the State no longer allows for the supply of services directly administered by the State.

Tensions and ambiguities

As we have seen, the idea that child care should be integrated into the educational system and carried out by educational professionals acquired the force

---

[18] These are institutions with equal representation of civil society and government which have a deliberative character and function together with the State and Municipal Secretaries for Education, evaluating and proposing public policies.

of law and stimulated a broad social mobilization on the issue of child care. The transformation of this orientation into systematic and consistent public policies is, however, still quite modest.

The new Guidelines and Foundations of Infant Education Law of 1996 imposed the need for regulations at national, state, and municipal levels, to be established and put into practice in a way that guaranteed quality standards in the pre-school services. Responsibility for the management of infant education was attributed to the municipal level, which was called on to establish norms for the authorization, registration and supervision of the infant education institutions of its teaching system. The municipalities also have the responsibility for organizing, maintaining and developing the appropriate bodies and institutions for the system, integrating them into the educational policies and plans of the states and at the federal level.

The municipal and state-level educational councils, composed of members of the Government and civil society on a parity basis, are responsible for elaborating criteria for the registering of public and private institutions. This body has become a privileged sphere for the population's struggles for changes. However, given that civil society is made up of different actors with differing and sometimes opposing interests, the registering of pre-schools has been conducted in an atmosphere of ambiguity and tension. We will now identify some of the tensions present in today's debates on the regulation of infant education establishments.

The private institutions are those which most resist the regulatory controls of the State, since they must now make themselves accountable for their activities and submit themselves to monitoring. They tend to react negatively to the adoption of democratic management practices within the education system, involving the participation of families, communities and teachers. They campaigned for a regulation which would authorize pre-schools to function with a larger number of children under the responsibility of one teacher, using the argument that, if not, their establishments could become financially unviable. The teachers, for their part, reacted against this and wanted to guarantee the lowest number possible of children per teacher, using pedagogical and workload arguments.

The "community" or "subcontracted" network supports the proposal of democratization, given that its own conception of pre-schools focuses on the importance of the interaction between families and their local social environment. A strong sense of community participation, however, and the collective dynamic which the management of these institutions assumes, comes into conflict with the guidelines on the conditions of registration; these impose a clear division of labour and responsibilities between the different professional sectors of managers, directors, coordinators and teachers. This definition of differentiated identities goes against the very idea which inspired these initiatives: "everyone together for the benefit of the children".

Finally, the presence of NGOs in the pre-school education sector also creates tensions for the militants, who have fewer professionals and are less formally organized. For many women who are leading the movement to create popular "community" pre-schools, the discourse on the "education" and "professionalization" of the pre-school workers seems to disqualify the work which they do, together with their practical knowledge.

These conflicts tend to increase, given the new definition of pre-schools as education institutions with the consequent demand by the public authorities that these institutions stop being informal and register themselves with the competent public bodies.

Various leaders of the pre-school movement fear that the "educational" discourse which has come to prevail will point the pre-schools exclusively in the direction of preparing children for basic education. The force which the educational discourse begins to assume might lead to the adoption of a standardized pedagogy which undermines the role of the pre-school as a space giving importance to play and to popular culture.

The group which has shown itself to be the most cohesive in the debates on infant education is that represented by teachers who, independently of the school for which they work – public, private or sub-contracted – converge in the defence of their interests, which include training, the definition of a career structure, promotion and wages.

On the campaign agenda of those actors involved with infant education, the demand for an increase in the investment of public funds heads the list. In fact, public funds for the education are meagre: in 1997 only 4 per cent of the funds for education were invested in programmes specifically for the education of children from 0–6 years, amounting in Brazilian *Reals* to R$1,970,043,000 (Kappel, 2000). If we divide the amount by the number of children who constitute the potential public (21,096,000) this would represent an investment of R$93 per child/year. The greater part of these funds (82.7 per cent) comes from the municipal budget, which is the body responsible for the education of children from 0–6 years. The funds dedicated to training teachers in this sector are also negligible (1.1 per cent).

Some public policies point to reversals in the new conception of child care as a right to an education of quality. Programmes of "family pre-schools" inspired by the experience of developed countries are being implemented by state and municipal governments. Supported by funds from the Secretaries for Social Assistance and international organizations such as UNICEF, mothers look after children in their own homes, on the basis of a small payment. Here again, the notion of a policy of caring for small children as that of compensating for the deficiencies of the family comes to the fore, playing down the idea of the right of the child to education.

Conclusion

In all areas of public policy Brazil is passing through a period of major changes in the relation between the State and the private sector, profit and non-profit. The production and distribution of social goods and services are increasingly being transferred to the private sector, with the State assuming the role of subsidizing and regulating their functioning. New forms of social solidarity (NGOs of the most varied types) have come to assume an important role and reflect changes in the relation between the State and the market, between the public and the private sectors.

The reduction in the scope of the State's activity is justified as a form of limiting bureaucratic and clientelistic control over the State, thereby increasing individual or collective options. In the past, this perspective was endorsed exclusively by liberals but has since become incorporated and disseminated into the most diverse contexts, even among socialists and social-democrats.

The emerging model of public policy for child care is, on the one hand, that of increasing the regulatory action of the State, expressed in the registering and formalization of these institutions. On the other hand, there is an evident stimulus to the privatization of this supply, to the extent that the State transfers funds to the market (private pre-schools), to NGOs, which have now become the principal instruments for implementing child care.

Institutional decentralization is also one of the principal factors in the reorganization of public policies in Brazil and its democratic potential can be perceived, especially in the increase in the degree of popular participation in different aspects of the adoption, elaboration and implementation of policies. Nevertheless, if the decentralization of social policies is not accompanied by adequate funding, the supply of these services will be called into question. The country's poor municipalities, in particular, will have great difficulty in supplying the quality services demanded by law and by the social movements. This is especially so in the case of demands for qualified pre-school and nursery teachers, which involve large investments for broadening access to and increasing the quality of all levels of teaching.

The emergence and consolidation of a new discourse which regards the care of small children as an object of public policies, was a task carried out, particularly, by women. Justified in many different ways, such as "a mother's right", "a right of the poor" and "a right of children", this vision has gained wide legitimacy in Brazilian society. More recently, the idea that it is not simply a matter of caring for children has gained in strength. On the contrary, the demands with respect to this service are becoming increasingly exigent. The inclusion of child care as a service integrated into the educational system indicates that a new quality threshold for this type of service has been established.

The general context of deprivation and great social inequalities characterizing the Brazilian social structure, especially families with small children, present a great challenge to any public policy, and in particular to social policies directed at infancy. One of the ways to break the vicious circle of poverty is to prevent the poor children of today becoming the poor families of tomorrow.

SOCIAL SUPPORT FOR HOME-BASED CARE IN THE RUSSIAN FEDERATION

7

Liana Lakunina, Natalia Stepantchikova and Tatyana Tchetvernina

Introduction

This chapter focuses on the provision of state-funded benefits, income allowances and social services to those providing or in need of care in the Russian Federation. To date, there is little information available on the embryonic market for non-governmental services. However, it is relevant to note that the Government intends to create the conditions necessary for the development of non-governmental social services. To this end, a specialized department is to be formed by the Ministry of Labour and Social Development. It will work out the legal framework and establish a licensing procedure for the providers of social services.

The chapter begins by outlining the legal and institutional background to both the provision of benefits and services and the responsibilities of family members for one another's welfare and care. It then focuses on benefits and privileges for those providing care, with a particular emphasis on child care. We then present the income benefits and social services available to those either in need of care or those providing it. Following this, the text discusses the efficiency of existing provisions, drawing attention to the gap between what is purported to exist and what people actually receive. The final section considers some necessary reforms.

The background to social protection policies as they relate to care

The Constitution of the Russian Federation, adopted in December 1993, declared Russia a social state, thus stressing the utmost importance of human values and a commitment of assistance to needy members of society. Its provisions laid the foundations for the social policies of the Russian Federation and formally brought the nation into line with the relevant principles of a range of international statutes. Federal agencies adopted regulations on the principles of social policies and established a unified system of statutory minimum standards on wages, pensions, benefits, health care, education and cultural services. However, the resolution of specific social problems is the responsibility of the regional agencies and local authorities (the municipalities), which have to take into consideration local developments and conditions. These authorities play a key role in developing and implementing the regional social programmes, providing targeted social assistance, ensuring the functioning of the social infrastructure agencies and resolving problems in the areas of employment and social protection.

During the 1990s, social protection in the Russian Federation evolved into a system of emergency responses to worsening social and economic problems. Social allowances and benefits inherited from the Soviet past were indexed; new allowances and benefits were introduced at federal, regional and local levels. New forms and methods of social protection have emerged, such as the establishment of bodies responsible for the social support of the most vulnerable groups and social extra-budgetary funds. Above all, these measures have been designed to mitigate the emergence or aggravation of social problems. As a result, there are over 1,000 forms of social support for the population in the Russian Federation at the present time. The majority are funded from the State budget. At the federal level, there are 156 forms of social benefits and subsidies and 236 eligible categories of people (veterans, children, disabled, young students, etc.). For all practical purposes, the system of provision of all these benefits is based on the principle of eligibility of certain categories of population. Only two types of assistance established at the federal level – a monthly children's allowance and housing subsidies – require means-testing and are paid to households with a per capita income below the subsistence minimum.

The legislative framework of the social benefits system embraces a huge number of laws, presidential decrees, government regulations and other legal acts adopted at federal, regional and local levels. Quite often these are poorly coordinated and fail to define sources of funding and responsibilities. The Federal Law "On Providing State-Funded Social Assistance", designed to restructure the entire system of social protection, was adopted in the summer of 1999. However, lack of proper implementation mechanisms, including those of funding and information gathering, have to a considerable degree prevented people from obtaining allowances to which they are entitled by law.

Another essential part of the background to social provision for care in the Russian Federation is the approach taken to the family. The Constitution declares protection of the family to be a concern of the State. A fundamental principle of family policy is the use of a differential approach to providing a socially acceptable standard of living for incapacitated family members and creating conditions that enable economically active members to achieve prosperity through work. This means that different categories of family members – children under 18, the disabled, war veterans, senior citizens over 80, single parents, parents with three or more children etc. – have a right to special benefits. Against this background, stronger guarantees of employment are included for workers from families in need of higher social protection, including disabled persons and pensioners, through encouraging efforts to generate specialized jobs, organize vocational training and re-training for these workers and by providing tax and other concessions to the organizations that employ them. The development of institutions providing family-oriented social services (care of children, the elderly and sick family members), material support and advice to families in need of outside help is another official priority.

The Family Code, enacted in 1995, sets out the duties of family members to each other. For example, children over 18 are responsible for incapacitated parents. Able-bodied grandchildren must also support their grandparents, just as each citizen has to support under-age siblings or family members who are unable to work. At present, the typical Russian Federation family is composed of a husband and wife with or without children. This type of family represents about 67 per cent of all families. Another 12 per cent of families live with parents or other relatives. The number of non-traditional families is growing and now accounts for 13 per cent of all families. For the most part these families are made up of lone mothers, divorced women and widows with children.

Privileges to workers providing care for family members

The labour legislation of the Russian Federation makes provision for a range of "privileges" for "domestic reasons" relating to work and leisure arrangements. These include entitlement to shorter than standard working hours, additional days off, unpaid leave, favourable treatment with regard to the termination of employment and special rules for the calculation of length of service. A temporary disability allowance is paid for providing care to a sick family member. For children under 7, this is paid for the entire period of illness, for children between 7 and 15 usually no more than 15 days are covered; in the case of an adult family member three days is the norm, although this period may be extended for up to seven days for serious cases – normally issued when hospitalization is necessary.

Caring for young, sick and disabled family members is also treated as a valid reason to terminate employment. For example, a woman with children under 14 and workers with three or more dependent children under 16 (for children attending educational institutions the age limit is 18) may terminate an employment contract. It is illegal for an employer to dismiss women with children under 3, workers with disabled children under 18 and lone mothers or fathers with children under 14. In addition, workers with two or more dependants have a right to retain the job in the event of lay-offs.

Women are granted child-care leave until the children are 3 years old. This leave can also be granted in full or in part to the child's father, grandmother, grandfather or other relatives or guardian. The period of child-care leave is treated as unbroken service and is included in the total years of service. The equivalent of two minimum standard wage rates (MSWR) per month is paid from the Social Insurance Fund (SIF) until the child is 18 months old. The employer pays for child-care leave until the child is 3 years old at 50 per cent MSWR per month; this is included in the payroll. The job is protected for the duration of the leave.

Provision is also made for children being reared without their mother. Maternity privileges granted to women (such as limitations on night shifts and overtime, holidays and rest-days, additional days of leave, favourable working conditions among others) extend to fathers raising children without mothers (in cases where the mother has died, or has been deprived of her parental rights by a court decision, or is in a medical institution or in a number of other circumstances) as well as to the guardians of minors.

Apart from the benefits guaranteed by law, additional allowances for workers with dependants and providing care for family members (minors, old people and the disabled) may be contained in branch tariff agreements[1] and collective agreements of enterprises. For the most part, these concern parents with underage children and include regular leave at convenient times, additional leave to parents with large families, unpaid leave in the period of school holidays, and so forth. Similar agreements for workers taking care of the elderly and disabled are much less frequent.

Parents of young children also have care responsibility time recognized as length of service. The general length of service, for pension purposes only, is calculated to include such periods as taking care of a Group 1[2] disabled person – a disabled child under 16 and an old person in need of permanent care.

---

[1] A type of collective agreement.

[2] All disabled persons in the Russian Federation are classified in three groups: the most serious cases constitute Group 1.

For mothers who do not work, taking care of a child under 3, the child-care period plus 70 days before the date of the birth of each child is included in the general length of service for up to a maximum of nine years. There is also a provision for pensions on preferential terms for women who have borne five or more children and have raised them to the age of 8. The length of service for women with children under 14 (or 16 if the child is an invalid) remains uninterrupted, irrespective of the number of employment breaks, provided they find new employment before the child's age limit is exceeded. This is relevant when calculating the amount of sick leave payment.

System of state support for persons in need of care

In relation to care, one could summarize the ethos of the social protection system by saying that it is oriented to creating conditions favourable for providing home care to incapacitated people and granting social assistance through government and NGOs.

Income benefits

State agencies are responsible for implementing statutory social protection policies. These bodies register incapacitated persons with the right to pensions, allowances, compensations and other social benefits. They also calculate entitlements and make payments from the relevant sources of finance. In this section we discuss the social protection and support provided through a network of social services institutions, including locally based centres, emergency services, night shelters and child centres, among others.

The most common allowance is a monthly one paid for the period of leave granted to provide care for a child under 18 months. The leave can be given to the child's father, grandmother, grandfather, other relative or guardian, provided they are the main carers of the child. In order to provide financial assistance to families with children, a lump-sum equivalent to 15 MSWRs, is paid to one of the parents (or foster parents) of a newborn child. This one-off birth grant is paid irrespective of whether the leave is taken or not; grandparents or other relatives are not eligible. The other allowance (2 MSWRs) is paid as partial compensation for lost wages to the person actually taking care of the child.

One more common allowance introduced in 1990 is a monthly allowance for a child under 16 (18 years when the child is still in education). This allowance, equivalent to child benefits in Western countries, amounts to 70 per cent of MSWR and is paid from regional budgets. In 1998 an upper limit for eligibility was set at 200 per cent of the subsistence minimum per family member. From the outset, the efficiency of this change was questionable. According to data from the Minister of Labour and Social Protection, this reform would guarantee the allowance to 80 per cent of all households. In 1999, the income limit was reduced to 100 per cent of the subsistence minimum. However, from January 2000 the social protection bodies at municipal level began to implement the 200 per cent cut-off to limit the number of eligible families to those in real need. Table 7.1 summarizes the principal allowances for child care.

It came as a surprise that, according to the data of the survey "Women and Labour Market Reform in Russia" (Russian-Canadian CIDA-funded project), a high percentage of women employees (almost half of the respondents) answered that they would not be able to use the aforementioned benefits. The reason for such a state of affairs may be explained in the following manner:

a) some women, not intending to have children, preclude the benefits;
b) informal agreements between the employee and employer not to use the maternity leave entitlement for mothers with children under 3 years old;
c) fear of losing their job, skills and qualification if they were to use this benefit; and
d) the economic conditions of the family – maternity leave paid during this period providing an insufficient living wage.

Care payments also exist for ill adults and the elderly. A monthly allowance of 60 per cent of the minimum wage is paid to the persons receiving care (the elderly and the disabled) as an increment to their pensions for the period that they need care. This allowance is payable regardless of whether the person providing care is a relative or a co-resident but only on condition that he or she is not working for this reason. The allowance ceases upon employment of the carer or the death of the incapacitated person or the person providing care, when the disabled child reaches the age of 16 or when the incapacitated person becomes fully supported by the State.

Of particular importance for the issue under discussion are the so-called "care-provision increments to pensions". In accordance with the Federal Law "On State Pensions", such increments are awarded to:

a) pensioners who are disabled or in need of permanent care (assistance, supervision) or over 80 years;
b) non-working pensioners with disabled dependants unless these dependants draw some kind of pension;
c) Second World War veterans who do not receive a disabled pension in addition to the old-age pension.

Table 7.1   The most widespread social benefits and allowances for child care
(Russian Federation)

	Benefit, allowance	Amount	Beneficiary	Duration and/or conditions of payment	Source of finance
1	Maternity leave	100% of average earnings	Mother	70+70 days (before and after date of child's birth)	Social insurance fund (SIF)
2	Birth-grant (lump sum)	15 MSWR	Mother/father (foster mother/ father)	One-off payment	SIF
3	Child-care leave (under 18 months)	2 MSWR	Mother/father or other relative	Paid monthly until the child is 18 months old	SIF
4	Child-care leave (under 3 years)	50% MSWR	Mother/father or other relative	Paid monthly until the child is 3 years old	Employer (included in payroll)
5	Allowance for a child under 16 years (18 years for students)	70% MSWR	Mother/father	Paid monthly up to 16 (18) years	Social institutes from the regional budget
6	Lone mother allowance for a child under 16 (18 for students)	140% MSWR	Lone mother	Paid monthly up to 16 (18 for students) years	Social institutes from the regional budget
7	Temporary disability allowance and care of a sick child	According to length of service, but only first 7 days, then 50% of wage	Mother/father or the other family member who is involved in the child care	Children under 7: the entire period of illness; Children 7-15: 15 days	SIF

Normally, the amount of care-provision increments should not exceed that of a state pension.[3] The purpose of care-provision increments is to enable pensioners either to hire somebody who will take care of them, or to

---

[3] This is a minimal pension guaranteed to every citizen of pensionable age, irrespective of his or her length of service.

compensate the family members if the care is provided within the family, or to compensate their own caring for a disabled dependant.

Apart from the above allowances, Russian legislation provides a range of housing and other privileges for socially vulnerable groups, including families with disabled members. Those who suffer from certain diseases also have the right to additional housing space to make the necessary care possible. Free medicines are provided to families with children under the age of 3. There is a discount drug purchase scheme for certain categories of the population. Most of these discounts are awarded to such groups as Second World War veterans and persons of similar status or to those who are regarded as having provided exceptional services to the State. To a lesser extent the scheme covers people with acute and chronic diseases in need of permanent expensive treatment.

Social-service-related assistance to the elderly and the disabled

On the basis of various estimates, 5 to 6 million elderly people in the Russian Federation fall within the categories of unattached persons (without relatives) and persons living alone (persons who have no relatives living in close proximity). Some 1.5 million elderly people need outside help and social services. About 300,000 people need social and medical home care. To provide such assistance, various state-run institutions have been set up.

By far the most widespread type of social-service institutions are the Social Service Centres. These are non-profit-making organizations reporting to the social protection authorities of the municipalities. They organize and coordinate the provision of social services for the elderly and the disabled in their area. Partly funded by federal and local funds, income from fees and revenue from business operations, the centres have the following general functions:

a) to identify and register persons in need of social services;
b) to provide social, medical, psychological, consultative and other forms of help;
c) to assist people in a more active search for opportunities to meet their needs through their own efforts;
d) to assist those who benefit from the centres' services to exercise their legislative rights.

Disabled veterans, Second World War veterans, persons of similar status and people who worked during the war have the first call on a centre's services. They are followed, sufficient staffing permitting, by surviving spouses of those killed in action; spouses of disabled veterans and Second World War widowed veterans who have never remarried; unattached incapacitated persons and the disabled, including those who are forced migrants.[4]

There are six units within the Social Service Centres. The first units, "departments of home-based social services", provide temporary (up to six months) or permanent social services at home to those who have fully or partially lost their capacity for self-help and need outside support and social/household assistance. This type of social support is regarded as most promising, because

a) it requires fewer financial resources; and
b) it enables persons in need of care to live a life as close to normal as possible, and to maintain an adequate social, psychological and physical status.

Social assistance, consulting and other services, included in federal and regional standard lists, can be provided in accordance with the extent and type of care required. Home-based social-services departments can be set up when there are at least 120 potential recipients in a city or 60 in a rural area or in a city district lacking adequate facilities. Services are provided by social workers who are responsible for eight recipients in a city and four in a rural area. The exact areas covered by social workers and their work schedules is defined on the basis of the character and extent of the recipients' needs, distances, transport, availability of food and repair shops and a public catering system, taking into consideration the necessity of making home visits at least twice a week.

The second type of unit, departments of home-based social and medical services, provide temporary (up to six months) or permanent social and household assistance and paramedical services at home to those who have lost fully or partially their ability for self-help and suffer from severe diseases. They differ from the first type in that medical care is provided for seriously ill people, including those suffering from oncological diseases. Specialized departments coordinate their activities with those of the territorial health-care services and the Red Cross committees. These departments provide recipients with high-quality general care, social and household assistance and general nursing at home. They also monitor recipients' health and take measures to prevent exacerbation of chronic diseases, provide moral and psychological support and train the client's relatives in nursing. Specialized departments can be formed when there are at least 60 potential recipients in a city or 30 in a rural area or a city district with inadequate communal facilities. Services are provided by social workers with special training and nurses.

---

[4] It is difficult to obtain benefits for this category, due to complicated legal regulations. This is a new problem for the Russian Federation and remains unresolved both in legislation and in practice.

Unfortunately, only scattered data are available on the activities of the home-based social services. No special studies have been undertaken. Table 7.2 provides figures for the period 1990–93 aggregated for both types.

Day-care departments, the third type of service unit, provide social, house-hold, cultural and medical services for persons who retain their capacity for self-help, transportation, organization of their own meals, leisure and active living. The facilities include paramedical (medical) consulting rooms, clubs, libraries, workshops and dormitories where possible. The staff include organizers of cultural activities, nurses, labour therapy instructors and auxiliary personnel (25 to 35 people altogether). Recipients of care come in the morning and leave in the evening. Such a schedule may last for a couple of weeks or longer and depends on the number of people on the waiting list.

Emergency social-services departments, the fourth type of provider, support persons in need with emergency assistance aimed at maintaining their vital functions. Persons living in extreme poverty are provided with meals, clothes, footwear and other essential items, emergency paramedical assistance, assistance in obtaining temporary shelter, legal advice, emergency psychological support including access to "hot lines", information and consultation on social support issues. The departments employ social workers, psychologists, and lawyers who work in close contact with the Government, the public, charitable and religious organizations and associations, foundations, and with volunteers.

Fifth, social rehabilitation departments help their recipients to maintain vital functions through measures aimed at keeping them in good health, making them more physically active and improving their mental health. To perform their activities such departments can rent premises in health-care institutions, rest houses and sanatoria. Rehabilitation programmes and procedures are worked out by departmental doctors or public health bodies, on an individual basis.

Finally, social canteens provide hot meals and foodstuffs for the impoverished or those incapable of self-help. Only persons living permanently or temporarily within the area serviced by the Centre have the right to use the canteen. Social canteens are supposed to operate a means test but, in practice, they quite often provide services to whoever applies for help, irrespective of income levels.

Apart from these service-oriented providers, there are a number of institutional services.

Residential state-run institutions – boarding homes – take care of persons not capable of self-help or who have medical grounds for residing in specialized institutions. Boarding homes offer a range of services including household assistance, meals, recreation, socio-medical and sanitary services, educational services for the disabled and job placement services.

Table 7.2   Evolution of home-based social services

	1990	1993	% increase
Offices providing home help	3 360	7 833	233.1
Social workers per office	32.0	97.9	305.9
Recipients cared for per office	315.0	724.2	229.9
Recipients per social worker	9.9	7.4	−27

Source: "The concept of social care for aged and disabled people under the market economy", Ministry of Labour and Social Development of the Russian Federation, Moscow, 1994, pp. 17–18.

At the beginning of 2000, according to the Ministry of Labour and Social Development, there were 1,160 boarding homes for the elderly and disabled. Although the number of beds increased between 1980 and 1990, the situation was reversed in the restructuring of the mid-1990s, when the number of beds fell. However, there is some evidence that the numbers began to rise again in 1998 and exceeded the 1991 level, although no official data have, as yet, been released.

An important distinguishing characteristic of boarding homes is that they developed as socio-medical institutions. As a result, they are staffed by medical personnel and are equipped with medical facilities. In most other countries such institutions fall within a purely social category and their medical personnel is made up uniquely of nurses: should more serious medical needs arise, patients resort to the help of the nearby city or municipal hospitals or clinics. The Russian system evolved in the period when it was more convenient to concentrate all the services in one place. However, the quality of medical services in such homes is lower than in specialized medical institutions. Medical staff employed in these homes receive lower wages than their colleagues working for the Ministry of Health. Doctors' positions in homes are considered of low prestige and the staffing had become a problem until the pressure of unemployment forced many doctors to take any available vacancy.

There are also special homes intended to serve as boarding homes for elderly persons (married couples) with full or partial ability for self-help. These facilities aim to create the conditions necessary for the inhabitants to satisfy their basic needs. Such homes are municipal or government property. They are part of the "housing reserve for social use". Normally, boarding homes have a number of one or two-room self-contained flats and facilities which include a medical check-up room, a library, a room for club activities, a canteen or cafeteria, a workshop, a laundry, a dry-cleaner's and a shoe-repair shop. The homes have all the facilities to make them "elder friendly". Repairs and upkeep costs are paid from regional and local budgets. Again, access is on a priority basis. Unattached pensioners (those without relatives) on the list for better housing, veterans of the Second World War and persons with similar status, parents and widows of servicemen killed in action or while performing state and public duties have first priority to move into boarding homes. Persons suffering from chronic alcoholism or drug-addiction, sexually transmitted diseases (STDs), psychological problems and cancer require treatment in specialized hospitals and are not accepted in boarding homes. People moving into boarding homes are obliged to transfer their house or apartment to the local authority. The privatization of apartments in boarding homes is not permitted.

Efficiency of the social protection system

In that pensioners have very limited opportunities for gaining income from other sources (employment, small business, subsistence farming, interests on savings), the benefits and allowances they can draw on can increase their pension by a maximum of 20 per cent.

The 1998 crisis resulted in drastic reductions in social benefits and allowances and an increase in the number of those in need of social assistance (table 7.3).

Table 7.3 shows pension calculations. According to data from the Ministry of Labour and Social Development, the minimum old-age pension with allowances (lump-sum compensation not included) amounted to 46.5 per cent of the subsistence minimum in July of 2000. The Goskomstat (State Statistical Agency) data for 1998 demonstrate that 6.4 million disabled people eligible for benefits were receiving on average 23 roubles per month (4.6 per cent of the 493.3 roubles subsistence minimum) and 13.4 million veterans were getting on average 19 roubles per month (3.9 per cent of the subsistence minimum).

A comparison of average amounts of the most widespread benefits and allowances with average resources of households shows that the ratio is: 2.8 per cent of subsistence minimum per family for food and travel allowances and 1.4 per cent for housing allowances. By the second quarter of 1999 the ratios had become even worse. The ratio of monthly child allowance to average per capita household resources dropped from 4.2 per cent in the fourth quarter of 1998 to 3.2 per cent in the second quarter of 1999.

The number of people eligible for various social guarantees, privileges and payments specified by the legislation of the Russian Federation amounts to about 70 per cent of the population in Russia. Hence about 100 million people have the right to claim social benefits and allowances. Federal-level privileges and benefits alone will require over 15 per cent of the gross domestic product (GDP) to meet payments, which is much more than the actual social expenditure of the federal budget (1.6 per cent of GDP in 1998).

Table 7.3   Ratio of minimum social guarantees to the subsistence minimum
(1996–98) (as a percentage)

	1996	1997	As of 1 Jan. 1998	As of 1 Jan. 1999
Minimum wage	13	19	18	13
Standard rate for starting grade in the civil service	19	18	19	14
Minimum pension (without allowances)				
old-age pension	27	25	29	21
disability pension:				
Group 1	38	35	40	29
Group II	19	18	20	15
Group III	13	12	13	10
survivor's pension (per incapacitated family member)	13	12	13	10
Social pensions to persons disabled since childhood (including allowance for provision of care)				
Group I	38	35	40	29
Group II	19	18	20	15

Source: Statistical Bulletin 1998/1999, pp.199–201.

A 1999 survey by Goskomstat demonstrated that 33.6 per cent of households had members eligible for benefits and allowances in accordance with the law or to be provided by various institutions in cash or in kind (Statistical Bulletin, 1998/1999, pp.187–190).

Data from the Russian Longitudinal Monitoring of the Economic Situation and Health of the Population (RLMS) show that in September–November 1996 about 44 per cent of households qualified for monthly child-care benefits and over 11 per cent were eligible for medicines at discount prices. However, about 83 per cent of these households were not receiving child-care benefits and only 7 per cent of the households that qualified for housing subsidies actually received them. The discrepancy between the number eligible for benefits and the number in receipt of benefits is due to the budget deficit and arrears in social payments.

As mentioned earlier, income level is the criteria for making a decision on eligibility for child and housing allowances. As a result the lion's share of resources allocated for social protection at every level is spent on supporting groups with incomes above the subsistence minimum. Hence a substantial part of the social protection resources is not spent on those in real need.

According to a number of assessments of the efficiency of social support programmes in industrialized countries and some Eastern European countries, the share of social transfers reaching families below the poverty line is as high as 50 per cent. In the Russian Federation the equivalent figure is only 19 per cent (World Bank, 1996). Data from Goskomstat prove that the share of recipients of benefits and allowances in poor households is lower than in families located elsewhere on the income spectrum. The total sums received by the population through various social protection channels are distributed in such a way that only one-fourth of all benefits and allowances comes into possession of the households below the subsistence minimum while households above the subsistence minimum get the remaining three-quarters (RLMS).

Interestingly, the probability of getting a monthly child allowance is higher for families that are not poor (ibid.). In 1996, for example, the probability of getting this form of allowance was about 45 per cent for families that were not poor, 36 per cent for the poor and only 25 per cent for the poorest.

This mode of redistribution is neither fair nor efficient if the importance of social assistance for poor households is taken into consideration. The value of the ratio of benefits and allowances to the income of poor households is extremely low and gives no grounds to evaluate the existing social protection system as providing real support for the poor. By way of example, the monthly child allowance covers a meagre 8 per cent of a poor family's budget deficit (ibid.).

Reforming the social protection system

Among the factors hindering the formation of effective social policies in general and an effective policy of social protection in particular are an oversimplified perception of the status of the Russian Federation as a social state enshrined by the Constitution and the attempts to equate a social state with a paternalistic state. Social legislation, irrespective of the changes made to it in the 1990s, still bears the hallmarks of the pre-reform past. The principle of eligibility, giving the right to receive allowances and benefits to whole social groups, has been retained and strengthened; it is the most vivid example of the fact that the State's liabilities are unrealistically high, given its resources. As a result, the actual benefit distribution is out of line with the principles of social justice and with the real economic and financial capacities of the State. During periods of transition and crisis, the system of social protection should be, first and foremost, aimed at ensuring the protection of socially vulnerable groups and supporting those unable to support themselves. We suggest that a wider and more efficient use of targeting and means-testing should form the basis for the re-structuring of the social protection system. The transition to providing targeted social assistance would see a higher share of resources allocated to the most needy households. A modernized system of social payments would make it possible to establish an integrated database covering all the recipients of social allowances and benefits. In turn, the individualized recording of payments would reduce the amount of resources needed to fund the system.

However, when advocating the principle of means-testing, one should realize that existing methods of such testing, based on legal income (wages, pensions, stipends), are imperfect. The probability of including families that are not poor into programmes is high. In the immediate future, searching for relatively inexpensive means-test methods should become a top priority of social policy reform. Another aspect of reform should be the simplification of the existing system when introducing the means-test procedure for poor households and the social insurance principle for households which do not fall below the poverty threshold but are in need of social support.

At present, most of the decisions that result in liabilities concerning payment of social allowances and benefits and providing other types of social assistance are made at the federal level in the form of laws, while most of the responsibilities for making the payments rests with the regions. At the same time, regional agencies have a limited capability to modernize the privileges and adjust them to their specific needs. The existing situation is inconsistent with the principles of federalism. Given this, one of the most important tasks for the Russian Federation is to give the local authorities as much freedom as possible to decide what types, size and forms of payments are necessary and to which categories of the population they should apply within their territory.

PART III

CARE IN INDUSTRIALIZED COUNTRIES

THE POLITICS OF SOCIAL CARE IN FINLAND: CHILD AND ELDER CARE IN TRANSITION

8

Anneli Anttonen

Introduction

In all affluent societies governments are seeking new solutions and strategies to meet the increasing service and care needs of the growing elderly population. Concurrently, the feminization of labour market participation, increasing mobility of workforce and overall individualization of lifestyles and family patterns have reduced informal care resources. All this has led to a situation where caring has become a major social policy issue in the new millennium. More than ever before, informal care-giving work needs to be replaced by formal arrangements of care. At the same time, informal caregiving has started to constitute a new policy area of modern welfare states.

The aim of this chapter is to look at social care policy in the Scandinavian context. It focuses on two major areas of social care policy: child care and elder care. Finland, alongside the other Scandinavian countries, differs from most post-industrial welfare societies in the extent to which informal care has already been transformed from a private to a public matter. The comparative literature on the welfare states shows that in the Scandinavian societies there exists an extensive public provision of social care services for adult citizens who need regular help in their daily lives. The Scandinavian societies are also fairly generous in their support of families with small children.

The present chapter pays special attention to the recent changes and trends concerning public policy on social care. In this context, it is of great importance to look at the changing boundaries between private and public responsibilities. Indeed, social care as a concept comprises care work done in both informal and formal settings (Daly and Lewis, 2000). It is also evident that innovations in the field of social care often represent a new welfare mix, where there are no clear borderlines between private and public responsibilities. This is true even in Scandinavia, which since the 1960s has relied strongly on public services for child and elder care provision. The situation is, however, changing quite rapidly.

The Scandinavian social care regime

In the field of social care services there are many important similarities between Finland, Sweden, Norway and Denmark. To begin with, Sipilä et al. (1997, pp. 39–40) have argued that in all the Nordic countries (with the exception of Iceland) social care services are widely available. Secondly, the middle and upper classes are prominent users of public social services; this is related to the fact that service systems in general respond most specifically to the interests of women. Thirdly, the municipalities are responsible for service provision; they are independent in terms of their right to levy taxes and are supported by the State in this task (Alber, 1995; Kröger, 1997). These similarities allows us to speak of a Scandinavian social care regime (see Anttonen and Sipilä, 1996).

When describing the Scandinavian social care regime, reference is often made to the principle of universalism as opposed to selectivism and particularism (Anttonen and Sipilä, 2000). The label of universalism is however often used vaguely, although it is a multidimensional concept (e.g. Sainsbury, 1988). Universalism means, first, that all citizens have access to the same service system; second, that this system offers uniform services all over the country; third, that the services are available to all citizens, irrespective of their economic status; fourth, that a majority of citizens actually use these services when in need. Universalism may also include the idea that citizens have a right to services.

The grand idea of universal social services was brought into public political discourse by Swedish social democrats in the 1920s ("society as people's home"). It was closely connected to the promotion of gender equality and the work society. Universalist solutions, both in the field of income security and social services, have received much support in Scandinavian politics, especially since the 1950s. In Finland though, this has been more a result of a political compromise than an explicit political aim. Universal social policy has been a pragmatic consequence to this situation: social democrats have promoted the interests of employees and agrarians have put the interests of farmers first. Neither group has wanted to exclude better-off people. In particular, the agrarians' demand for regional equality has favoured solutions that cover all citizens on the same terms.

Another strong source of support for the development of universal social services has been the women's movement. Nordic feminism often sees the equal availability of social services for all as a guarantee of women's right to paid labour and as a way of reconciling home and work. It is also important to note that the feminization of labour market participation has been paralleled by the expansion of social services (Anttonen, 1997). In 1997, 41 per cent of employed women worked in the Finnish public sector. The field of social care is especially female-dominated: in the mid-1990s more than 90 per cent of care workers were women (Kolehmainen, 1997, p. 21).

To understand the distinctive nature of the Scandinavian social care regime, it is important to note that municipalities are much more than administrative regions (Kröger, 1996). Although the State provides the framework through its legislative power, municipalities have the main responsibility for running such social services as education, health care and social care. In these tasks they are subsidized by a central government grant, but the Government does not control local activities in detail. It is also important to mention that municipalities are democratic and self-governing institutions in the sense that their representatives are elected in municipal elections and they have the right to levy taxes.

Tax financing is one of the cornerstones of the Scandinavian social care regime. Municipal taxes create a bond among people living in the same community with respect to the funding of social services. Among Scandinavians it has been common to think that taxes are the best method of funding in that a certain benefit can be systematically made available either to all people or to those who, according to certain criteria, are judged as being in need. Tax revenues are a useful means of income transfer where the taxpayer does not benefit from the outlay immediately or personally. Taxes also allow for the common good to be taken into account and moral criteria are not as pressing as they are in other forms of funding. Therefore tax-based services and benefits are of great importance for poor people and other marginal groups. Indeed, the countries with extensive and universal service provision rely mainly on tax revenues for funding.

Universalism has been a leading principle of welfare state development. However, it is important to stress that even in Scandinavia universalism is not complete. It is more like an ideal or never-to-be-reached goal as Lehto (1998) says. However, many Scandinavians appreciate equality and tend to think that similarity produces an equal outcome, whereas differences (in service production) easily lead to inequality. There is also a strong reliance on professionalism and expert knowledge, which gives at least indirect support to the national standardization of services. Of course, the policy of universalism is also supported strongly by the extensive public sector and its interest groups.

Many feminist scholars (Anttonen, 1997; Hernes, 1987; Siim, 1993) have pointed out that universalism has brought into being a woman-friendly welfare society, where women's needs as mothers and workers are widely acknowledged. National as well as comparative studies show that the Northern European democracies have the most advanced welfare systems for safeguarding citizen's social care rights. In Finland, it is legitimate to speak of established social rights in regard to children's day care and the care of disabled, but only to some extent when it comes to elder care. Elder care lacks the characteristics of social rights and is thus only partly shaped by the policy of universalism.

In Finland, the universalist principles in the field of social care encountered problems during the economic recession of the early 1990s. The recession of 1990–94 was unparalleled in Finland's economic history, with unemployment up to the 20 per cent level. This particularly unbalanced the central government budget, which was heavily cut. One of the main victims of cost containment was the state subsidy to local government, which strongly impacted on municipal social services. Services for the elderly suffered as a result. Currently, central government grants cover only a minor part (about 20 per cent) of local government expenses in social and health care. This means that municipalities carry the main responsibility for financing and providing social services.

The economic recession together with the growth of a liberal ideology has led to a profound restructuring of social policy. However, even before the economic collapse, Finnish social welfare authorities had opened up some important routes to developing new strategies. A major reform of social welfare legislation in 1984 allowed local authorities to use state subsidies for the purchase of social services, not only from the municipal authorities but also from voluntary and private organizations or to make payments for informal care. The Social Welfare Act (1984) obliges municipalities to provide services according to need, but also gives them freedom to decide how these needs are met.

Another major change took place in 1993, when the system of earmarked state subsidies for social welfare came to an end. This reform gave even more freedom to the municipalities in governing social service policy; however, financial resources were at the same time much more limited. In spite of these legal changes, social services are today mainly financed by tax revenues and only partly by users and other sources. In the 1990s, the tendency was to increase service fees. In Finland, as in many other countries, the Government tries to reduce the costs of tax-funded social care services that are provided according to high professional standards. In particular, there has been a strong tendency to reduce the costs of institutional care.

Scandinavia is typical of affluent societies in that social care arrangements are currently being reassessed and reorganized, and pressures towards convergence are growing. Many scholars and politicians have pointed out that, with the continued trend towards economic globalization, the Scandinavian countries will be hard-pressed to maintain their high standards of social welfare (Andersen et al., 1999; Lindbeck, 1994; Stephens, 1996). These countries therefore have a special interest in evaluating the so-called Nordic welfare model and in looking for alternative ways to provide social care.

A number of changes have already taken place in Finland. This chapter argues that the municipality as a producer of services often turns to private companies, voluntary organizations and households to purchase social care or to support its care provision. Besides institutional care and home-help services for the elderly, the so-called home care allowances represent a new type of social care. Instead of providing social services directly to elderly and disabled persons, the State pays relatives and other lay persons to take care of those who need regular help and attendance. In the field of family policy, home-care allowances are even more important in that they function as an alternative to municipal child-care institutions. All these developments indicate that care regimes are undergoing rapid change.

Finnish child-care policy: Universalism and pluralism

Finnish childcare is a good example of recent changes in social care policy. In the mid-1980s Finland adopted a new policy line by introducing home-care allowances to parents with children under three. Moreover, in 1997 families started to receive a special allowance if children were cared for in private day-care institutions. In this way nearly all forms of child care now benefit from public financial support. The case of child care clearly shows that innovations were created and implemented before the 1990s. Thus, economic recession and the growth of a liberal ideology do not explain all of the changes.

In Finland, the first calls for public day care were made at the beginning of the twentieth century. Yet, it took more than 50 years for the first national law on day care to come into force, in 1973. As late as the 1950s the number of municipal kindergartens and crèches was very low; however, the pattern of women's labour market participation started to change rapidly, as did the pattern of women's political participation. In the 1940s, 70 per cent of women stopped working on the birth of their first child, while in the 1960s more than half returned to work within 12 months (Rissanen, 2000, p. 40). At least as important was that in the 1960s the proportion of women in the Finnish parliament rose from 15 to 22 per cent. These factors combined to set day-care reform into motion. Children's day care became one of the most debated social policy issues in the 1960s and early 1970s.

Following a series of inevitable political disputes and compromises, the first National Day-Care Act (1973) came into force. Local authorities were charged with the responsibility of supporting, first, the building of day-care centres and, second, supervised day care in families. The latter option was included in the law partly because the advocates of the so-called mother's wage remained in the minority: the alternative suggested was that all mothers with children under school age would be paid a flat-rate allowance so that they could themselves decide who would look after their children (Anttonen, 1999a).

Debates around a mother's wage in Finland have been closely associated with the policy of municipal child day care. Two contradictory policy lines have been put forward: the agrarian Centre Party has promoted the idea of a mother's wage, while the political left strongly supports building up a nation-wide system of child day-care centres. The pleas of the Centre Party to support families directly through flat-rate allowances were left unanswered in the 1970s. After the introduction of the National Day-Care Act, the municipal day-care system expanded very rapidly (see table 8.1).

Up until the 1990s children's day-care places increased steadily, with Finland gradually catching up with coverage levels in Sweden and Denmark (Kröger, 1997, pp. 492–497). The recession of the early 1990s, however, put a brake on this development, and the family day-care service was in particular greatly reduced. In the late 1990s child-care services started to grow once again. Generous public support to municipal child-care has left very little room for private provision. Whereas in 1974 private providers employed 20 per cent of all personnel in children's day care, the proportion had shrunk to 3 per cent in 1990. However the staff numbers in private day care dropped by half during this period (Päivärinta, 1993, p. 51).

In the mid-1980s child-care legislation was revised quite radically. There was still a chronic shortage of day-care places and municipalities were unable to meet the increasing demand. Moreover, the debate on alternative ways to provide child-care had been going on since the first Day-Care Act was enacted in 1973. The Centre Party persisted in advocating cash benefits to families which could make no use of day-care services.

The child-care reform implemented in 1985 represented a historic compromise between the two competing policies. By accepting a proposal for a revised day-care act, the Centre Party won the backing it needed to get a system of child home-care allowances (CHCAs) adopted. The new legislation consisted of two major parts. The new Day-Care Act required local governments not only to organize day-care services according to demand, but also established day care as a legal right for parents (or guardians) of children under 3. This right became fully effective in 1990, and in 1996 was extended to cover all children under school age.

The second part of the reform was equally radical. In 1985, the Finnish Parliament passed a law which stipulated that, as an alternative to a municipal

Table 8.1   Publicly funded day care for children in Finland, 1965–98
            (number of places)

Year	Day-care centres	Family day care	Total
1965	19 750	0	19 750
1970	28 195	0	28 195
1980	83 670	47 970	131 640
1990	118 030	95 850	213 880
1995	125 031	65 580	190 611
1998	142 776	75 746	218 524

Source: Anttonen, 1999a, p. 65.

day-care place, the parents of children under 3 were to be given the option of claiming a CHCA, either to look after their children themselves or to pay for private care (Sipilä and Korpinen, 1998, p. 263). At the same time the situation of parents who opted to stay at home was facilitated by an amendment to the Contracts of Employment Act, which gave parents of children under 3 the right to take child care leave with full job security.

Almost as soon as it was introduced, the CHCA became immensely popular, even though the new law was to be implemented gradually and would not cover all children under age 3 until 1990 (table 8.2). Already in 1987 the number of children of families choosing the allowance surpassed the number of children in the same age group in municipal day care. The peak years in the popularity of the CHCA were the early 1990s, when the unemployment level started to climb to a record high level of around 20 per cent. At the same time, the amount of the allowance was at its highest to date. Moreover, a number of local governments were paying additional supplements to those receiving the CHCA. At that time, nearly 70 per cent of children under age 3 were covered by the CHCA system, while less than 20 per cent of children in this age group were in municipal day care.

Given the improving employment situation, the need for day care has risen since 1994 and, correspondingly, the number of children on CHCA has decreased. Moreover, in 1996 the Government, led by the Social Democrats, cut the CHCA by more than 20 per cent, making it considerably less attractive. However, even at the end of 1997, 45 per cent of children under 3 were in care arrangements subsidized by the benefit and the majority (more than 90 per cent) were looked after at home by a mother or father.

Table 8.2   Care of children under age 3 in Finland, 1985–98

Year	Children in day-care centres	Children in family day care	Total children in day care	Families on CHCA[1]	Children under age 3 on CHCA[2]
1985	13 103	27 299	40 402	25 890	n.a.
1990	17 594	25 173	42 767	81 210	n.a.
1993	15 488	16 139	31 627	95 820	103 360
1995	16 392	16 296	32 688	84 476	89 807
1998	18 745	22 245	40 990	74 359	80 683

n.a. = figures not available.
[1] In 1997 the CHCA was reformed and, thus, later figures are not wholly comparable with earlier ones.
[2] Until 1992 recipients of CHCA were registered only as families.

Source: Sipilä and Korpinen, 1998, p. 268; Anttonen, 1999a, p. 67.

In 1997, the CHCA was accompanied by a new benefit, the children's private care allowance (CPCA), to be used by families preferring to purchase private day-care services. The CPCA is paid to families with children under school age. With its introduction, nearly all forms of care arrangements for small children are now covered by public support. The CHCA can be used to purchase private services or hire a child minder, even though only 5 per cent of the CHCA recipient families have done this (Rostgaard and Fridberg, 1998, p. 250). However, the introduction of the CPCA signifies that the Government now openly encourages private child-care provision.

In the European context, the number of children under 3 cared for in day-care centres is relatively high in Finland. However, in Sweden and Denmark nearly half the children under 3 were in public day care in 1996 (NOSOSCO, 1998). When looking at the figures for children over 3, it is easy to arrive at the conclusion that the coverage of day-care provision is low in Finland, not only in comparison to Scandinavia but also to countries such as France, Belgium, Germany and Italy, where nearly all children over 3 are within some sort of day-care provision (Rostgaard and Fridberg, 1998).

Overall, three-quarters of Finnish children under 3 are cared for at home, as are nearly a third of all children over 3 years of age. Most families choose to take care of their children at home at least some of the time before the child is 3 years old. More than 90 per cent of parents staying at home after parental leave is over are women, although one of the explicit aims of the childcare reform of 1985 was to promote gender equality. The end result is that small children are cared for mainly at home by their mothers. Yet, it is important to remember that in

Finland women do re-enter the labour market. The number of women staying out of work at the time when their youngest child turns three is internationally very low (Salmi, 2000). Moreover, as the option of part-time work does not really exist in Finland, around 90 per cent of working women are in full-time work. The legal right to children's day-care services guarantees that women have the choice of re-entering the labour market.

The Finnish case confirms that there have been profound changes in the field of child-care policy. The new allowances (CHCA and CPCA) have brought plurality into a one-dimensional system. The principle of universalism has been transformed: whereas earlier it included the idea of providing nationwide services for all in need, today's universalism means that all modes of child care are covered by public financing. The change is best described by two phrases: "'particularism in provision" and "universalism in financing".

Elder care in transition

When looking at the development of elder care in different countries we can identify some common features. Evers and Sachsse (1999) have suggested that welfare states are constructed on two main pillars. On the one hand, benefits and services developed from the poor law and social assistance tradition are often means-tested, targeted at poor citizens or citizens at risk, and financed and provided by local governments. On the other hand are the benefits and services which have their roots in welfare state-ism and are tax or insurance based. These are designed to cover the social risks of wage earners and to finance and run large-scale (and often universal) service systems such as health care and education so as to promote the welfare of the entire nation. The level of centralization, standardization, legal codification and professionalization is high among these services, while those developed from the poor laws have remained decentralized, unprofessional and patchy, and their legal status is often weak (Evers and Sachsse, 1999).

Social elder care has its roots deep in the poor law tradition. In Finland, there is a huge difference between the status of child care and elder care. The former is today a universal service with clear social rights. The modernization of elder care has been much slower. Accordingly, the rights of citizens and duties of local authorities are not as clearly written into the law as in the childcare legislation, and the right of appeal is seldom used. Access to care services depends on professional assessment and there is considerable variati⸳⸳ between different municipalities. Care for the elderly is even ⸳ regarded as a family obligation, whereas care by formal organiz⸳ stood to be more or less complementary to the informal systen to the other Scandinavian countries too, with the exception of Denmark (Sundström, 1994).

Finnish elder care has its roots in institutional care designed for poor elderly people. Institutional care has been in the hands of municipalities. It was not until the 1980s that old-age homes began receiving regular state subsidies in addition to municipal budgets. Moreover, it can be argued that only with the Social Welfare Act of 1984 was poor relief thinking finally supplanted. The new law made old-age home residents equal and obliged them all to pay for their care. Before 1984 there were two categories of residents: the welfare clients who did not pay any fees (but lost their assets if they had any) and the so-called self-paying patients who paid nominal fees.

In Finland, as in the other Scandinavian countries, the proportion of older people living in institutions has been traditionally somewhat higher than in most other European countries. In the early 1990s the proportion of elderly people (65+) receiving long-term care in different institutions was around 7 per cent (OECD, 1991, table 3.1). Since the early 1980s, the absolute number of older people in institutional care has been falling due to the policy of deinstitutionalization. Between 1981 and 1991 the supply of beds in residential homes decreased by 6 per cent. In 1991–96 the reduction in places was nearly 20 per cent in the age group 75 and over (Noro, 1998, pp. 77–78).

Long-term residential care has been replaced by serviced housing, home-help services and payments for informal carers. Moreover, the primary health-care system has taken on a major responsibility for people needing long-term institutional care. With the number of very old people increasing in the future there will be more demand for institutional long-term care, although on average elderly people are healthier than people used to be at a given age. Moreover, older people often live alone and prefer to stay in their own home as long as possible. It is also important to stress that in Finland there is an unusually high difference in longevity between men and women. Thus, the share of women of the older population is high, which makes elder care a highly gendered phenomenon. In 1997, there were 469,024 females aged 65 and over in Finland, while the figure for men was 283,464 (*Statistical Yearbook of Finland*, 1997, p. 82). In the same year, the overall share of older people was 14.6 per cent out of the total population of 5.1 million. It is estimated that the proportion of older people will rise to 22.7 per cent by the year 2020 (Vaarama and Kautto, 1998, p. 7).

All Western countries have adopted a policy of deinstitutionalization in favour of community care. In Finland, home-help services, service housing and home-care allowances represent the main alternatives to institutional care. Municipal home help constitutes the most important part of community care for older citizens. It has a fairly long tradition in Finland, the first law of Municipal Home Help dating back to 1950. A significant extension was introduced by the Municipal Home Help Act of 1966 when municipalities began to receive higher state subsidies to provide home-help services to the older population.

According to the law, home-help services are available for all those who need them, irrespective of age and financial position. The overall status of municipal home help for the elderly has, however, been changing. Earlier it was more or less a universal service given in small amounts to nearly every applicant. Nowadays the aim is to enable old people to live at home as long as possible. In 1970, around 7 per cent of the population aged 65 and over received home help; by 1980 this figure has increased to cover 20 per cent. In 1990, Finland was in the top position internationally with the coverage of 24 per cent (OECD, 1991, table 3.6). However, the average time that was spent with one client was only 1.5 hours a week. At the beginning of the 1990s the Finnish system of home help provided services for many, but for most this service was minimal.

By 1995, however, the situation had rapidly changed, with home-help services covering only 12 per cent of the elderly population. Between 1988 and 1995 the number of older home-help clients decreased by 39,000 (31 per cent). There are now fewer old people receiving home help, but the time spent with one client has increased. Home-help services are provided to those who need lots of help and, despite cuts, to some extent they help compensate for the decline in institutional care. Concurrently, the service fees for home help have gone up and more people use private services (Vaarama and Kautto, 1998, pp. 36–38). Yet, in 1997, 80 per cent of home-help services were provided by municipalities and the rest by voluntary organizations or private companies.

In addition to home help there is a wide range of other supportive services available for the elderly: municipal meal services, transport services, and bathing services. These services are organized differently according to municipality. Usually, the services are provided by the municipality's own institutions such as schools and old people's homes. The tendency has been for municipalities to increasingly use private enterprises and voluntary organizations as subcontractors.

The only service for the elderly that expanded in the 1990s was serviced housing. Serviced housing has tripled in a decade, in 1998 covering 2 per cent of the elderly. There are flats especially designed for the elderly, and service centres where elderly people have access to home help, home nursing and a 24-hour emergency call service. Serviced housing is run mainly by non-profit organizations heavily subsidized by grants from the Finnish Slot Machine Association. As far as health services are concerned, home nursing is an important part of community care. The basic principles of home nursing are more or less the same as in home help: together they form the backbone of elder care for those living at home.

Support for informal caring: The system of home-care allowances

The public sector has assumed a wide-ranging responsibility for care in Scandinavia. Yet the family and close relatives play the most important role in helping older people to cope with their day-to-day activities. Recent studies show that informal care has been increasing in Finland, while social service provision has been declining. According to the study by Forss et al. (1995) the family is the main source of help for older people. Children are the most important group of helpers, followed by municipal home help. Among men, spouses are the second most important source of help, while among women, spouses are even less significant than friends and neighbours (table 8.3).

According to the old-age barometer first conducted in 1994, one-third of the population aged 60 or over was in need of daily help. When this survey was repeated in 1998, the proportion needing daily help remained unchanged. However, some very interesting changes had taken place in the four-year period. In 1998, half of those who needed daily help received it from their spouses. The corresponding figure in 1994 was as low as 26 per cent, very close to the 24 per cent found by Forss et al. The two surveys also tell us that home-help services dropped from second to third place as a primary source of help (*Vanhuusbarometri*, 1994, p. 21 and 71; *Vanhusbarometeri*, 1998, pp. 50–51).

How then should we explain this upward change, when the overall tendency seems to be that informal care resources are declining in importance? One reason is that home care and home nursing services are today much more strictly assessed than in the early 1990s. In practice, there are as many municipal home-helpers at work as before, but they no longer cater to those with minor caring and helping requirements. Thus, along with the policy of deinstitutionalization, the number of older people receiving social care services has declined. The new situation has been partly offset by the system of home-care allowances that are paid to relatives and other lay persons to take care of those who need regular help and attendance.

Home-care allowances (HCAs) are a fairly new innovation in Finnish old-age welfare. When placed in a historical context, care allowances represent a new discourse on the policy of care. Some municipalities were already paying allowances to relatives taking care of their elders in the late 1970s. At the beginning of the 1980s a national experiment of HCAs was launched by the

Table 8.3   The primary sources of help among people aged 65+ in Finland in 1994

Source of help	Percentage of all persons over 65+ receiving help	Percentage of women aged 65+ receiving help	Percentage of men aged 65+ receiving help
Children	57	59	52
Home help	33	36	23
Relatives	19	21	14
Spouse	24	9	39
Neighbours	16	15	16
Friends	15	16	10
Total numbers in 65+ bracket	411,000	311,000	100,000

Source: Forss et. al., 1995, p. 61.

Ministry of Social and Health Affairs. The aim was to encourage close relatives and friends to assume responsibility for the care of older and disabled persons (Anttonen, 1999b).

During the early 1980s payments to carers of frail, elderly and disabled persons increased substantially. The reform of social welfare legislation defined these payments as a form of home-help service, making it possible for the municipalities to receive state subsidies for this purpose. In 1984, when HCAs were integrated into the Social Welfare Act alongside such services as municipal home help and service housing, municipalities were allowed – but not obliged – to pay allowances for relatives. Nevertheless, in 1989 HCAs were in use in each of the 452 municipalities.

The Finnish system of supporting informal care remains somewhat variable and inconsistent, chiefly because it has been developed in a piecemeal manner without strong statutory coordination. From the very beginning the system of HCA was organized on a municipal basis, and eligibility for the allowance has varied from commune to commune. Some national rules were stipulated in 1993 when the Social Services Act was amended (Anttonen, 1999b).

The aim of the law was to bring some uniformity to the variety. Under the new law the HCA may consist of money or services or both but they have to be specified in a care and service plan drawn up by the municipal authorities. The local government grants HCA to a person who is being cared for but the monetary benefit is paid to the caregiver. The law also sets a minimum allowance and some other requirements. Moreover, a contract between the municipality and caregiver is required for specifying the rights and duties of both sides. One of the most important achievements is that, since 1993, the caregiver is entitled to a pension arranged by the Municipal Pension Institution.

The only restriction concerning the status of caregiver is that he or she has to be over 18 years old. Other restrictions, common in other countries, do not exist. The carer can be a spouse or a relative or anybody accepted by the care recipient. The caregiver is not required to stay outside the labour market and he or she can also be an unemployed person. The income or property of the carer or care-receiver does not affect the allowance; this is graded depending on how binding and demanding the care work is. According to the law the minimum fee is 1,070 Finnish Marks (FIM). However, it is possible to pay smaller allowances if the care need is not very demanding. In some municipalities the highest allowance paid for a relative of a patient in need of continuous care in 1997 was 7,000 FIM, while the average monthly payment was around 1,500 FIM. These figures remained at the same level throughout the 1990s. Since 1997 a monthly day off has become obligatory.

In the early 1990s the Finnish system of home-care allowances for carers of older people was one of the most comprehensive in the whole of Europe, although no law required the municipalities to pay HCAs (Sipilä and Korpinen, 1998). In 1990 the number of home-care allowance recipients was at its highest, but since 1992 it has steadily declined due to heavy cuts in public budgets and new regulations. In 1990, there were about 13,000 older persons receiving home-care allowances, which means that about 2 per cent of the age group was covered by HCAs. In the mid-1990s the number had dropped to about 2,000 recipients, but at the end of the 1990s the number of recipients began to rise again.

There have been some significant changes in the structure of old-age welfare. Home help and home nursing as well as housing services for the elderly expanded very rapidly during the 1970s and 1980s. In the 1990s only service housing expanded, while home-help service provision declined. If we look at the situation in 1998, only one-tenth of people in the 65–74 age group used any kind of external services, while the corresponding figure was three-quarters in the age group of 85 and over. Table 8.4 sums up the usage of the most important social care services among different age groups.

Besides home help and home nursing, the system of HCA has been of great importance in limiting the expansion of institutional care. However, the system of HCA has been seen as an alternative not only to institutional care but also to home help. Since the recession of the 1990s the Government has tried to reduce the costs of long-term care financed by tax revenues and provided to highly professional standards. In spite of these developments, among social care services institutional care is the most extensive part of expenditure, while less than 1 per cent of total social expenditure on old-age welfare is used for HCAs.

Table 8.4 Care service provision for older people in Finland in 1998 (as a percentage of age group per type)[1]

Type of provision	65–74 years	75–84 years	85+ years	All 65+ years
Hospitals	1	2	7	2
Residential care	1	3	14	3
Service housing	1	3	8	2
Home help[2]	7	26	26	15
Home-care allowances	1	2	5	2
Total	11	36	60	24

[1] The numbers include private services that are purchased by local authorities. An older person may receive more than one of these services. Therefore, the sum totals are only indicative.

[2] The proportion of households of older people receiving home-help services from all households of older people. Figures are not available separately for age groups 75–84 and 85+.

Source: SOTKA, 2001.

Conclusion

The Scandinavian social care regime can be described as a combination of service arrangements funded by tax revenues and organized by municipal authorities under the democratic control of citizens. Municipalities must have the backing of the citizens, who in the end foot the bill in the form of heavy taxes. All this suggests that families have neither very strong normative nor legal obligations to care. Yet, when looking at social care policy in detail, it is clear that child care has been made a public issue on a much larger scale than elder care. In Finland, elder care has been developed in an uneven and piecemeal manner. Subjective rights to social care services are vague and universalism was weakened in the 1990s.

The weakness of universalism in old-age welfare is at last partly connected to the fact that the supply of services available for the frail elderly, whether institutional or home-help services, has never met the demand. Accordingly, citizens' access to municipal social care services does not entirely depend on the elderly person's functional capacity (the need); the availability of care by relatives also enters the equation. The municipal social care system puts pressure on relatives to take more responsibility for caregiving, even though they have no statutory obligation to do so. This is a fairly strong cultural and social norm in most parts of the world. Likewise, the idea of equal services for poor and rich does not always work in practice. The well-off elderly have always found private solutions: domestic servants, cleaners and even private residential homes. Gender is another important dividing line: men can rely more on informal care than women, while older women and particularly women living alone have had to rely on public services.

In the 1990s the dream of universal services seemed to be less real than previously, at least as regards elder care. A new tendency is that access to public services, not only residential care but also home help and home-care allowances, has become more medicalized than before. It is important to notice that the financial crisis in the health sector is spreading to the social service sector: "no access except in illness!" Social needs are not as valid as they used to be. Moreover, social care has become a subcontractor for health care with its strong professionals, scientific technology and ever-growing demand for resources. The overall status of social care services in the whole package of old-age welfare is changing and medical expertise is becoming more and more dominant.

Yet, it is worth mentioning that in Finland social care workers are well-educated professionals with strong unions and professional organizations. This is true both in child care and in elder care. During the last few years, however, there has been a shortage of labour, especially in elder care. At the same time, elder care should be developed in such a way that older people can live at home and have easy access to social care services that are diversified rather than uniform. Moreover, social care should be sustained as an autonomous field of municipal service provision. It is important that the care needs of the elderly are negotiated in the social context – not only in medical terms. Diversified home-help services and payments for care as the right of every citizen might be topical post-modern solutions. All this means that the overall status of elder social care has to reach the same level as child care in Finland.

Against the background of elder care, contemporary Finnish child care policy represents a totally different policy line. Social rights are well established and universalist principles have become stronger during the last decade. Furthermore, there is a tendency to pluralism in service provision. Indeed, there is a huge gap between the status of elder care and child care. However, it is interesting that in both fields the system of home-care allowances has been introduced. It tells us that informal care has increasingly come to the public's attention. It also indicates that innovations are needed in the field of social care.

CARE WORK: INNOVATIONS IN THE NETHERLANDS

9

Trudie Knijn

Introduction

Once "care" became a keyword in the feminist analysis of gender equality, it acquired a problematic character. Without a strict empirical or theoretical object, the term is a container concept, with many interpretations and associations. A further complication is that the concept of care found its way into the academic world as well as into the domain of social policy before it had time to crystallize. As a consequence, manifold interpretations and definitions circulate. Care is, thirdly, problematic because of its specific but different meaning across countries (Ungerson, 1990). Yet it still proves to be a catchword. All over the Western world "care", the "C-word" has been used in the context of social problems related to state-dependency, ageing, the division of paid and unpaid work, the reconciliation of work and family life, women's invisible work, the quality and valuation of "people's work" and even the specificity of women's ethics (Graham, 1999; Hochschild, 1996; Tronto, 1993; Lewis, 1998).

Indeed, the "C-word" appears to fill a linguistic and conceptual gap at a time when the self-evidence of women's unpaid work in the family and community as well as their low-paid work in the serving professions are being brought into question. The associated process of diffusion and generalization of the "C-word" has caused some confusion among academics and policy-makers in the Netherlands. Currently at least six, partly overlapping, discourses on care can be identified.

Welfare state and care discourse

This discourse focuses on welfare state dependency and the "over caring" welfare state. Care is used here negatively, connoting dependence on welfare state provision, including social security, social assistance and health care. This use, which dates from the 1980s when it was suggested that the welfare state traps citizens in dependence, continues to the present day. In contrast to the British debates about ending welfare state dependency which were inspired by the New Right and within a few decades became part of New Labour's "Third Way" (Giddens, 1998), the Dutch debate was less politically inspired and articulated. It was social scientists, not necessarily linked to political parties, who formulated criticism about welfare dependency and urged a return to care by the community, self-help and a revaluation of autonomous voluntary organizations. Their pleas were mainly inspired by the tendency towards the centralization and bureaucratic nature of public services and a negative view of the power of professionals working in these services. In formulating their critique, they drew upon the assumptions of the corporatist welfare state based upon the "good old" combination of autonomous voluntary organizations and community care. However, some are of the view that the old preference for these institutions should not set the example for the future (Hattinga-Verschure, 1977; Achterhuis, 1978; Van Doorn and Schuijt, 1978; Adriaansens and Zijderveld, 1983). Nowadays all political parties support welfare pluralism in the domain of care. Under the rubric of "shared responsibility", the view is widespread that, in addition to the State, the market, the family and the community have a role in providing care.

The care-gap discourse

This, concerned with the supply and demand of care work, is a debate echoed all over the developed world. On the one hand, because of the greying population, the demand for care has increased and continues to grow. On the other hand, more paid carers are needed, due to women's entry to the labour market and their consequent withdrawal as informal carers. This gap is not being solved by women's entry to the caring professions since the shortage of home carers, nurses and other caring professionals has increased in the past few years. As a consequence, long waiting lists exist in all domains of care, whether in child care, home care for the chronically ill, the disabled and the dependent elderly, or institutionalized (health) care. Interestingly, the care-gap is hardly addressed in the welfare state debate. Yet many social reports focus on this issue, albeit that their conclusions are not unanimous. Some conclude that no real problem exists, given huge reservoirs of informal carers while others anticipate an enormous shortage of carers in the near future. De Boer et al. (1994) have calculated that 66 per cent of all disabled people receive only informal care, 22 per cent receive no care at all and only 12 per cent receive publicly provided care. People who live alone receive less care than those sharing a household.

Substitution of formal by informal care discourse

Questions arise as to which is better: professional care or informal care given by parents, children or friends. In this discourse such issues as "cold and warm" care, control and support are discussed, often without reference to the political consequences of such preferences. It is hard to unravel what comes first in this debate: the wish of people to be cared for by relatives and friends or the social policy which provides care only when the informal networks cannot. This kind of ambivalence is to be found in many social reports such as, for instance, the recent *Social and Cultural Report* by the Social and Cultural Planning Bureau (SCP). From a starting position that people in need of care are dissatisfied because of the long waiting lists for home care and the poor quality of care, this report then goes on to say that informal care workers are dissatisfied with the accessibility of public care provisions. And it concludes: "Citizens in general at first try to solve care problems themselves. This fits well with the Government's intention to prioritize informal care above public care." (SCP, 2000, p. 237).

The care and work discourse

It hardly seems possible that the issue of care can be discussed in isolation from the already mentioned discourses, but this often happens. The care and work discourse is well developed in the Netherlands, especially now that women's wish to enter the labour market parallels the demand for new workers in the context of the booming economy. Care is formulated in terms of women's work on behalf of the members of their families, relatives and friends and includes the substitution of that work by formal, paid care provisions. This care and work discourse is, in contrast to the other discourses, explicitly gendered and has been on the agenda of the Dutch feminist movement since the end of the 1960s. It finally secured political attention when feminist scholar Jeanne de Bruijn proposed a National Care Plan in 1993. The social liberal coalition coming into office in 1994 invited de Bruijn to be one of the experts on an advisory committee to develop "Future Scenarios concerning the Re-division of Paid and Unpaid Work". It was this committee that developed the Dutch "Combination Scenario", described below.

The care and citizenship discourse

Citizenship rights are seldom mentioned in Dutch debates on care. Only now and then do some authors refer to this particular aspect of gendered care (Knijn and Kremer, 1997). This type of discourse is also – but not from a gender perspective – to be found in some court cases taken up by elderly people on waiting lists for home care. In these cases disabled elderly people who are in need of care but who have been put on the waiting lists of their home-care offices have claimed the right to receive care. Interestingly, it is not immediately clear who in the end is responsible for the provision of care. Although all Dutch citizens compulsorily pay insurance premiums, it is unclear whether the ultimate responsibility rests with the public regional home-care offices, the National Health Insurance that coordinates the purchasing of home care, or the Government that decides on the yearly budgets for home care. Several court cases were needed to reach the conclusion that the National Health Insurance is responsible for the delivery of care, and that the Government should ensure the purchase of sufficient insurance premiums to cover care costs. Although one might expect the care and citizenship debate to include the social citizenship rights of care workers – the right to give care, earn a decent income and perform quality work – this aspect of social citizenship is seldom discussed in the Netherlands.

The ethics of care discourse

This academic discourse found the ear of politicians by stressing that a holistic orientation of responsibility, attentiveness and reciprocity is required when political governance is decentralizing towards local levels and new communities. Care has a very broad meaning in this discourse. Not only does it include care work or informal care but it is defined as "all social activities that maintain, continue and repair the world and enable us to live as well as possible" (Tronto, 1993). This discourse mainly focuses on social morality and reciprocal care in order to promote "a climate of compassion and trust and sustainable forms of cooperation between diverse individuals" (Svenhuijsen, 1999).

It is worth noting that all these discourses in one way or another involve gender issues such as female wages, the large numbers of housewives and women's gender identity. The gender dimension is, however, less articulated than the more gender-neutral care issue. The practice is to speak about carers or about the division of work and care without referring to gender. It will come as little surprise therefore that neither gender equity nor women's citizenship rights are very much in the forefront in the Netherlands. It is not unusual to read articles in the newspapers or to hear politicians talk about care with no reference made to gender inequality. This chapter looks at the question from a gender perspective, taking two of the above discourses to analyse the currently changing Dutch policies. First, the care and work discourse is described, since this is central to the employment policies of the Dutch Government and has been developed into a unique model – the "Combination Scenario" – as the best way to reconcile work and care. Second, the transformation of public care provisions for children and the elderly is analysed. This transformation relates to the welfare state and care debate and was perceived to offer a solution to the over-spending welfare state as well as to the lack of care recipients' choice. Currently these transformations are debated from the perspective of the substitution discourse (the borderline between private familial care and public care) as well as from the perspective of the care-gap discourse (because of the enormous lack of personnel in almost all care professions).

Envisioning both pillars of care and employment policies in combination results in a striking conclusion: on the one hand Dutch employment policy aims to get more women into paid work via the "Combination Scenario"; on the other hand an adequate public care policy is lacking. This contradiction can only be understood in terms of an overall tendency to shift more responsibility to the private sector, the family, the community or the market. This is indeed a major tendency on the part of the current governing coalition of social democratic and (social) liberal parties. The term "shared responsibility" is a favourite in the context of the Dutch poldermodel. Its main characteristics are what Duyvendak (1997) calls the three Cs – Consensus resulting from Consultation and based upon Compromise. Its main drawback is that in the end no one bears responsibility.

Care as a dimension of the "Combination Scenario"

After years of pleas by the feminist movement in the Netherlands to have women's labour market participation supported by means of social policy, a political breakthrough was reached by the creation in 1994 of the government Committee for the Re-division of Unpaid Work (Commissie voor de Herverdeling van Onbetaalde Arbeid). This committee was given the task of developing options for future work policies on the basis of a so-called re-division of paid and unpaid work. In 1995 the committee presented four alternative scenarios: the first, known as the "Perpetuation Scenario", stated that if nothing changed it would take a very long time for the labour market participation of Dutch women to reach European levels. The second scenario was named the "Re-division Scenario" and implied that it is mainly the responsibility of individuals to re-divide work and care, although some new laws would be needed to stimulate part-time work among men. The third scenario, "outsourcing", held the view that full-time work for both men and women is the best option and has to be supported by numerous new care provisions, adjusted taxation laws and an altered social security system. The final scenario, favoured by the committee itself, is the "Combination Scenario". The underlying view here is that future work and care policies should be based upon three principles:

a) the combination of work and care by every individual adult in an average 32-hour working week;
b) the sharing of work and care in individual households;
c) the outsourcing of a small part of care to institutionalized (by definition not state provided) provision.

This scenario would promote the growth of labour participation in a way that best fits the Dutch care culture, which is founded on a preference for family care for at least part of the week (Commissie Toekomstscenario's Herverdeling Onbetaalde Arbeid, 1995). The introduction of the "Combination Scenario" would demand greater adjustments in employment laws and policies than the outsourcing scenario but it would also mean less extensive investment in care provisions. Among the incentives mentioned by the Committee are: a legal right to work part time and to paid care and paid parental leave; individualization of taxation and social assistance, extension of child-care facilities and lower taxation of personal services such as housekeeping and childminding.

The "Combination Scenario" can be evaluated as a typically Dutch phenomenon. In contrast to the social-democratic model of the Scandinavian countries, no primacy is given to the State in care and employment policy, while at the same time the purely individual responsibility of the liberal model is avoided. The "Combination Scenario" stresses that care work should be partly carried out by parents, relatives and friends and that to do so they should limit their involvement in employment. This will, in effect, be unpaid care work, which leads to the additional effect of reducing individual incomes. Care is, therefore, only a limited citizenship right to the extent that it is unpaid and is provided for only limited periods (Emancipatieraad, 1996; Niphuis-Nell, 1997). In the event of people being unavailable to care, the gap should be filled by paid services, although not necessarily public ones. Indeed, private services are rapidly developing, including private child-care centres, private home-care offices and contracted private nurses and childminders. The "Combination Scenario" will therefore inevitably result in private interdependence. Care receivers as well as carers will depend on a wide configuration of people and institutions to fulfil their needs. Family members who choose to live in accordance with this scenario will first have to negotiate among themselves about who will care and when. Then each will have to negotiate with his or her employer for reduced hours of work and eventually for an employer's contribution to the care. Finally, they will have to depend on the care centres to provide care on the days when they need it.

The Dutch Government rapidly embraced this "Combination Scenario". As early as 1997, the Department of Social Affairs and Employment presented the White Paper *Kansen op combineren: Arbeid, zorg en economische zelfstandigheid* (Opportunities to combine: Work, care and economic independence). In this paper it is stated: "For the Government the following objective serves as a guideline: to reach a situation in the domain of work and income where every adult person, whatever form his family takes, earns his own living and fulfils his own care responsibilities." (Ministerie van Sociale Zaken en Werkgelegenheid, 1997, p. 9). This kind of philosophy, which is in line with the "Combination Scenario", was also supported by many governmental advisory boards such as the Sociaal Economische Raad (Social and Economic Council), Emancipatieraad (Equal Opportunities Council) and the Vereniging Nederlandse Gemeenten (Association of Dutch Municipalities) (Niphuis-Nell, 1997). The White Paper includes several concrete incentives to stimulate the realization of the combination of work and care. First of all single parent families, obliged by the 1996 welfare law to work when their youngest child reaches the age of 5, are supported by an extra tax deduction (from 6 per cent to 12 per cent) and their earnings are overlooked if they accept a part-time job. In addition an extra child-care budget for lone parents is given to the municipalities. The White Paper also announces new leave schemes for working parents, such as parental leave and adoption leave. Finally it proposes improving use of time over the whole life span, by suggesting that people work more or take fewer holidays during some stages of the life-course in order to work less in other periods (for instance when they have to take care of children, need a sabbatical year or when they are nearing the end of their working life). However, no concrete regulations have so far been made. The paper only mentions options, holding that further research is needed and that the social partners should include the suggestions in negotiating collective agreements. With respect to child care, the paper signals an enormous shortage, especially for school-age children, but announces no new measures. The stated wish of the Government is to extend child care under the following conditions: it should be accessible to all workers' children, meet quality standards and be related to schools' locations and timetables. It is suggested that parents and employers will be the main purchasers, eventually supported by tax reductions.

It is worth stressing that this, as well as the subsequent white papers, rhetorically support the re-division of work and care and put this in the context of gender equality. Nevertheless, the committee that made the first national report about the implementation of the United Nations Convention on the Elimination of all Forms of Discrimination against Women concluded: "None of the recommendations of several committees on work and care are implemented: the results have not found their way into policy. Yet this should be done: the Agreement obliges national states to develop concrete and measurable objectives" (Commissie Groenman, 1997, p. 138). The Dutch Government has instead procrastinated. In the meantime, it has responded to the growing dissatisfaction of many working parents, feminist national organizations and the Equal Opportunities Council by creating a Committee on Daily Arrangements. Assigned the task of developing visions for organizing the practical aspects of the combination of work and care, this committee was greeted by much cynical comment and laughter when it was introduced in 1996. With a limited budget the committee is to stimulate local "good practices" for combining work and care, such as child-care centres linked to schools for developing after-school care, or community service centres for the elderly. No structural change could be expected from this initiative.

The next White Paper *Op weg naar een nieuw evenwicht tussen arbeid en zorg* (On the way to a new balance of work and care), published in 1999, prioritizes work over care and, interestingly, broadens the definition of care to include all kinds of non-work activities. Care for one's own development, schooling and social participation is added to care for one's family. Another shift away from the "Combination Scenario" is in this White Paper's stress on freedom of choice: "The Government's preference for the "Combination Scenario" does not interfere with men's and women's freedom of choice. By contrast, the "Combination Scenario" improves people's choice of work and care.... People themselves decide what is the right balance between work and care and this may vary during their life-span" (p. 9). Finally in 2000 the long-expected *Meerjarennota Emancipatiebeleid* (Long-term Equal Opportunity Policy) was presented. In the paper, entitled *Van vrouwenstrijd naar vanzelfsprekendheid* (From Women's Struggle to Self-evidence), it was concluded that the combination of work and care is stagnating. In particular, both men's contribution to care work and women's economic independence are lagging behind. Therefore once again work, care and income are the major items for the future, with the aim of reaching "a sustainable situation in which as many people as possible can combine economic independence with care responsibilities during their life-span" (p. 17).

Despite these confusing formulations, the Wet Arbeid en Zorg (Work and Care Law) came into force in mid-2000. This law outlines the role of the state in providing the conditions for the combination of work and care. These include paid pregnancy leave (16 weeks, formerly included in health insurance), paid care leave (maximum ten days a year and limited to care for members of the nuclear family), adoption leave (four weeks) and two days' paid leave for men who become fathers. The social partners can, however, decide that all leave, except for pregnancy (which is exempted because of international agreements), can be offset against the employees' holidays. The only new leave is the paid care leave and this was fought for by Parliament against the will of the Government. The additional law which came into force in 2000, the Wet Aanpassing Arbeidstijden (Law Adjusting Working Hours), was enforced by Parliament through a complicated political process spanning several years. It gives employees a right to reduce or extend weekly working hours, important for many part-time working women. Employers can only refuse on the grounds of certain recognized reasons such as the continuity of the company's production or a lack of available overtime.

Any evaluation of the current Dutch policy towards the reconciliation of work and care has to acknowledge that the Netherlands maintains its breadwinner model and adds to it aspects of the "outsourcing" and "combination" scenarios (Ministerie van Sociale Zaken en Werkgelegenheid, 2000). The breadwinner model still exists in single-earner privileges such as tax reductions, free insurance for housewives and housewife additions to unemployment benefits and old-age pensions. Every year about 25 billion Dutch guilders are invested in maintaining this model (Bekkering and Jansweijer, 1998). It seems that no government to date has intended to withdraw these privileges, at least not for married and cohabiting couples. As long as women are married, their employment is costly, to such an extent that less educated women hardly gain anything from working part time (Ministerie van Sociale Zaken en Werkgelegenheid, 1997). At the same time, the "outsourcing scenario", which assumes that every adult earns his or her own income, has been introduced into social assistance. Lone parents are especially confronted by the contradiction between these two models: they are no longer protected by the breadwinner-motherhood model but at the same time lack a spouse to share work and care as well as the means to outsource child-care (Bussemaker et al., 1997; Knijn and van Wel, 2001). By contrast, the Dutch welfare state still financially discourages married women's paid work. Though they have no obligation to work, by staying at home or working part time they remain financially dependent on the breadwinner. Of the 60 per cent of mothers of school-age children that are employed, an overwhelming majority (70 per cent) work part time. This increase in women's employment is mainly due to changing social and cultural assumptions about motherhood. Currently 80 per cent of the population find no issue with the fact that mothers of school-age children have a paid job, compared with 56 per cent in 1970; 66 per cent do not object to child care compared with 36 per cent in 1976. Nevertheless the tendency is towards the one-and-a-half earner family, mainly because the majority prefer to work part time (table 9.1). Mothers'

Table 9.1   Types of families with children, 1998 (percentage of families where parents are aged between 20 and 50)

Family type	%
One-earner family	**41**
Male breadwinner	39
Female breadwinner	2
Two-earner family	**57**
Women > 32 hours, men < 32 hours	1
Men full time, women < 12 hours	12
Men full time, women 12 to 32 hours	32
Both for 32 hours	3
Both > 33 hours	9
Both unemployed	**3**
Total (rounded down)	**100**

Source: Keuzekamp and Hooghiemstra, 2000.

preparedness to take a part-time job can be explained by a combination of three phenomena:

a) shortage of child care for pre-school children and after-school child care;
b) an overwhelming majority of Dutch mothers prefers to combine (part-time) work with private care:
c) part-time work is well regulated in the Netherlands (SCP, 1998, 2000).

Do women gain?

Currently the Dutch Government faces an enormous labour shortage in almost every branch of industry as well as in public services, schools, home care and hospitals. The booming economy in combination with the greying population casts the contradiction between family policy and employment policy in sharp relief. The policy of combining work and care does not help to promote women's full-time employment. As only a modest effort to alter the bread-winner model, it has resulted neither in women's economic independence nor in improving men's involvement in care. As Plantenga and Schipper conclude: "Concerning equality in work, care and income between women and men the Netherlands takes the last place [of all EU countries]" (2000, p. 23). So, while part-time work might be a nice perspective for the reconciliation of work and care – and even helps women to get back more quickly into the labour market –

some disadvantages are obvious. First of all, part-time jobs are mainly for women, which hampers gender equity; second it enforces the glass ceiling[1] for women because working part time does not enable promotion. Finally, the "Combination Scenario" strategy assumes that men and women share care privately and therefore only limited care provisions are developed.

In reflecting on the progress made since she announced her National Care Plan in 1993, Jeanne de Bruijn wondered what had happened to the gains associated with the increased employment of married women. Although they often work part-time – the private solution to the care and work dilemma – this has been very profitable for the Dutch economy. The SCP has even stated that the rising rate of female part-time work is the major contribution to the current booming economy. Good protection for part-time workers was agreed upon in the so-called Akkoord van Wassenaar (Wassenaar Agreement) in 1982, an agreement between the social partners. In response to high unemployment rates and the increasing flexibility of the labour market, part-time workers were guaranteed steady contracts, a right to minimum wages, holidays and inclusion in the social security system (Visser and Hemerijck, 1997; SCP, 2000). Unintentionally this agreement perfectly matched the desire of mothers to get a steady but part-time job. However, during the 1990s some economic downside to this development became evident. Women's increasing labour market participation left high unemployment rates virtually unchanged. In addition, part-time working women occupied many new jobs, in particular in the post-industrial economy. The high unemployment rates put a downward pressure on wages, which barely increased at all in these years. In addition, had the extra income of part-time working married women not improved family income, the trade unions might have demanded an increase in male wages (SCP, 2000, pp. 292–293).

So, while women work for many kinds of social reasons, this brings us back to De Bruijn's question: what happened to the financial gains of married women's employment? The State gained extra tax revenue, paid by working married women who formerly received tax reductions. These employed married women also paid work-related premiums for pensions and health insurance that they would get anyway. Finally they paid extra for services such as contributions to child care and schools. De Bruijn and Verhaar (1999) explain the very slow development of public investment in care provision by the fact that the State benefits from the private solutions to combining work and care (see also Knijn, 1999). It is very profitable for the State when no public funds are invested in care provision while women's financial contribution to the State

---

[1] "Glass ceiling" is a term coined in the 1970s in the United States to describe artificial barriers, created by attitudinal and organizational prejudices, which block women from senior executive positions.

increases. De Bruijn and Verhaar, (1999) also argue that women's employment in the Netherlands is always envisioned in terms of women's work-related wishes rather than as a labour market demand. As a consequence, care provision has for a long time been perceived as a women-specific need rather than something critical to social and economic interests. It is only since the recent labour shortage due to the booming economy that investment in care has been specifically linked to market supply and demand.

Two other arguments are also of importance. First, the "Combination Scenario" itself is in accordance with the private solution adopted by Dutch women for combining care and part-time work. While this might be a rather unique approach from a gender equality perspective in that it challenges not only women's gender position but also men's, it does not promote public services. The "Combination Scenario", at least in intent, tries to stimulate men to a greater involvement in care as a condition for women's labour market participation. Such an approach demands less state investment in public care because the family retains primacy for care. Instead it demands more in the way of labour market regulation and employment laws (which indeed have been recently adopted). Such a strategy can, however, hardly be expected to improve women's economic independence. When the family retains primacy for care, it will almost always be the woman who will reduce her working hours, thereby remaining dependent on her husband's earnings. Indeed this is the main trend and subject of debate in the Netherlands where politicians agree that women's labour market participation should increase, but not their economic independence nor men's share in care (Ministerie van Sociale Zaken en Werkgelegenheid, 2000). Second, Dutch women entered the labour market at the time when neo-liberal thoughts about the welfare state were gaining in popularity, especially among social-democratic parties in Western Europe. The political climate was not in favour of extending public provision, especially not in such new domains as child care. As a consequence people had to look for private solutions, including expensive private child-care centres or take cheap private child-minders. Private markets of care are therefore expanding rapidly, bringing many women into new unprotected and unregulated forms of paid work. The per centage of private childminders for instance rose from 9 per cent in 1987 to 31 per cent in 1999 (Keuzenkamp and Oudhof, 2000).

Care work: Another private solution

Care work has been a hot issue in the Netherlands since the beginning of the 1990s. Long waiting lists for all kinds of services including hospitals, home care, elderly homes and child care appear almost daily on the public agenda.

Also, work-related pressure, burn-out of care workers and recently an enormous shortage of care workers have all attracted the attention of politicians and policy-makers as well as ordinary people confronted with care needs for themselves or their relatives (Boeije et al., 1997). According to opinion polls, Dutch citizens blame the Government for its reluctant attitude and are even willing to pay more taxes to improve public services (SCP, 1998). However the Dutch coalition of social-democratic and (social) liberal parties is not very receptive to this position. Together with Sweden, the Netherlands has had the highest tax decrease of all European countries, and along with Ireland, it has seen the greatest relative reduction of collective expenditure since 1990 (SCP, 2000). Public investment in education and (health) care is especially low in comparison to other European countries. This is a rather striking development in the context of rapid economic growth. It is not an exaggeration to say – at least in regard to care work – that the public has reason to complain.

The problems of care work are mainly due to the ambivalence of the Dutch Government about being involved in a process of transformation from a hybrid welfare state, based upon a mixture of social-democratic and corporatist principles, to a model which includes liberal principles as well. This process is all the more complicated because of the strength of the still corporatist voluntary organizations (in education, health care, home care, housing and the media), which only reluctantly accept market principles and do not wish to lose subsidies. The Government itself, being caught between the dilemma of losing control of public services and privatizing them, opts for a diffuse concept of "regulated competition" (Knijn, 1998, 2000b). As a consequence, many ad hoc decisions are made about restructuring these services while budgets are increasingly limited. Meanwhile market principles are gaining influence in the field of care in three ways:

a) a welfare mix of payments;
b) private corporations operating in the domain of care;
c) the development of informal labour markets.

With regard to the first, a mix of payments has rapidly developed in both home care and child care. In home care this has been introduced through the individual income-related payments per hour of home care. These payments have to be made despite the fact that everyone has paid premiums for the Algemene Wet Bijzondere Ziektekosten (AWBZ – General Law of Specific Health Costs), a collective insurance to which every citizen contributes by way of wage- or benefit-related premiums. These additional payments are assumed to limit the access to home care by preventing people in need of care claiming it too readily. In addition, they reduce the public costs of home care in that they appear to have caused the withdrawal of two groups of care dependants: low-and high-income wage earners. Although low-income earners have the right to social assistance if they cannot afford the individual payments themselves, they increasingly try to find informal unpaid care instead of claiming for what they experience as humiliating social assistance. The second group, high-income earners, try to find their own solution in the care market, which often offers them better quality care than that available in the public services. This kind of situation has led government advisory boards to the conclusion that the AWBZ is tending to lose its character as a collective insurance (CSED, 1999).

Child care has only recently developed in the Netherlands and has hardly any history as a public service. It developed at a time when the Dutch Government endorsed "shared responsibilities" and its financial structure shows all the particularities of this idea. Since the beginning of the 1990s, when for the first time child-care policy was on the political agenda, the Dutch Government described its role in terms of being "a stimulator" of a child-care policy which should be based upon shared responsibilities between the state, employers and parents. After the first large investment in child care in 1989 (Eerste Stimuleringsmaatregel Childcare), the state contribution was reduced from 53 per cent of the total costs of child care in 1990 to 33 per cent in 1998. Over the same period the contribution of parents in the costs of child care decreased from 34 to 19 per cent, while that of employers increased from 11 to 45 per cent (SCP, 2000). One of the problems is that the financial structure of child care is very complicated. First of all, municipalities have discretionary power in founding and running child-care centres themselves or in recognizing private child-care centres. For children of lone parents, municipalities can apply for additional state subsidies. Although employers' investment in child care is subsidized by tax reductions, employers retain the discretion to decide which category of their employees benefit from these child-care places. It is assumed that such matters will be arranged through collective agreements between employers and trade unions. Finally, parents pay for child care (according to their family income) as do employers (Ministerie van Sociale Zaken en Werkgelegenheid, 1997). This purchasing system resulted in some growth in the number of child-care places, from 6 per cent of all children below school age in 1990 to 15 per cent in 1998 (SCP, 2000), although the waiting lists did not shorten. It also resulted in a huge polarization of parents making use of child care: 90 per cent of higher educated, one-and-half earner families compared with hardly any children from ethnic minorities and lower educated parents (Ministerie van Volksgezondheid, Wezlijn en Sport, 1997– Ministry of Health, Welfare and Sport).

With regard to the second form of encroachment of market principles into care – private corporations – most political parties, including the Social

Democratic Party, are convinced that the shortage of care cannot be solved without the help of the market. This acknowledges the failure of the Dutch welfare state to provide adequate care. In the domain of child care and home care, private providers are filling the gaps left by the State. In home care this is a contested issue since the voluntary organizations have long resisted competition from private home-care offices. Given this, the Government took the decision in 1998 to freeze the number of private organizations until 2001. Currently all political parties agree that privatization is inevitable but that the companies involved will have to follow strict regulations concerning quality, accessibility and working conditions, which will be monitored by the insurance companies. In child care, voluntary and private companies have gone hand in hand from the beginning. All providers have had to be approved by the municipal health and safety organizations and treated equally. Hence every parent can make use of each kind of child-care centre, and no extra conditions for receiving subsidies were imposed on private centres. However, an emerging phenomenon indicates that current arrangements are leading to another polarization in the parental use of child care. High-quality child-care centres are developing rapidly. These centres offer extremely good professional care in luxurious centres and are very expensive. Well-off parents not needing subsidies tend to buy child-care places in such centres partly because they like their children to be raised among equals, partly in order to avoid waiting lists (Knijn, 1999).

The development of informal labour markets is the third way in which market principles infiltrate care. The informal labour market of care is a reaction to the lack of good quality public services. There are also other reasons for its growth. People in need of care, such as chronically ill and older people, also prefer some informal care above or in addition to paid professional care. Furthermore, Dutch parents scarcely rely on public child care; they actually share the Government's opinion that parents, or informal substitutes such as grandparents or childminders, should themselves provide care for a few days a week. Nevertheless, in home care the responsibilities are often the other way around: home-care services frequently use the criterion that no informal care is available before approving a person as being in need of care (Keuzenkamp and Oudhof, 2000, Kremer, 2000). One solution for improving the quality and quantity of home-care services, is the introduction of a personal budget which, paid by the AWBZ, gives care receivers money instead of in-kind services (Kraan et al., 1991). The money can be used to buy services from public or private home-care offices or, as many do, to pay informal carers. It is this last option which occasioned resistance among insurance companies and public home-care offices; they felt that they were losing control of care and successfully prevented the extension of personal budgets for a time. Care dependants however were satisfied with their budgets, finding increased autonomy: the recipients proved to be very creative in spending the money in accordance with their needs and liked to pay their formerly unpaid carers (Woldringh and Ramakers, 1998). The number of private childminders has also increased rapidly in the last decade. Several surveys show that the shortage of child-care places in combination with the increase in women's employment has led to an expansion of private childminding. While children making use of child care increased from 5 per cent to 15 per cent between 1987 and 1999, the proportion cared for by a private childminder increased from 9 per cent to 31 per cent in the same period, (SCP, 2000).

Conclusion

The conclusion of this overview might be that the marketization of care in the Netherlands is a process of "shared responsibility" on the purchasing side (private payments for home and child care) and of giving private corporations entry to care services. However, the marketization of care also proceeds because carers and caregivers, often in reaction to the shortage and poor quality of publicly provided care, prefer to make their own private care arrangements (Knijn, 2000a). In the case of home care this is, although contested, supported by insurance-paid personal budgets; with regard to private child care it is not supported by public policy. In both domains informally paid carers fill the care gap. Commodification of care, therefore, takes shape in a process of transformation of public to private and marketized care as well as in the transformation of unpaid family care to informal paid care.

ACCOUNTING FOR CARE IN THE UNITED STATES   10

Nancy Folbre

Introduction

Among the advanced industrial countries the United States is an outlier in its low level of public support for the care of dependants. Perhaps as a result, much of the scholarly attention devoted to care within the United States has struggled to define "care" in the broadest possible terms and to explain why neither individual families nor market forces are likely to provide an adequate supply. A broad interdisciplinary research agenda is emerging, but the economic dimensions of care, or analysis of what we might call the "care sector" of the economy, remain underdeveloped. As a result, it is difficult to explore the relationship between expenditures, outcomes, and the social organization of care.

This chapter presents a case study of the provision of care in the United States to help develop a systematic theoretical framework for international comparison. Elsewhere, we have emphasized the role that gender inequality plays in lowering the costs of care (Folbre, 1994; Folbre and Weisskopf, 1998; Badgett and Folbre, 1999). Here, we focus on growing problems in the provision of care that are associated not only with changes in traditional gender roles but also in overreliance on market provision and the increasingly anachronistic structure of welfare state policies.

The first section explores several different definitions of care, distinguishing among criteria based on motives, activities, forms of payment (or non-payment), and recipients. While it is important to acknowledge conceptual complexity and leave room for philosophical debate, it is equally important to develop ways of "operationalizing" care in ways that allow us to incorporate it into economic accounting frameworks. The second section illustrates this point by reviewing available information concerning the empirical dimensions of care within the United States, outlining a picture of the "care sector" of the labour force and how it is evolving. The third section describes emerging problems in three particularly important care areas: health care, elder care, and child care, emphasizing the ways that market incentives fail to guarantee high quality. The final section describes some salient features of the distribution of public spending on care, including special consideration of the role of "tax-expenditures" or targeted tax breaks. Consideration of public spending patterns reveals the urgent need to develop a better analysis of the distribution of care resources over time.

Defining care

In Chapter 2, Mary Daly writes that care is defined as "the activities and relations involved in caring for the ill, elderly, and dependent young", This conventional definition serves admirably for a broad overview, but raises some interesting questions with respect to the development of an accounting framework. Notice, first, that the concept is defined in terms of who benefits (ill, elderly, or dependent young). Activities devoted to the care of other adults are excluded. Do we really want to draw such a sharp distinction? Meeting the needs of dependants may be a particularly urgent aspect of care provision, but able-bodied adults also require attention to their personal – and especially their emotional – well-being.

Furthermore, it is often difficult to draw a clear line defining dependancy. At what point is a child no longer a "dependant"? At what point does a sick or elderly person become one? Indeed, at what point does a person become "elderly"? This is not an irrelevant question, since a large proportion of individuals over the age of formal retirement are perfectly capable of taking care of themselves. The tendency to define the elderly simply as those beyond the formal retirement age both begs the question and imposes a definition traditionally applied to male workers in all groups of society. A housewife aged 70 often undertakes activities for the care of her husband that are quite similar to those she undertook at age 60.

Next, consider the term "activities". These could be construed in terms of labour time. Much of the economic literature on care focuses on "care services" or "caring labour" as a way of calling attention to this active dimension. Time-diaries and other types of time-budget surveys offer some potential for quantification. However, further specification is required. Which activities, exactly, should be counted? A very broad interpretation might include all the labour time that affects the well-being of the ill, elderly and dependent young – time spent preparing meals, cleaning houses, and purchasing goods and services. Much of this time, however, is blended with time devoted to the fulfilment of the needs of able-bodied adults. Furthermore, it is difficult to clearly distinguish care activities from others. Purchasing goods and services, for instance, is an important form of provisioning in an advanced market economy. But if we count this as a care activity simply because it benefits dependants, why shouldn't we also count the activity of earning the money necessary to purchase these goods and services? After all, much of the market work that individuals perform is motivated by a desire to provide for dependants. In a kind of *reductio ad absurdum*, one could argue that virtually all work is care work.

At the other extreme, one could define care activities quite narrowly as those that involve personal contact and emotional content. In more technical terms, these are activities in which the identity of the care provider matters, because it has implications for the very nature of the transaction and/or the quality of the service. We might stipulate, for instance, that doing laundry is not really a care activity, but that bathing or reading aloud to a dependant is. In terms of the paid labour force, we might argue that hairdressers and retail clerks are not providing care services, while child care workers are. Such boundaries will always be fuzzy but they can nevertheless prove useful.

Some boundaries are clearly necessary for empirical analysis. A useful illustration emerges from consideration of a growing debate among social scientists concerning the effect of increases in mothers' hours of paid employment on time devoted to child care in the home. Many empirical studies operationalize maternal child-care time as a "primary activity" – an activity whose primary purpose was care of the child – such as physical care or reading to or teaching a child (Robinson and Godbey, 1997). These primary activities can be further disaggregated to include "developmental time", such as reading aloud and playing with a child, versus "low-intensity" time (Bittman, Craig and Folbre, 2001). Many time-use studies also include consideration of "secondary activities" – such as preparing a meal or doing laundry while also tending to child-care responsibilities. Still others define child care as all activities in which a child is present, such as time spent in eating meals together, even in a restaurant (Hallberg and Klevmarken, 2000; Almeida and McDonald, 2000). Not surprisingly, child care defined in narrow terms shows far less variation than child care defined more broadly – mothers who work for pay make explicit efforts to defend "high-quality" time with their children. But are they able to fully compensate for the reduction in overall hours spent with children? Whether or not we think that paid work creates a parental "time-squeeze" depends largely on how we choose to define parental care time, which is affected in turn by our definition of care activities.

Nor should we always take people's own designation of care activities for granted.

A fascinating study entitled *The time Americans spend working for pay, caring for families, and contributing to communities*, reports results from a large random survey asking Americans how much time they spent engaged in the following activities:

a) providing informal assistance to anyone such as shopping or free baby-sitting;
b) providing emotional support to anyone such as comforting them, listening to their problems, or giving them advice;
c) doing things with their children such as help with homework, playing with them, or doing other things with them;
d) volunteering at a community organization such as a church, hospital or senior centre (Almeida and McDonald, 2000).

This is an interesting list of activities, but it excludes assistance routinely provided to family members, such as shopping or laundry, perhaps because this is usually construed as a domestic "responsibility" rather than a "giving behaviour".

At the other extreme, some researchers include within their definition of "caregivers" those who have at least one child under age 18 who lives in his or her household at least part of the year, assuming that co-residence implies responsibility (Heymann, 2000). In some cases this may be true. However, the gender division of labour in parenting is sufficiently strong to suggest the possibility that many fathers would not actually qualify as caregivers if a quota of weekly hours of actual contact with children was required.

A more common boundary used in empirical research is the "commod-ification" line: some caregivers provide care within the family or the community outside any direct cash nexus; others work for wages in the occupations and sectors in which caregivers are paid a salary. Western social science, influenced by the Marxian tradition, has long made a distinction between "production for use" and "production for exchange" that treats the former as intrinsically less alienating than the latter. The obvious implication is that "commodification" will have negative consequences for caregivers and the quality of care they provide. But this conclusion is too simple by far (Folbre and Weisskopf, 1998; Nelson 1999; Folbre and Nelson, 2000).

Much of the care work that has traditionally been provided outside the market has been structured by highly gendered norms that require "compulsory caring" (Ward, 1993, p. 92) or "socially imposed altruism" (MacDonald, 1995). As Diemut Elizabet Bubeck explains, this represents a distinctive form of exploitation: "The exploitative mechanism is what I have called the circle of care, an interlocking set of constraints and practices that channels women into doing the bulk of care that needs to be done in any society" (Bubeck, 1995, p. 181). One implication is that the line between commodification and non-commodification may be less important than features more difficult to locate and subject to empirical scrutiny. To what extent is care undertaken as a genuinely voluntary choice (whether paid or unpaid)? Is it structured in ways that encourage the development of positive long-term relationships? Are caregivers and care-receivers in an egalitarian, reciprocal relationship, or an unequal hierarchical one? As Clare Ungerson puts it, "the social, political, and economic contexts in which payments for care operate and the way in which payments for care are themselves organized are just as likely to transform relationships as the existence of payments themselves". (1997, p. 377).

A final concern about the conventional definition of care as "activities and relations" is that it does not include financial resources. Yet the amount of money that we privately and publicly devote to the care of dependants is surely an important dimension of the economy of care. We also "care" about the distribution of financial resources among dependants, particularly about the ways these may impinge on inequalities in standards of living or in the development of human capabilities. Taking this issue seriously means paying much closer attention to income flows between parents and children and men and women within the family, as well as public expenditure and taxation. The growth in families maintained by women alone and consequent residential separation of fathers from children is particularly relevant.

The discourse of care has emerged partly as a response to the well-documented inadequacies of the conventional welfare state literature (Lister, 1990, 1997; Orloff, 1993). The conventional literature of public finance is even more unsatisfactory, offering endless rows and columns of numbers describing various programme expenditures, while ignoring the less obvious transfers of resources within family relationships and non-market work. But it is precisely because conventional public finance accounting systems are so incomplete that we need to move beyond critiques to develop explicit alternatives. This requires us to leave the abstract realm of conceptual debate and enter the even messier world of empirical surveys, imputed values and rough estimates.

The care labour force in the United States

The two most conspicuous trends shaping the historical organization of care in the United States economy have been fertility decline and women's entrance into paid employment, both under way for more than 150 years. The first of these trends has reduced our overall demand for caring labour by reducing the number of children relative to the working-age population – an effect increasingly countervailed by the increasing proportion of the elderly. The second of these trends has reduced the supply of caring labour outside the market by raising its opportunity cost: women now have access to better paying jobs than they used to – as a result, the cost of not working for pay has increased. On the other hand, caring occupations such as teaching, nursing, and home health care have increased dramatically as a percentage of the paid labour force in recent years.

The harder one thinks about these trends, the more arbitrary and misleading our conventional picture of economic development begins to seem. We look back on a history of economic growth that we have carefully constructed by "cooking the books". We divided the economy into two parts: the family (considered, like environmental assets, a part of nature) and the market. Household labour was simply not included in the GDP. When women reallocated their work from an arena in which it wasn't measured to the market economy, where it showed up in money terms, we registered significant economic growth. But what happened to the underlying quantity and quality of care services? We don't know.

Still, we can patch existing bits of data about the composition of the labour force together with time-use data in ways that help explain why caring labour is likely to become an increasingly important economic concern. William Baumol (1967) predicted long ago that we would suffer a "cost disease" of the service sector, with increases in relative costs resulting from less adaptability to technological change. His predictions have not been completely borne out. In recent years many services, including banking, retail, and entertainment, have been transformed by waves of innovation. But in an important respect, his prediction was spot-on. Productivity growth has been and is likely to continue to be slowest in care services requiring personal and emotional contact (Donath, 1998). These services have simply been redistributed and in some ways, concentrated, as other dimensions of work have been transformed.

The decline of home-making

Economists have just begun reconstructing quantitative estimates that reveal the magnitude of mismeasurement over time (Folbre and Nelson, 2000). We can deploy the somewhat anachronistic term "home-making" to describe women's non-market work, because it conveys the nature of the caring activities intertwined with the household production involved. Both men and women typically combine some home making activities with paid employment. However, many women have historically specialized in full-time home-making. Historical research and early census surveys show that women worked about the same hours per week providing goods and services for family members as paid workers did in their formal jobs, and women typically worked many more hours when young children are present in the home (Folbre and Nelson, 2000).

One way to make this work visible is to quantify it. If we assume that women devoted about as much productive effort to paid and unpaid work combined as men did to paid work, we can construct estimates of the total labour force, including both paid and unpaid workers (Folbre and Wagman, 1993; Wagman and Folbre, 1996). This rough estimate shows that even today home-makers represent a significant percentage of all paid and unpaid women workers – slightly less than 30 per cent. Overall, home-making occupies over 16 per cent of all workers (paid and unpaid) in the United States. The significance of this category has been obscured by conventional accounting categories.

Time-use surveys

An alternative way to look at the shift of caring activities into the paid labour market relies on time-use surveys, which are now becoming widely available. Canada and Australia, as well as most countries within the European Union, now conduct regular time-use surveys. By contrast, what we know about time-use trends in the United States is based on relatively small and unrepresentative surveys.

A theme emphasized in much of the historical literature on time-use is "the endless day" – home-making seems to expand whatever time is available, and standards of cleanliness and quality have ratcheted up over time (Cowan, 1980). An alternative (and not necessarily inconsistent) interpretation is that the income elasticity of demand for home-maker's services is relatively high. Technological innovation has clearly reduced the time necessary to perform many domestic tasks. In 1975, for instance, home-makers worked about 30 hours less per week in preparing meals and cleaning up than they did in 1910 (Lebergott, 1993, p. 59). On the other hand, activities such as shopping have become more time-consuming.

Fertility decline and the expansion of education have reduced the total amount of time devoted to child care. But in an analysis of historical time-use data, Bryant and Zick (1996) show that parents may also have increased the amount of time they spend per child. It seems that paid child care tends to displace "on-call" time when most of parental attention was already elsewhere, rather than primary care time. As families purchase more services, they may reallocate their non-market time and effort away from material production towards the personal and emotional. Increased freedom to explore career opportunities outside the home means that the time that women devote to home-making is given more freely – and perhaps more joyously – than before.

Whether improvements in quality of non-market work have been sufficient to compensate for declines in quantity we cannot say. But the greater the role that personal and emotional care play in non-market work, the greater the downward bias in market-based estimates of its value. There are some things you cannot buy perfect substitutes for. Nowadays the personal and emotional content of home life is becoming more and more concentrated in a relatively small number of activities, such as sharing meals or telling bedtime stories. Past a certain point, which we have yet to carefully define or negotiate, family time cannot be reduced without adverse consequences for all family members.

On the other hand, efforts to combine paid work and family responsibilities lead to stresses and strains. Pressure on lone mothers has increased, with provision of public assistance now largely conditional on paid employment. When married mothers increase their hours of market work, husbands seldom increase their hours of non-market work to help compensate (Hartmann, 1981; Bittman and Pixley, 1997). The time and effort that women devote to home-making tends to lower their earnings, even net of effects on labour force experience and job tenure (Waldfogel, 1997; Hersch, 1991). Widespread awareness of this pattern has contributed to a proliferation of studies of how men and women bargain over the allocation of time and responsibility as well as money in the household (Mahoney, 1995; Deutsch, 1999).

The difficult circumstances faced by single parents and dual-career families with young children help explain the heated debate over whether Americans are working longer or shorter hours overall (Schor, 1991; Robinson and Godbey, 1997). Surveys suggest a mismatch between individual preferences and work schedules (Jacobs and Gerson, 1998), largely generated by the difficulties of combining paid employment with responsibilities for the care of family and community.

Employment in care occupations

The growth of service jobs is a much remarked-upon feature of modern economic development, associated with the expansion of women's labour force participation. Services vary considerably along the dimension of personal contact. Some involve working purely with information, and some involve working purely with people, with many permutations in between. Women tend to move into jobs that resemble their traditional responsibilities for family care, a factor that contributes to occupational segregation. According to one recent estimate, 53 per cent of workers in the United States would need to change jobs to equalize the occupational distribution by gender (Blau, 1997).

The exact distribution of workers in jobs that involve care is difficult to specify.

Hochschild (1983) estimates that about one-third of American workers have jobs that demand emotional labour. But not all emotional labour is caring labour – some requires relatively shallow affective performance. Such performance may be stressful for workers but does not have serious consequences for consumers. It matters less – and is more difficult to ascertain – if an airline attendant is faking cheerfulness than if a nurse is faking concern for patients.

The two high-skilled occupations that most distinctly require care are nursing and teaching, two subcategories within the Professional, Technical and Related category that are poorly paid considering the amount of education they require. In the United States in 1991, almost one-half of all women in professional and technical work were either nurses or teachers. Throughout the world professional women are over-represented in these two occupations (Anker, 1998, p. 163). Among occupations with lower education requirements there are two within the category of Service Workers that clearly embody care – child-care workers and elderly care workers.

But caring responsibilities are not limited to the most explicitly caring occupations. Ethnographic studies of work show that secretaries are expected to protect their bosses from stress and construct a supportive and reassuring environment (Alexander, 1987; Kanter, 1993). Waitresses are encouraged to be kind as well as personable (Spradly and Mann, 1975). Airline attendants are expected to be heroic in crises as well as cheerful in serving beverages (Hochshild, 1983). Paralegals are expected to mother the lawyers engaged in tough-guy litigation (Pierce, 1995). Conventional categories cannot be used to tally up the exact percentage of jobs that fit the profile of caring labour.

Furthermore, the forms of personal contact involved in jobs are strongly affected by technological innovation and industrial organization. Both urbanization and increased geographic mobility probably reduce the likelihood that employers form personal relationships with workers or workers with consumers. But in the market as well as in the family the reduction of opportunities for personal interaction may heighten the importance of those opportunities that remain. Relationships among workers may acquire increased significance. Services requiring relatively long-term relationships, such as those provided by psychotherapists and personal athletic trainers, become conspicuously sought-after luxuries.

The nature of caring work is often defined by professional standards and cultural norms that value and reward intrinsic values of care. As competitive pressures intensify, however, employers may be forced to reduce expenditures and increase work intensity. The difficulties of measuring and monitoring quality of care mean that the negative effects of cost-cutting may not be immediately apparent.

Employment in care industries

Women are also segregated by industry, a pattern which has received less attention from economists than segregation by occupation, but which is even more relevant to a consideration of sectorial trends. To illustrate, it is helpful to create a category we will call "professional care services" by combining the standard industrial classifications of "Hospitals," "Health Services except Hospitals," "Educational Services," and "Social Services." In 1998, about one-fifth of the paid labour force was engaged in a professional care service (Folbre and Nelson, 2000). Today, hospitals and schools should now count as much in forming our image of wage employment as factories and construction sites.

Women remain concentrated in professional care industries. In 1998, they constituted 46.2 per cent of the paid labour force over age 16, but 76.3 per cent of those employed in "Hospitals," 79 per cent in "Other Health Services," 68.7 per cent in "Educational Services," and 81.8 per cent in "Social Services." (US Bureau of Labor Statistics, 1999 table 18.) The way in which these care industries are structured has especially important implications for women workers, as well as for the welfare of children, the sick, and the elderly.

Three care industries

Good illustrations of the negative impact of competitive pressure on quality emerge from even a brief consideration of health-care, child care, and elder care in the United States. Expenditures in these areas have risen significantly over the past 30 years, while institutional restructuring has created new openings for profit-oriented providers. There can be little doubt that the introduction of profit-based competition helps reduce the escalation of costs. What is at issue is whether it also reduces the quality of services in ways that consumers may be slow to recognize, and unable to effectively respond to.

Health care

The reorganization of the health-care industry in the United States away from "fee for service" toward Health Maintenance Organizations (HMOs) significantly reduced the escalation of health costs for a brief period. But the overall quality of care is rapidly deteriorating. Market competition is having negative effects that are becoming a focus of protest by doctors, nurses, and other professional health care workers. HMOs charge their members a fixed amount, creating obvious pecuniary incentives for them to cut costs and to discourage unhealthy applicants. Most of their cost savings come from lower rates of hospitalization (Gordon, 1999, p. 11). In recent years, many HMOs have eliminated coverage for senior citizens on Medicare (Hibbard, 1998). A recent study published in the *Journal of the American Medical Association* found that several measures of the quality of care are significantly lower in for-profit than non-profit HMOs (Stolberg, 1999).

Hospitals have dramatically reduced the length of stay by sending patients home more quickly than ever before, usually offloading care costs onto family members and friends. Measures of cost-effectiveness do not take these hidden costs into account. Nor have the health effects been closely scrutinized (Gordon, 1999). Forced cut-backs in hospital stays created so much bad publicity that Congress passed legislation in 1996 requiring insurance companies to reimburse at least two days of hospital care for a normal childbirth.

These well-publicized issues, however, are not as troubling as less visible deterioration in the emotional dimensions of care. As a recent *New York Times* article put it, "Critics say 'hit and run' nursing has replaced Florence Nightingale" (Kilborn, 1998). Bedside nurses have been replaced by unlicensed "care technicians". A survey of over 7,500 nurses released in 1996 reported that 73 per cent felt they had less time to comfort and educate patients (Gordon, 1998, p. 255). At the same time, reimbursements to home health-care workers have been cut back. Deborah Stone, who has extensively interviewed home health-care workers, reports "The more I talked with people, the more I saw how financial tightening and the ratcheting up of managerial scrutiny are changing the moral world of caregiving, along with the quantity and quality of care" (Stone, 1999, p. 62). These are ominous signals.

Child care

Paid child care can serve as a very good complement for parental time. Although there is some controversy over the amount of time very young children should spend away from their parents, there is no evidence that paid child care per se has negative effects. It is the quality of both custodial and parental time that matters most. But experts and parents differ widely in their assessments of quality of paid care. The time and effort required to monitor quality is quite costly, especially for parents constrained by a tight budget. A recent comprehensive survey argues that the physical and emotional environment in many child care centres remains relatively poor, partly because of poor regulation in many states (Helburn, 1995). Pay levels for child-care workers are seldom much above the minimum wage, and high turnover rates in the child-care industry, averaging about 40 per cent per year, preclude the development of long-term relationships between caregivers and young children.

Voluntary accreditation by the National Association for the Education of Young Children tends to improve quality. A recent California study, for instance, rated 61 per cent of accredited centres as good in 1997, compared with only 26 per cent of those seeking accreditation the previous year. Nationwide, however, only 5,000 of the nation's 97,000 child-care centres were accredited (Whitebook, 1997). Furthermore, many children in paid child care are in small informal family settings, rather than centres, where quality is even more variable. In the rush to expand child-care places to accommodate the exigencies of welfare reform, some states have provided child-care vouchers that can be used virtually anywhere and may actually have a negative effect on quality by segregating low-income users.

The links between regulation, industrial organization and quality of care are just beginning to be explored. In general, for-profit child-care centres do not seem to emphasize "curb-side appeal" at the expense of more difficult-to-monitor aspects of quality. However, for-profit child-care centres that are part of national chains do seem to follow this strategy (Helburn, 1995). What looks attractive to the parent is not necessarily what is best for the child. Shiny new toys matter less than the skill and commitment levels of the workers providing care.

Elder care

Quality issues are even more salient, even shocking, in elder care. Nursing homes now employ more workers in the United States than the auto and steel industries combined. Almost 95 per cent of these homes are privately run, though most are subsidized with public dollars. Turnover rates among workers are high, amounting to almost 100 per cent within the first three months. According to consumer reports, about 40 per cent of nursing homes repeatedly fail to pass the most basic health and safety inspections (Eaton, 1996). In a 1999 study, the General Accounting Office (GAO) reported government inspections of nursing homes across the country showing that more than one-fourth cause actual harm to their residents (GAO, 1999).

Given their poor track record at meeting even basic needs, it is chilling to consider how poorly nursing homes meet the emotional needs of the elderly. Susan Eaton describes the things companies "can't bill for, but that make all the difference if you're living in a nursing home: time to listen to somebody's story, time to hold their hand, time to comfort somebody who is feeling troubled. And you can't exactly put that on your bill; imagine finding 'holding hands' on the bill. You have to have a 'treatment,' you have to have some formal procedure" (Eaton, 1996, p. 7). One could hardly ask for a better example of the difficulty of commodifying care.

Public support for care in the United States

We tend to assume that public support for care in the United States is lower than in most European countries because welfare state expenditures are lower. This comparison, however, is somewhat misleading, because tax exemptions and credits play a larger role within the United States system. The following sections show that overall, qualitative differences in the organization of funding are probably more important than differences in spending levels. These differences have important implications for inequalities based on race and class, as well as on gender.

Support for child rearing

The United States stands out among the advanced industrial countries in its failure to provide paid parental leave from work. The only benefit currently available to parents is an unpaid family leave of up to 12 weeks, that is guaranteed only to employees of firms with more than 50 employees. The Clinton administration urged individual states to use unemployment insurance funds to fund their own parental leave programmes, but with little success.

The United States does provide some benefits to families with children through the tax system, which are comparable to family allowances. The complexity of the United States tax system, however, means that different families get different amounts per child. Few citizens and probably few policy-makers really understand who gets what. The overall pattern of support is inconsistent, benefiting both poor and affluent families far more than those in the middle of the income distribution (Folbre, 2001b).

Families who earn enough income to owe federal taxes can subtract an exemption for every dependant from their taxable income. In 1999, this exemption was US$2,748. Because federal income taxes are set at higher rates for families with higher incomes, the value of this deduction varies. It saves families in the 15 per cent tax bracket about $412. It saves families in the 31 per cent tax bracket (with adjusted gross income between $104,050 and $158,550 for a married couple filing jointly) more than twice as much, $852. Families can also claim a $500 tax credit per child that can be subtracted from their actual taxes. The overall benefit for a family with two children in the 31 per cent tax bracket is $2,704; for a family with three children it is $4,056. In higher brackets both these benefits are gradually phased out.

Families with income below the poverty level pay no income taxes, so do not benefit from these features of the tax code. Instead, they can take advantage of the Earned Income Tax Credit (EITC), which gives them a refund greater than the taxes they are liable for. This benefit applies if only one or both parents are working for pay; the levels increase sharply for families with one child, and less sharply for families with two. No additional benefits are provided for families with three or more children. In 1999, the maximum EITC credit was $3,656. A low-income family with two children which obtained the maximum credit would derive more tax benefits for child rearing than a family with two children in the 31 per cent bracket. Among families with three or more children, however, the benefits are greater for the affluent.

Relatively few families receive the maximum EITC benefit, however, because it phases out quickly as the family earns income over about $13,000 a year. This phase-out has the same effect as a higher tax rate. Combined with the effect of progressive income taxes on the value of the dependant exemption, this means that tax benefits linked to child rearing follow a U-shaped pattern: they are highest at either end of the income distribution and lowest in the middle. A family in the 15 per cent tax bracket with two children that is not eligible for the EITC enjoys a tax benefit of only $1,824.

This obvious inequity has prompted some policy-makers to argue that eligibility for the EITC should be expanded in a way that increases public support for child rearing among near-poor and middle-income families. David Ellwood of the Kennedy School at Harvard University supports this basic argument, and Robert Cherry and Max Sawicky of the Economic Policy Institute have developed a detailed proposal for Universal Unified Child Credit that would combine the dependant exemption, child credit, and EITC into a single credit that would initially rise along with earnings, and then phase down to a minimum benefit of $1,270 per child for all families. This proposal however, has been eclipsed by the tax cut proposed by the new Bush administration.

Child care

The United States provides relatively little public support for child care. The only federal programme that actually provides care, Head Start, is targeted exclusively at low-income children. Despite its political popularity, the programme has never enrolled more than about 40 per cent of eligible children; and because it is typically organized on a half-day basis, it does not meet the needs of many mothers who work for pay. Furthermore, as families earn more income, they lose their eligibility for Head Start in a phase-out similar to that of the EITC.

Federal block grants have enabled states to increase spending on child care by over 50 per cent since the welfare reforms of 1996, but places remain scarce. Less than 15 per cent of families eligible for child-care assistance actually receive it. Efforts have been targeted at mothers leaving the welfare rolls, so almost-but-not-quite-poor families are least likely to receive assistance with child-care costs. Many states have opted for quantity over quality, providing vouchers to large numbers of families but setting voucher levels so low that they cannot pay for high-quality centre-based care.

The higher its income, the more likely a family can afford child care with an explicitly educational component. Only about half of four-year-olds from households with incomes of $10,000 or less attend centre-based programmes. Attendance is even lower among working-poor families who do not qualify for Head Start or state assistance. By contrast, more than 75 per cent of four-year-olds from households with incomes of $50,000 or more are learning their ABCs in centre-based programmes. And affluent parents are more likely to be able to make use of the Child and Dependent Care Credit, which is worth as much as $720 for families with incomes of $75,000 or more with two children (Shore, 2000). Upscale professional and managerial parents are also well-positioned to ask their employers for pre-tax accounts that allow them to set aside up to $5,000 per year for dependent care; this money is exempt from income and payroll taxes (a subsidy worth about $2,000 a year per child to families in the highest income bracket).

The low level of public support for child care means that in many cities it actually costs more to send a four-year-old to an early-education programme than to send an 18-year-old to college. The subsidies built into community college and state university tuition rates, combined with the extensive financial aid available for enrolment at private colleges, cover about 60 per cent of total expenditures. Students at public universities enjoy a subsidy of about 80 per cent. By contrast, only about 30 per cent of the total costs of child care are subsidized by the Government (Heckman and Lochner, 2000; Graetz and Mashaw, 1999).

This huge difference in public support has momentous distributional implications. Children from low-income families generally attend poor schools, with lower levels of per student spending than children from affluent families (schools are largely financed by local property taxes). As a result, they are less likely to graduate from high school and go on to college, where they could take advantage of higher education subsidies. In 1992, only about 28 per cent of high school graduates from the poorest quartile of families enrolled in a four-year college within 20 months of graduation, compared with 66 per cent from the richest quartile. Family income had a significant effect even among graduates with identical high school records and test scores (Ellwood and Kane, 2000).

Elder care

The social security system in the United States has successfully reduced poverty among the elderly, and some argue that its success lies in its universality. A very large proportion of the population is eligible either through work or marriage. However, the privileged place that it has long held within United States social policy has increased public spending and future budgetary commitments to levels that may threaten its political viability. President George W. Bush campaigned on promises to partially privatize the system.

Support for the elderly comes in several forms. As with other areas of American social policy, the tax relief often goes unnoticed. However, the practice of exempting employer-provided pensions from taxation effectively subsidizes high-earners above and beyond their eligibility for social security benefits per se. It is estimated that the top one-third of wage earners receives about two-thirds of the overall subsidy, which costs the United States Government nearly $80 billion a year (Graetz and Mashaw, 1999, p.109). By comparison, Head Start, the early childhood education programme targeted low-income children, cost $4 billion in 1998.

Social security itself has several components. Of greatest relevance to the elderly are the retirement and health-care provisions. The retirement provisions are based on a regressive tax but have a progressive payment structure. On net, the payments individuals and their spouses receive are roughly proportional to their earnings. The spousal benefit essentially subsidizes marriage, and one could argue that this represents a subsidy for a form of care. Among the elderly, in particular, spouses are crucial care providers for one another. On the other hand, the spousal benefit almost certainly does more to reinforce the traditional gender division of labour than to reward care for dependants.

The health-care provisions, known as Medicare, are funded not only by specific contributions but also through a federal subsidy for physician expenses. The overall effect is to provide virtually universal health-care coverage for individuals over age 65, with two major loopholes: no coverage (as yet) for prescription drugs, and no support for long-term care. Nursing home care is funded only for the indigent through Medicaid, forcing those elderly who require it to "spend down" all their assets, such as home ownership, in order to qualify. This helps explain the vulnerable position of nursing home residents, described above.

As in many European countries, the combined effect of growth in the relative size of the elderly population and improvements in medical technology have been a rapid increase in the fiscal burden of elderly care. Retirement and health benefits together account for more than half of the total annual outlays of the Federal Government (Graetz and Mashaw, 1999, p. 93). Projections of future deficits in the system by the year 2030 are forcing consideration of changes in the overall tax/benefit structure. They may also help call attention to a fundamental inconsistency in the structure of the welfare state: it socializes the benefits of child rearing to a far greater extent than it socializes the costs (Folbre, 1994).

Conclusion

Most economic analysis of the welfare state in the United States has largely ignored analysis of the way in which it intersects with non-market care provided in the family and the community. The so-called "intergenerational accounting" systems developed by Laurence Kotlikoff and others are based on extremely narrow comparisons of the tax rates projected on current and future generations, with no consideration of the "investment" component or of the overall size of transfers between generations as a whole (Kotlikoff, 1992). Furthermore, these estimates completely ignore the ways in which social policy is influencing both the size and the educational attainment of the next generation. In short, they are based on a fundamental lack of understanding of the economy of care.

The United States represents a particularly striking example of problems in the quality of care that can be exacerbated by the rhetoric of reliance on market provision. These problems are far less visible – especially to a public informed only by an uninformed and unmotivated mass media – than the more easily measured successes of growth in GDP. Hence the importance of insisting on more meaningful definitions of economic success that emphasize long-run sustainability and quality of life.

The development of better accounting systems for the provision of care can contribute to this effort. There is a pressing need to bring scholars doing important conceptual and qualitative work into more sustained contact with those engaged in the more quantitative measurement of labour force, time-use, and social expenditure trends. International collaboration will be required to develop the tools required to make the "care sector" of the economy a central focus of research. International collaboration will also be required to develop a compelling vision of new and better ways of sharing the costs of care.

PART IV

REPRESENTATION FOR CARE WORK

FROM PRIVATE CARER TO PUBLIC ACTOR: THE CARERS' MOVEMENT IN ENGLAND

11

Marian Barnes

Introduction

A growing recognition of the significance of "informal care" was a major factor in the development of community care policy in Great Britain during the 1980s, culminating in the passage of the 1990 National Health Service (NHS) and Community Care Act. Carers were "discovered" by policy-makers and were urged to "come out" by organizations such as the Carers National Association (CNA) and by local carers' organizations. This chapter discusses the collective organization of unpaid carers at local and national levels and describes the way in which this has impacted on policy and service delivery.

It is important to consider the growth of such action in a sociological as well as a policy context. Why should the position of "family carer" have come to be regarded as something around which collective action should develop? In order to answer this question we need to explore broader sociological critiques of "the family", as well as considering both the demographic and policy shifts affecting the particular experiences of families with a disabled or frail older person.

The National Council for the Single Woman and her Dependants

It was in 1963 that the first organization was established to represent the interests of those subsequently to be known as carers. This resulted from an initiative taken by the Reverend Mary Webster, an unmarried woman who had given up her work in the early 1950s to care for her elderly parents (McKenzie, 1995). After the Second World War there was a plentiful supply of women who had never been married and thus were "available" to provide care to older people whose numbers were increasing because of improved social conditions and more accessible health care. Mary Webster recognised that her experience was unlikely to be an unusual one and when her parents died she started to explore the experiences of other single women in similar circumstances. She wrote a letter to *The Times* and sought to engage the interest of the churches:

I am anxious to mobilize the redoubtable energies of the Federation in what I consider to be a very neglected social matter. More than ten per cent of the women in this country who are over 40 are unmarried. Because of changing economic circumstances, most of them follow a salaried occupation. Many of them also have responsibilities for dependants. Because they have to earn their living, as well as undertaking the tasks of caring for others, life for them is often difficult. (Webster, 1963, p. 13).

Once she had started to make visible the experiences of women like herself she received an enormous response from others in a similar situation, or who recognized that they were likely to be so in the future. It was suggested that the scale of the response was not only evidence of the extent of single women's involvement in informal care, but also of the opportunity it provided for a group who felt ignored, unvalued and powerless to organize on a collective basis. Baroness Seear, who later became President of the CNA, observed that "many women saw the organization as a kind of single women's trade union" (Kohner, 1993).

Elizabeth Wilson (1977) described the post-war period as a time during which the task of rebuilding the family in the context of a protective welfare state meant that the role of women as wives and mothers was given particular prominence. Those who had been neither wives nor mothers were excluded from the ambiguous benefits of a return to traditional roles for women after their experience of work in factories and land armies during the war. Women were seen to be liberated from much of the drudgery of housework by the availability of new household appliances. They were also to be relieved of the anxieties caused by poverty and ill health by the post-war settlement which resulted in the establishment of the NHS and the welfare state. Prime Minister Harold Macmillan's assertion that "You've never had it so good!" represented the dominant perception of the 1950s and early 1960s as a period of increasing prosperity and ease. In this context the dominant image of women was that of wives and mothers happy to return to their domestic roles. However much such an image might have been at odds with the reality of women's experiences, single women who were combining paid work with responsibilities for looking after elderly relatives did not share in it. An organization which represented their experiences and interests was not only welcome for the specific improvements it sought in their practical and financial circumstances, but also as the start of a more fundamental critique of assumptions about the nature of the family which underpinned the welfare state and which were picked up in later feminist critiques of community care (e.g. Finch and Groves, 1985).

The National Council for the Single Woman and her Dependants (NCSWD) sought to achieve legislative and policy changes which would benefit single women carers, and to provide support and advice to them. The NCSWD commissioned research into the experience and circumstances of single women carers and hosted conferences to publicize results, as well as campaigning and lobbying at national and local levels. From an early stage the organization was successful in gaining the support of powerful public figures. This was considered to have been important in its success in achieving financial improvements in the lives of many carers. At a local level "branches served as the eyes and ears of the organization at the grass roots". (McKenzie, 1995, p. 86). Whilst the national organization primarily focused on the need for legislative changes in relation to the financial circumstances of carers, local branches were more directly concerned with the availability of health and social care services.

The major achievements of the NCSWD were the introduction in 1971 of the Attendance Allowance, payable to those needing constant care at home, and, in 1976, the Invalid Care Allowance, paid directly to carers. The origins of these benefits in campaigns led by an organization representing single women is evidenced by the fact that the Invalid Care Allowance was payable only to single women. The assumption was that the allowance was remuneration for lost earnings resulting from women giving up work in order to care. Married women were assumed not to work but to be dependent on their husbands' earnings. In this, as in other parts of the benefits system, the welfare state was based on profoundly sexist assumptions about women's roles and positions within the family (Land, 1985). It was only in 1986 as a result of an appeal to the European Court of Justice that entitlement to the Invalid Care Allowance was extended to married women.

The successes of the NCSWD started to prompt contact from married, widowed and divorced women who identified themselves as being in similar positions to that of single women carers. Eventually it became impossible to sustain such an exclusive membership and the title of the organization was changed to the National Council for Carers and their Elderly Dependants (NCCED).

This still separated the experience of those who cared for older relatives from those who cared for younger ones. Whilst the experience of adults in mid-life taking on the care of an elderly parent for many years could be constructed as a more than usual family responsibility, looking after a disabled child or providing a quasi-nursing service to a partner impaired as a result of an accident or chronic ill health were assumed to be "natural" responsibilities of marriage or parenthood. In the case of older parents who needed additional support because of advancing frailty there is implicit if not explicit negotiation over where this responsibility should lie (Finch and Mason, 1993). When it is a child or partner, it is almost entirely taken for granted where responsibility lies (Parker, 1992; Ungerson, 1987).

The AOC was founded in 1981 on the principle that it should represent all carers, regardless of sex, age, marital status or relationship to the person they cared for. There was some opposition to this – not only from professionals who wanted things organized around the "condition" of the person receiving care, but also from some members of the National Council who were unhappy about a shift of focus away from carers of older people. The NCCED in fact remained in existence until 1988 when it merged with the AOC to form the CNA.

"A stronger voice"

These early activities had established the identity of "carer" and laid the basis for a new social group – carers – to become a subject of public policy. During the 1980s the carers' lobby became increasingly influential at a national level as well as continuing to provide a focus for self-help in the expanding network of local groups. The AOC was founded both on personal experience (its founder was Judith Oliver, whose husband was disabled) and on the analysis of research into the experiences of carers which demonstrated that "if you broke the experience of caring down into the emotional issues, the physical issues, the environmental issues, the financial issues, then all carers were really experiencing the same kind of stresses and suffering the same kind of problems" (Kohner, 1993, p. 8).

Subsequent research would suggest that such a claim ignores important differences in the experiences of women and men carers (Ungerson, 1987), of black carers (Atkin, 1991), of those caring for partners rather than for parents or children (Parker, 1992), as well as differences in the extent to which caring is experienced as a "burden" (Braithwaite, 1990). But shared experiences and shared identities are important in establishing a constituency, which can form the basis of a powerful pressure group. The subsequent successes of the carers' lobby would have been less likely had there not been a single organization representing the interests of all carers.

By the mid-1980s community care policy was receiving increasing attention not only from policy-makers but also from researchers. Academic interest in "the family" was starting to include consideration of the way in which families were assumed to be the natural source of care for elderly and disabled members, as well as of the socialization of children. Informal care offered a substantial new area for research and the number of research projects exploring the experiences of informal carers and their relationships with formal services burgeoned (see e.g. Parker, 1992; Twigg, Atkin and Perring, 1990). Policy assumptions about the potential for interlinking formal and informal care started to be questioned by academic analysts (Bulmer, 1987; Waerness, 1987), whilst others looked more closely at the notion of "caring networks" and the resources available within communities to provide care (Walker, 1987; Wenger, 1991).

Research and pressure group activity developed hand in hand in some instances. In 1985, following an initiative launched by the Department of Health under the heading "Helping the Community to Care", the King's Fund Informal Caring Unit was established in London. This unit combined information giving and gathering, research and service development. Ten years later Carers Impact, the successor to the Caring Unit and an alliance of local authority, health authority, and voluntary sector organizations, held its first national conference entitled "Carers in the Mainstream?".

The focus on the financial circumstances of carers which had been a primary concern of the NCSWD continued to be pursued by the AOC in the campaign for the extension of the Invalid Care Allowance to married and cohabiting women. In 1982 a steering group was established to pursue this campaign, which stood to benefit 96,000 women if it were successful (Kohner, 1993). The campaign was based on a test case brought by a married woman caring for her mother who had dementia. This woman was selected by the AOC and invited to pursue her case with the support of the Association. The case was based on a directive issued by the European Economic Community (EEC) requiring equal treatment in social security systems. As in other cases, the United Kingdom government was reluctant to accept European rulings on social policy and it took an application to the European Court of Justice to force a change of policy. The Government backed down the day before the European court ruling in 1986.

The Caring Costs Campaign, launched in 1992 by the CNA to secure an independent income for carers, continued to emphasize both the personal financial implications of caring and the amount which informal carers save the State by providing unpaid care. But during the latter part of the 1980s attention shifted to the policy review process which culminated in the passage of the 1990 NHS and Community Care Act. The 1986 Disabled Persons Act provided the first legislative recognition of the role of carers when it required local authorities to take account of carers' abilities in assessing the needs of people seeking support from social services departments.

At a local level the late 1980s and early 1990s saw an increase in campaigning on the part of carers. The recognition which carers had achieved by this time is reflected in action from within service delivery agencies to engage with carers in developing the policy and practice of community care.

One example of this was in Birmingham where a project to develop user-led community care services gave priority to engaging carers in determining the shape and direction of community care services. In this instance a project instigated by the local authority in collaboration with local NHS agencies was proactive in creating a local carers' lobby.

The Birmingham Community Care Special Action Project (CCSAP)

The Birmingham CCSAP was a wide-ranging initiative designed to promote user involvement and cultural change in services within a large metropolitan area. Supported by the city council and the (then) five health authorities within the city, a high-profile director was appointed to lead a small team to encourage collaboration across agencies, and to develop user and carer involvement in decision-making. The main initiatives undertaken during the three years of the project included work focusing on advocacy for people with mental health problems, service reviews and service developments involving people with learning difficulties and disabled people. But the most high profile and extensive of its activities was a series of public consultations with carers and a programme of developmental work arising from this.

The carers' consultations formed the subject of a number of articles in the professional press (Jowell, 1989; Jowell and Wistow, 1990; Prior, Jowell and Lawrence, 1989), of presentations at conferences, and of representations to government ministers. During the preparation of the White Paper *Caring for People* – the forerunner of the 1990 NHS and Community Care Act – both David Mellor and Virginia Bottomley visited Birmingham in their role as health ministers and met with carers and project staff. A lasting outcome was the establishment of a Carers Unit, at first within the Central Executive Department of the city council, and later transferred into the Social Services Department. Two panels of carers established during the evaluation of the CCSAP continued to meet as a forum through which carers' views could regularly be fed into both health and local authorities. These panels produced a Carers Charter, which was adopted by statutory authorities within the city. Carers Weeks continued to be an annual event within the city and became the focus not only for information sharing and support for carers, but also the opportunity for social events to give carers a break from providing care.

The Birmingham Carers Charter asserted ten rights of carers:

a) Carers have the right to recognition of their contribution, their own needs and that they are individuals in their own right.

b) Carers have the right to be consulted and to be involved at every stage of service delivery in order that services are provided which reflect their own and the users' individual circumstances.

c) Carers have a right to a service which reflects their racial, cultural and religious backgrounds, is anti-discriminatory and ensures that carers are not disadvantaged.

d) Carers have the right to accessible information on services, welfare benefits, financial assistance, policies and procedures.

e) Carers have the right to have time to themselves and their own needs addressed. They should have opportunities for a break, both short term and long term.

f) Carers have the right to practical help to ease the task of caring. This help could include such things as domestic help, nursing care, equipment and adaptations, continence services, respite and day care and help with transport. Help can be required 24 hours a day.

g) Carers have the right to guidance and in some instances training in how to cope with the particular condition of the person they are looking after.

h) Carers have the right to receive support for what is most often a stressful and isolating experience. The support networks should be identified at the outset and should continue during and after the caring task is over.

i) Carers have the right to explore alternatives to family care based on informed choice, both for the immediate and long-term future.

j) Carers have the right to make comments, suggestions and complaints in relation to any service received.

There was a broad consensus amongst those taking part in CCSAP initiatives that a major purpose of involvement was achieving service improvements. The carers' consultations identified 11 issues on which action was promised, including action to improve information, to improve respite care and to improve access to help outside office hours. A performance review group was established to monitor progress on these issues. Two panels of carers working with the author as the evaluator of the CCSAP, both monitored action and became actively engaged in prompting developments. For example, panel members took part in work to produce a directory of information for carers, and produced a "respite care quality checklist" to assess the quality of care homes.

Carers in Birmingham clearly judged the consultations in terms of their effectiveness in securing change in the quality and responsiveness of services (Barnes and Wistow, 1995). Whilst there was considerable frustration on the part of some carers about the slow pace of change, others recognized that the actions which had been taken in response to consultations, the need for better information for example, plus the mechanisms which had been established for continuing involvement via the panels and the Carers Unit, constituted a real departure from the situation which existed prior to the CCSAP (Barnes and Wistow, 1993). In Birmingham, as elsewhere during this period, it was becoming increasingly difficult for decisions about community care services to be made without some consultation with or involvement of carers in that process. Whilst the Birmingham Carers' Charter emphasized individual rights to support and recognition, the collective recognition of carers as co-producers of care perhaps marks a more fundamental shift towards an emphasis on partnership between the State and citizens as a key means of delivering policy objectives (Barnes and Prior, 2000).

Consolidation

The second half of the 1990s can be seen as a period in which carers' organizations secured their positions both as service providers and campaigners. Carers' centres offering a combination of information and advice to carers, an opportunity for social contact and respite, and a base for local and national campaigning became widely established. The 1995 Carers (Recognition and Services) Act gave legislative force to the rights of carers to receive an assessment, but did not contain a right to receive services. The CNA has continued to campaign for that right. In 1999 the Government published *Caring about carers: A national strategy for carers,* setting out what was being done to support lay care and promising further action. The CNA has called for legislation which would give direct services such as training, emotional support and mobile phones to carers, and is involved in consultation with local carers' groups to produce a Carers Manifesto to urge government action.

The final section of this chapter reflects on what the experience of collective action by carers illustrates about the relationship between the State and the provision of lay care.

Informal care and the State

Collective action by carers has been influential in affecting national policy and local service delivery. There is evidence of considerable goodwill on the part of policy-makers and service providers who have sought to improve the support they offer to carers, or to involve them in policy-making. Service providers often find it easier to develop new ways of working with carers than with service users. There are a number of reasons for this.

The methods required for involving excluded groups and groups for whom talking is not an available method of communication can be very intensive and time-consuming. From a practical perspective it can be much easier to involve carers who, despite severe constraints on the time that they can be available and the need for arrangements to "cover" them whilst they are not available to provide care, can nevertheless get to meetings under their own steam. Carers are often very articulate in expressing their views based on their considerable experience of care providing and, in many instances, campaigning. They may need less support to articulate their views than those who have been subject to others' decision-making for much of their lives.

Carers do not threaten the professional authority and knowledge of health and social care workers in the same way that disabled people or people with mental health problems can. For example, in a study of mental health user councils, developed under the remit of the Birmingham CCSAP, it became clear that the angry voices of users who were highly dissatisfied with the way they were being treated in a psychiatric hospital in the city generated dismissive or defensive responses on the part of clinicians. The views expressed by service users went beyond specific dissatisfactions with particular aspects of their treatment and called into question the practice of psychiatry itself. That such challenges were being offered by people who could be deemed "incompetent" by virtue of their mental disorder contributed to the blocking response of some professionals. Similarly, disabled people have experienced professional defensiveness in response to their arguments for alternative service models. The social model of disability undermines the right of clinicians to own disablement as an arena in which to practise their professional expertise.

Whilst carers too have fought for their specific and particular knowledge to be recognized and valued by professional service deliverers, there is much less evidence that this has led to defensive responses. Indeed, there was a degree of surprise in Birmingham that carers were not being more challenging nor asking for considerably more than they were. There was a sense that what they were saying was entirely reasonable and that the inadequacies they were pointing out were system failures to which providers were grateful to be alerted. Much of what carers were saying indicated a wish to benefit from professional knowledge, rather than a questioning of it. It was only when there was a suggestion that some of what carers were saying implied that they be recognized as "care recipients" in their own right, with needs of their own which public authorities had a responsibility to meet, that there was a degree of alarm. And that alarm was prompted by the resource implications of such a position, rather than by a perceived threat to the authority of the welfare bureaucracies, or of professional groups within them.

Not only is there a higher likelihood of "professional" identification between paid and unpaid carers, there is also a potential for personal identification. Many paid care workers can anticipate that they too will experience being "informal carers". It is easy to think that as a daughter or son you are likely to be in the position of having to take on the care of an elderly relative. Many are already in that position. The *Carers in employment* report published by the Princess Royal Trust for Carers in May 1995 stated that 15 per cent of all people at work also care for someone at home. There is no reason to assume that at least 15 per cent of those employed within the caring professions do not also have personal caregiving responsibilities. Self-interest prompts action to ensure that services are sensitive to carers' needs.

But much of the success of the carers' lobby is because it was clearly in the Government's interest to acknowledge the role played by informal or family carers. The success of community care policy depended on informal carers being prepared to continue to undertake the primary caring responsibility for their relatives and friends. It was no accident that Jill Pitkeathley, Director of the CNA, was invited to become a member of the group advising Roy Griffiths on the Department of Health commissioned report: *Community care: Agenda for action*; nor that, during the deliberations which led to the publication of the Community Care White Paper, ministers from the Department of Health made their way to Birmingham to hear what carers were saying about their needs and their views of community care in practice (Barnes and Wistow, 1991). The apparent convergence of interests is clear in the following statements from the Griffiths report and the White Paper *Caring for people*:

Publicly provided services constitute only a small part of the total care provided to people in need. Families, friends, neighbours and other local people provide the majority of care in response to needs which they are uniquely well placed to identify and respond to. This will continue to be the primary means by which people are enabled to live normal lives in community settings. The proposals take as their starting point that this is as it *should* be, and that the first task of publicly provided services is to support and where possible strengthen these networks of carers (1988, para 3.2 – author's emphasis).

While this White Paper focuses largely on the role of statutory and independent bodies in the provision of community care services, the reality is that most care is provided by family, friends and neighbours [...] helping carers to maintain their valuable contribution to the spectrum of care is both a right and a sound investment (Secretaries of State, 1989, p. 9).

From the perspective of the State, informal care is to be preferred both because it is a more cost-effective option and because it is the "natural" and hence the best option. Underpinning an unwillingness on the part of the State to accept the full resource responsibility implied by meeting the needs of disabled and elderly people, is an ideological position on the relative role of the

State and the family (Dalley, 1988). This position can be sustained because there is little evidence of a powerful lobby arguing that collective forms of provision should be preferred over individualized services. Jill Pitkeathley is quoted as saying: "I've never known such consensus around a set of proposals as there was around Griffiths's. Everyone, on the whole, agreed with the proposals." (Kohner, 1993, p. 20).

Carers' organizations were campaigning for increased recognition of the role played by carers, and increased support for this role. They were not, with the exception of the National Schizophrenia Fellowship, campaigning for the extension of residential rather than community services, nor for a reassessment of the possibilities of alternative forms of collective provision such as that suggested by Dalley (1988).

What do carers want from community care?

There is little evidence from research into carers' needs and experiences, or from the campaigns of carers' organizations, that families are seeking to give up their role of providing care and support to older or disabled relatives. Whilst caring is a "labour", it is also very often a "labour of love" and the carers' lobby sought primarily to find an accommodation with the State which would enable genuine caring relationships to be maintained without the burden of care becoming overwhelming.

In some instances both those providing and those receiving care are asking for specific tasks to be undertaken by paid service providers, although which tasks vary according to personal circumstances and preferences. Some would not want personal tending to be provided by a stranger, but do want help with practical domestic work so that they can have the time to undertake more intimate tasks involved in personal care. Others, often spouses, find that having to deal with incontinence and other highly intimate physical needs can interfere with their relationships as lovers and partners (Morris, 1993). They would prefer such tasks to be undertaken by a professional in a way that separates physical tending from sexual relationships. Carers want to negotiate with services in order to reach an accommodation about who does what. They are not happy with a system that demands allocation to dependency categories which carry with them specified amounts and types of help which may bear little resemblance to their perception of their needs.

Those who provide intensive care over long periods of time to older people, disabled people, people with mental health problems and to those with chronic illnesses are asking for opportunities to have breaks which can benefit themselves and those they are caring for.

Carers are asking for their close and intimate knowledge not only of the person they are caring for, but also of ways in which they are able jointly to solve problems and find solutions, to be recognized and respected. For example, parents with daughters or sons with learning difficulties emphasize the importance of the understanding which comes from familiarity with their children's behaviour. The ability to recognize and interpret feelings which cannot easily be expressed in spoken language, and the development of different forms of communication with those for whom words do not come easily may be a particular advantage gained from living in close proximity for many years with family members. A frequent complaint is that such knowledge and the experience and skills which derive from this are ignored or dismissed by the paid workers with whom carers come into contact (Barnes, 1997a).

Yet many carers have not actively chosen to take on this role and, whilst some describe considerable satisfactions to be gained from caring (Grant and Nolan, 1993), many also feel that they are expected to do too much and that there is insufficient recognition for what they do (Barnes and Wistow, 1992). They are asking that their input be recognized and, if they have to give up jobs or the prospect of promotion in order to take on a role which saves the State a considerable amount of money, they should not be further penalized by the additional costs of caring. From her study of the costs of informal care, Caroline Glendinning found:

The analysis of household budgeting and expenditure patterns carried out in this study took full account of the resources contributed by the disabled person. Nevertheless, in many instances at least some of these extra disability costs still fell on carers to meet out of their own financial resources. In addition, some carers incurred extra expenditure because they provided their elderly or disabled relatives with a higher standard of living than s/he would have been able to afford from her/his income alone. In poorer households, hidden "costs" were experienced by carers, these included foregoing items of consumption in order to meet the disability costs of the disabled person, and the psychological "costs" of their own financial dependency (Glendinning, 1992, pp. 110–111).

The latter point reflects the fact that adult children can become financially dependent on the welfare benefits of their elderly or disabled parents because they have to give up jobs in order to provide care. They experience considerable difficulty in finding work following the death or admission to residential care of the person they cared for, and also in these circumstances lose the marginal advantage of the benefit income.

Caring is experienced as physically and emotionally demanding work. Those who care for people with mental health problems in particular can also experience the effect of the stigma attached to mental illness, and the impact of mental distress on family relationships can be devastating (Lefley, 1996; Smith and West, 1985). On top of the emotional and physical demands, obtaining benefits and services is experienced as a battle or an uphill struggle which may sometimes be too exhausting to attempt. Information about services and entitlements has to be sought out rather than being offered and, as carers have said in many studies of their experiences of services, you have to know what question to ask before you stand any chance of finding out a useful answer (Twigg et al., 1990). Those service providers to whom carers turn in the first instance, in particular general practitioners (family doctors), are themselves often unaware of other services which might be available or unwilling to share their professional knowledge in a way which would allow carers to develop their own problem-solving strategies. Some carers have suggested that lack of information is a deliberate strategy for rationing services (Twigg and Atkin, 1994), whilst others have expressed considerable distress at having to make complaints or threats in order to get access to services to which they know they are entitled (Ellis, 1993). The benefits system is complex and confusing, and appealing against apparently arbitrary decisions can be a humiliating experience (Twigg and Atkin, 1994).

In discussions in the Birmingham Carers Panels, as in interviews conducted for research purposes, carers reflected on their own needs as people with major responsibilities for meeting the needs of others, as well as on the direct needs of those for whom they care. Carers are often aware of the potential for conflict between their own needs and those of the people they support. Respite care is a good example of this. Carers need a break from caring but they know that often the person they care for does not want to be "pushed out" into a respite care home to enable this to happen. They face the dilemma of forcing their relative to do something which will make them distressed or unhappy, or risking their own health by not taking a break. But to what extent is this conflict inherent within caregiving and care receiving relationships rather than being a result of inadequate or insensitive services? If respite care provided positive experiences for those being cared for, would there be a problem?

Encouraging wives, daughters, lovers, husbands, or friends to identify themselves as carers was an important objective of the carer's movement. It was seen to be a vital means of raising awareness amongst those who provide care that they are entitled to services and financial support, and necessary to achieve legislative recognition for the work that carers do. By naming carers as an identifiable group it became possible to include reference to their needs and circumstances in community care legislation. But such naming can serve to disguise the other, very different relationships that carers may have with care receivers. It may also separate them from each other in ways which may result in competition between interest groups, rather than alliances between all who have a shared interest in ensuring effective "community care". Judith Oliver has argued that the carers' lobby has had common cause with the disability movement:

We were on the side of disabled people and acting in their interests too. Because from the start, we argued that disabled people deserved better than to be looked after by one (usually), exhausted (usually), possibly resentful person who was being used as a doormat by statutory authorities. We were saying that the system did neither side any good. It tied disabled people to one person who might not even be the person they would choose to have care for them (Oliver, quoted in Kohner, 1993, p. 16).

However, not all would agree that action taken on behalf of carers has benefited disabled people. There has been opposition from within the disability movement to the introduction of legislation aimed at carers because the demands of disabled people are based on notions of "rights" rather than "care".

In seeking recognition as experts, carers are challenging the right of professionals to define the nature of their "problems" and to determine the appropriate response to them. In this respect their project shares with user movements the aim of asserting the authority of experiential knowledge alongside and, if necessary, in preference to that of professional knowledge. The concept of "care" contained within policy pronouncements is beset by as many confusions as that of "community". Whilst in practice individual paid care providers often learn that the separation of physical labour from the emotional content of caring is not possible, the commodification of care in "care packages" seeks to define the provision of care on the basis of contract rather than trust (Barnes and Prior, 1996). The conflicts revealed between the interests of carers and those they care for derive from the problems of sub-ordinate relationships (Waerness, 1987). As long as caregiving is conceived as a one-way relationship, it will always risk the construction of one party as dependent on the other. But there is considerable evidence of reciprocity in caregiving and care receiving relationships. Waerness also argues that both rationality and emotionality, normally regarded as dichotomous and exclusive, need to be brought together in "the rationality of caring" in order to understand what "good caring" consists of.

This understanding is something which front-line paid care providers may learn, but which is likely to be frustrated by the rules and procedures within which "caregiving" bureaucracies require them to work. Home carers forbidden by their employers to undertake any task which involves dealing with electrical equipment, for example, changing light bulbs, or which involves climbing on steps, such as cleaning the top of cupboards, find themselves in a position of either having to refuse to do exactly the tasks which their elderly care recipients find most difficult to do for themselves, or disobeying rules and risking censure. Treating each care recipient differently is incompatible with rules which define the type and amount of support that can be provided by reference to allocation to particular dependency categories. The maintenance of reciprocity in caring relationships is threatened when public caregiving services are experienced as inflexible, stigmatizing and of poor quality.

Underpinning all that carers' groups are seeking to achieve in terms of practical improvements in community care services of benefit to themselves and those they care for, is a recognition of both the quantity and quality of work they undertake. Carers are claiming recognition as co-producers of care, and they are claiming recognition of the experiential knowledge which they bring to caring and from which they want professional carers to learn. Both factors provide legitimation for claims to be involved in public policy-making.

Conclusion

The emergence of collective action by carers is one aspect of a broader movement amongst users of welfare services to achieve both recognition and change (see e.g. Barnes, 1997b, 1999; Barnes and Bowl, 2001; Barnes and Shaw, 2000). Like these other movements, carers have used a combination of research, lobbying at local and national levels, and joint working with statutory officials, in order to achieve their aims. They have also prioritized direct support to carers – both to build a collective identity and to enable sharing of the experiential knowledge often hidden within private caring relationships. From the early campaigns to achieve recognition for a group of hidden women, undertaking a role which was taken for granted and unrewarded, through successes in achieving some financial support for private care, to a presence within national policy-making forums developing community care legislation, by the mid-1990s carers collectively had been recognized as a significant force within the production of community care. At the turn of the century the Government was proclaiming in its *National Strategy for Carers*:

We need to achieve a cultural change in the way society as a whole – employers, statutory services, members of the public, the media, the educational system, and friends, colleagues and neighbours – perceive caring. Carers should not be pitied, but respected and admired (Department of Health, 1999).

Carers – as well as disabled people, users/survivors of mental health services and older people – have succeeded not only in making the private experience of care a matter for public debate in the context of health and social care services, but also a matter for broader debate about our capacity to achieve an inclusive society.

CARING FOR CARERS: AN EXAMPLE FROM IRELAND **12**

Eddie Collins-Hughes

Introduction

In tracing the experience of the Carers Association of Ireland, this chapter explores the reality of caring and the effects of lobbying on caring. The presentation serves to reveal both the needs of Irish carers and the politics of care provision in Ireland. The chapter outlines the strategies pursued by the Association in relation to its own membership and also in relation to improving the treatment of care and carers in Ireland.

For the purposes of the Association, a carer is a person who provides care and assistance with daily living activities at home to a family member who is frail in old age, has a significant disability or is terminally ill. The great majority of carers in Ireland, as elsewhere, are family members – often a wife, daughter or female relative. It will come as little surprise therefore that almost 80 per cent of carers are women. One important feature of home caring in Ireland is that "good neighbours" may also be the providers of care (O'Shea, 2000). The Carers Association includes these carers in its membership. Thus, for the purposes of the Association's lobbying activities and services, the concept of "family" is broadened to include neighbourhood carers.

It is important to distinguish family members and good neighbours who care from those who provide care services on a professional basis. For this purpose the Association works with the concept of "family carer" as outlined above. This terminology has now been broadly accepted in Ireland, being used by the National Council on Ageing and Older People, the statutory advisory agency on policies and services for older people. The term is also used by a range of research and policy-development bodies, including the National Dementia Research Centre and the National University of Ireland.

It is difficult to estimate the numbers of carers. There is a general acceptance that many carers are "hidden", i.e. they are unknown to either the

Association or the statutory services. These carers often only present themselves in times of crisis. In the absence of a national database on carers, the number of current and prospective family carers is unknown.

The Association estimates that the figure is in the region of 125,500. The Department of Social, Community and Family Affairs estimates the number at 49,000. However, other Government departments and agencies have carried out various research studies that indicate the Association's estimates may be too low. The fact that there is no national database on carers makes planning for the future virtually impossible. The absence of figures about current and prospective family carers renders the development of suitable services and support a matter of guesswork. One solution would be to include relevant questions in a future population census.

The research situation with regard to carers in Ireland is generally poor. While a number of separate pieces of research have been carried out recently for different state agencies, there is little evidence of a coordinated approach to this research. However, there is a growing body of work, due to the political interest in family carers and the realization that carers were, until the last year or two, largely neglected by the State (O'Connor et al., 1988; O'Shea, 2000; Department of Social, Community and Family Affairs, 1998).

The Carers Association of Ireland

Founded in 1987, the Carers Association of Ireland is the national voluntary organization of family carers. Members include carers, ex-carers and people who work closely with carers. Over 95 per cent of members are carers or former carers. It was founded following a public meeting to emphasize the lack of attention and consideration given by policy-makers to the vitally important role of family carers in maintaining the health, independence and dignity of frail older people in the community.

From its own experience, as well as from the studies referred to above, the Association has identified the main needs of carers in Ireland:

a) Valorization: to feel that the work done at home is recognized by the State in a tangible way. In essence, this means that the great majority of carers want to receive the Carer's Allowance (the national social security income support for carers).
b) Recognition of and compensation for the additional costs arising from caring at home: e.g. extra heating for an incapacitated older or disabled person, incontinence products, special diets, additional medical care and problems with transport.

c) Protection of personal health: many carers suffer poor physical health as well as high levels of anxiety and emotional distress arising from long-term, intensive caring duties.

d) Respite care: to give the carer short breaks from caring at times which suit her (or him), which implies a greater emphasis on home-based support and social care services.

e) Involvement in service planning and delivery: to ensure that services are designed to meet the needs of the carer and not those of the service provision agencies, e.g. the availability of flexible, "out-of-hours" home support services. Training in technical skills required to care, and in caring for the carer's own health and welfare: e.g. back care, dealing with emergencies, special training in caring for people with very high dependency (such as people with dementia, severe learning disabilities or emotional disturbances), coping skills and stress management.

f) Information: on services, rights and entitlements.

g) Carers' support groups/social activities: such as weekly and monthly meetings.

h) Opportunities to develop work-related skills while engaged in caring at home: e.g. training in use of computers, personal development/confidence-building skills, part-time work experience and skills training in caring.

Taking into account these needs, the Association has developed two main thrusts to its activities: advocacy and service provision.

Lobbying and advocacy

The primary activities of the Association are lobbying and advocacy. When the Association was founded in 1987 many groups were already representing the interests of people with disabilities and older people in Ireland, but no separate organization existed to campaign for recognition of the existence and work in the home of family carers. The Association set out to raise awareness about family carers among government ministers, senior policy-makers and journalists working with national and local media. The Association's main message was the urgent need to address the requirements of family carers, many of whom had been providing care at home for several years in circumstances which were physically, emotionally and economically difficult. Two aspects were emphasized: first, that caring is a 24-hour job; second, that carers save the State millions of pounds each year by caring at home as opposed to calling on residential care, which, even if available, is extremely costly.

The principal objective of the initial information and awareness campaign was to secure some form of public payment for the work of carers in the home and in particular the abolition of the means test for the social security income support for carers.

In 1990, three years after the foundation of the Association, the Carer's Allowance – a social assistance (means-tested) payment to carers – was introduced. The Allowance recognized that some people in the community were unavailable for employment because of their caring commitments at home. It therefore allowed many carers to transfer from unemployment assistance, which required them to be actively seeking paid work, to the Carer's Allowance. This substitutional character continues to be a feature of the Carer's Allowance with as many as 65 per cent of people who qualify for the Allowance coming off other social assistance payments once they do so (Department of Social, Community and Family Affairs, 1998). The introduction of the Allowance also permitted carers who were not in receipt of any social assistance payment from the State to apply for one for the first time. The initial budget for carers in 1990 was £3 million Irish pounds (IR£) whereas today it is IR£108 million. The Department of Health provides an additional IR£24 million for various services supporting carers in the home.

A major problem with the Allowance is that it is means-tested. Carers are of the view that the Allowance should be paid not because the carer is on low or no income, but because she or he is a carer. In other words, the State should recognize the important financial and social contribution made by carers by automatically granting all those who care the appropriate payment, i.e., the payment should be universal. Moreover, because of the allowance means test, those who apply (principally women) are assumed under Irish social security legislation to "enjoy half their partner's income". This principle means that a married woman who is a full-time carer at home without any income of her own is assessed for the Allowance on her husband's gross income, even though she is the person who is providing the full-time care.

The Irish Government holds the view that the Allowance is not intended to pay carers for the work done at home, but is paid as a social assistance or anti-poverty support. Part of the Government's argument is that there is no precedent for the universal approach. This is to ignore the fact that such a precedent does exist in the case of child benefit, which is a universal payment for all families with children, regardless of means. The fact that a woman is a mother entitles her to the benefit and no other considerations are taken into account.

This continues to be the single largest issue for political change for carers. In the lead-up to the 2001 Budget, where the biggest issue for debate was the means test for the Carer's Allowance, the Government responded by making changes to the test which was to result in no more than an additional 5,000 carers receiving the allowance from April 2001. Given that at the time of writing there are approximately 16,000 already in receipt of some level of Carer's Allowance, the reforms will see a maximum of 22,000 carers in receipt of the Allowance. This means that on the Association's estimates another 100,000 carers get no financial payment for their activities.

As well as campaigning for changes in the Carer's Allowance, the Carers Association also lobbied in 2000 for additional public resources for support services for carers. This campaign was largely successful – special additional funds were to be made available in 2001 for national and local support services for carers. Given the performance of the Irish economy in the late 1990s and the IR£3 billion surplus which the Government had at its disposal for the Budget for 2001, family carers expected that a major "catching up" exercise would take place to ensure that the great majority of full-time carers received the Carer's Allowance and that a large investment would be made in community care services.

In the event, an additional IR£25 million was put into support and improvements for carers. At the same time, the changes to capital taxation and benefit in kind improvements cost the Irish Exchequer IR£350 million. Increases in child-care services cost another IR£300 and the private nursing home industry has received subsidies of almost IR£25 million.

Carers in Ireland are angrier than ever, given this lost opportunity and the seeming unwillingness of the Irish Government to make proper provision for community care and carers' supports.

Some forms of lobbying and protest are not available to the Carers Association. It is prevented under Irish charity law from operating as a trade union and cannot therefore arrange a strike. However even if a strike were legally possible, it is not feasible for other reasons. Against whom would carers strike? Furthermore, a strike would be more likely to have a negative impact on the people cared for than on the Government. Carers simply cannot leave the caring situation at home to engage in these forms of campaigning. Yet, there is a perception in Ireland that those groups – most recently farmers and the police – who can muster larger numbers of members onto the street are rapidly accommodated by the Government. The continuing challenge for the Association is, then, how to get politicians to publicly accept that much more needs to be done for carers and how to achieve rapid delivery of the required support.

Providing for the needs of carers

Because of the slowness of the State in responding to the needs of carers, the Carers Association has developed its own support services. These are designed to offer a local resource to improve the quality of life of carers and those cared for at home.

A national network of Carers Resource Centres provides facilities for carers in the community. The 20 centres, located in key towns and cities around Ireland, provide advice and support to carers. Their 180 employees reach over 20,000 people annually with activities such as:

a) "Carer-to-Carer", whereby a former carer is available to listen to an existing carer's concerns.
b) Carers Support Groups, where carers can share experiences and concerns.
c) "Pamper Days", offering relaxation days for carers, including massage, grooming, manicure and a meal.
d) The Carers Information Pack: on display at all centres, it provides details on available supports and services at national and local levels.

The concept of Carers Outreach helps to overcome the difficulties which carers may have in travelling to the Carers Resource Centres. Given the poor public transport infrastructure in many rural areas in Ireland, the limited time available to carers when out of the home and the need to create opportunities to interact with carers at local level, the Association enters into arrangements to provide part-time services at convenient times for carers in local communities. This mirrors the structures adopted by the political parties, who hold local "clinics" in their constituencies which have proved very successful to politicians in Ireland over the years.

A fundamental question relates to the representational role of the Association and how it can purport to represent the interests of family carers and ensure that the needs and desires of carers are articulated to policy-makers and service providers. The Association seeks to listen to carers and engage them in its daily work and activities. The tools used by the Association in supporting carers' views include a magazine (*Take Care!*), free telephone helplines operated from the Carers Resource Centres and Carers Outreach, conferences and seminars, training courses (certified by the educational author-ities), and information campaigns (including the Carers Information Pack, the Carers Web Site and local and national advertising). In addition, a number of innovative events and actions stimulate media and public attention to the problems faced by carers. These include the Carers of the Year Awards, the National Carers Clock-Out Day, a short story competition and special support for Young Carers (information pack and short film for teachers and professionals).

In focusing on the needs of carers, the Association endeavours to maintain an organizational culture of "ownership" by family carers. It seeks to stay as close as possible to its members. For example, all but one of the ten members of the Board of the Association are carers or ex-carers. The Association also invites carers each year to put views forward during the preparation of the annual Pre-Budget Submission to Government.

Many carers in the community do not feel that there is a mechanism for having their voice heard. It is generally accepted that many feel very isolated. They may lack opportunities to express their views or may feel that there is little point in doing so. It is this kind of situation which the Association seeks to redress.

Thanks to the Association's lobbying activities, many of these activities are now grant-aided by government agencies and departments. The services offered include:

a) Education;
b) Training;
c) Information – including the Carers Information Pack;
d) Home-based respite care;
e) Counselling;
f) The National Carers Information Technology Centre;
g) Part-time work outside the home for carers;
h) National and local telephone help-line services.

In fact, there is an acknowledgment at government level that much needs to be done for carers and that this involves cooperation between the two principal government departments, the health boards and the Association. There is a mutual exchange of information and, as appropriate, mutual referral. Other forms of partnership include sharing of premises and participation of health board personnel in the Association's training courses.

A key issue addressed by the Association over the years has been the fear that the move towards service provision might reduce the Association's capacity to promote the needs of carers and to lobby for change and improvement. Centre managers and other new personnel may be less interested in advocacy, lobbying and promotion, favouring rather the day-to-day issues of service delivery, personnel management and their own career development opportunities. Mindful of the strong local basis to politics in Ireland, the Association has addressed this issue by concentrating on the capacity of each Carers Resource Centre to act as a base in its community to increase the profile of carers and to lobby at the local level.

The future

When it was established in 1987, the Association was primarily concerned with carers of older people and was principally a Dublin-based organization. In the three-year period to December 2000 there was a major increase in membership. This is because carers of children with severe disabilities may now qualify for the Carer's Allowance and also because of the increased lobbying activities and profile of the Association. Over the last two years the Government has made very large additional resource allocations for long-term care services for children with severe intellectual, sensory and physical disabilities. A constant worry for many carers of children with severe disabilities is what will happen to their children after they themselves have died. These new members are drawn from a somewhat different constituency from the previous membership. Traditionally, many members were caring for older people and many carers were themselves in the later phase of life. Perhaps through a sense of the inevitable end to the caring situation in the foreseeable future, and being tired and lacking in energy, many of these carers were less politically engaged. The situation of many newer members is different. They tend to be younger, to be caring for children with disabilities and see themselves as "being in for the long haul". These carers are generally far more militant and insist on recognition, support and services as a right; they object to the State arbitrarily deciding how to treat carers. This "new blood" in the Association bodes well for future advocacy activities.

CREATING UNIONS, CREATING EMPLOYERS: A LOS ANGELES HOME-CARE CAMPAIGN

13

Jess Walsh

Introduction

In-home care for the elderly and disabled is the fastest growing sector of health and social service provision in the United States. It is also where American workers face some of the worst wages and conditions to be found across formal sector employment. As care of the frail elderly and people with disabilities has been brought out of nursing homes and into individual residences, employment standards for long-term care providers have deteriorated. Home-care workers in many parts of the United States are "stateless". Working in consumers' homes, they are isolated from each other and they often lack a codified employment relationship defining the obligations of government and home-care recipients to them.

In February 1999, 74,000 home-care workers joined the SEIU in Los Angeles County (LA),[1] after 12 years of campaigning. In order to bring these care workers into collective representation, the SEIU had to confront three key challenges presented by the specificity of home-care work:

a) the lack of any common worksite for home-care workers (the terms home-care workers, providers, and attendants are used interchangeably in this chapter);

b) the absence of a clear chain of employment responsibility between home-care providers, consumers of care, and the county, state and federal governments, the policies of which shape the programme; and,

---

[1] Unless otherwise specified, LA refers to Los Angeles County. The County is the largest in the United States, with 9.9 million residents. Los Angeles City is one of 88 incorporated cities in the County, containing around 3.8 million residents (California Department of Finance, 2000, table B–4). The SEIU represents approximately 1.4 million members nationwide, many of whom are low and moderate wages earners, across three industry groupings: building services, health care and public services. SEIU International devotes more than 40 per cent of its resources to organizing new workers, such as home-care workers (see SEIU President's Committee 2000, 1999).

c) the existence of a third party in the employment relationship – that of people with disabilities and senior citizens articulating their right to control how personal care work is organized in their homes (these individuals are variously termed consumers, clients and recipients in this chapter).

In confronting these challenges, the SEIU has built a strong political voice for thousands of previously "invisible" home-care workers. Drawing on an innovative political programme that linked worker and consumer issues, the union achieved major policy changes within the social services system. In so doing, the SEIU forged a unique and institutionalized long-term alliance between care workers and consumers, one which has traversed both the junctions and divergent paths of union and community politics.

As care work is moved from institutions back to the home, and as home-based care work is recognized as wage-worthy labour in the United States, SEIU's innovative work suggests a path forward to security of care for consumers and work security for union members. For workers this security is not based on the single-workplace job protection that American unions have traditionally sought to provide. Unions have generally defended members' jobs with "just cause" contract provisions that protect workers from arbitrary firing, and by enforcing work rules and conditions laid out in bargaining agreements. Instead, recognizing the specificity of the home-care workplace and employment relation, the SEIU has developed a union which offers a different kind of security for workers: representational security comprising a powerful voice in the political sphere; and work security through access to home-care employment, but not particular home-care jobs.[2]

This chapter tells the story of how the SEIU created a union and an employer, and wrote new rules for organizing low-wage personal assistance work along the way. The first section outlines the key characteristics of the home-care industry and the organization of home-care work. Next, the chapter documents the development of a union without a unitary workplace in the context of high worker turnover. The chapter then examines the creation of a union-community political voice and the extraction and delineation of a single home-care employer out of multi-tiered employment relations with action first at the state, and then county levels. The concluding comments consider the lessons of the SEIU campaign for providing security for home-care recipients and workers alike.

---

[2] This analysis draws loosely on Standing's (1997) notion of representation security as a strong voice in the labour market, although a different notion of job and work security from that suggested by Standing seems more appropriate to home care. This chapter distinguishes between a home-care job (with one consumer, with certain workplace conditions) and home-care work (comprising a job or a series of jobs with consumers), and related job and work security.

The home-care industry and labour market

Home-care workers are paid attendants for people who need assistance with the activities of daily living in order to remain independently in their homes. These services may include domestic work, such as cooking, cleaning and shopping, and personal services, such as feeding, bathing and dressing. In some forms of home-care provision (also referred to as Personal Assistance Services), routine medical procedures such as bowel and bladder care may also be part of a home-care worker's job. Higher order medical care is not provided through home-care programmes, but rather through home health care, and generally by nursing staff.

California's home-care programme, In-Home Supportive Services (IHSS), provides care within a "Consumer Directed Model" (CDM) (Doty et al., 1999). The key characteristic of CDM across the United States is that it is the consumer of home care – not a governmental or private agency – which finds, hires, trains, supervises and fires the home-care attendant. The attendant may be designated an "independent contractor" or an employee with multiple employers, each fulfilling a particular part of the employment relationship. Termed the Independent Provider (IP) mode in California, the CDM model is preferred by disability activists who argue that the primary alternative – provision of services through contract agencies – robs them of their ability to choose their own attendant, and therefore robs them of control over their bodies, homes and lives (NICDLTS, 1996; Doty et al., 1994). Although at times some government representatives and bureaucrats have advocated a contract mode of provision for California, the IP mode has received wide government support because available funds go directly to hours of care rather than to contract agency intermediaries. Further, whilst excluding private agencies, the IP mode nonetheless protects governments from the fiscal implications of adding tens of thousands of new workers to the public sector employment rolls. Together, the preferences of consumers and state and county governments for the IP mode have created a tripartite employment relationship for home-care workers in California. In this relationship, the state pays home-care workers, the counties control a provider's hours of work by determining how many hours of care a consumer can receive, and consumers hire, fire and supervise attendants.

In LA, which has California's largest IHSS caseload, the home-care programme currently serves almost 100,000 people with disabilities, around 60 per cent of whom are over the age of 65. The remaining 40 per cent are younger people with disabilities (DPSS, 2001a). Overall, between 70 and 80 per cent of clients are frail elderly senior citizens, and the remainder are people with long-term disabilities. The programme allows consumers to hire any family member: California-wide, 47 per cent of consumers hire a relative as their independent provider, with another quarter hiring someone with whom they were previously acquainted (Doty et al., 1999, table 5).

While empowering many consumers, the IP mode also places the burden of recruitment and retention of workers on consumers, who have no access to an immediate replacement if their home-care worker leaves, becomes sick, or if they themselves wish to terminate the working relationship. Fears of liability for the acts of providers have prevented counties from establishing their own full-service registries to clients to remedy the insecurity many face. More generally, IHSS maximizes consumer control, but it also fragments service delivery. Over the years, consumers have had little voice within the IHSS system and the processes for making complaints and appeals against cutbacks in hours of care received, for example, have been opaque.

For workers, the IP mode has also been severely limited. Prior to unionization, independent providers in California received the minimum wage and only 2–3 per cent of IP workers received any benefits such as compensation for travel time and costs, sickness and holiday leave or health benefits (Doty et al., 1999, table 8). In LA most home-care workers are women (83 per cent), two-thirds are 40 years of age or above, two-thirds are people of colour and half are immigrants. Most live in or near poverty, working an average of 25 hours a week in home care, with a third having a second job to make ends meet (Coisineau, 2000, pp.33–34). Many home-care providers cycle in and out of IHSS work. While the average tenure for a home-care worker in 1991 was two years,[3] a study showed that 49 per cent of home-care workers had been with their current recipient one year or less, while only 31.5 per cent of clients had been with the programme for that short a period (SEIU Research Department, 1994, p.4). These discrepancies between consumer and provider tenure in the programme suggest that there may be a core of long-term home-care workers, perhaps those looking after family members with disabilities, with higher turnover amongst another group of providers.

Home care presents a set of challenges, but also significant opportunities, for union organizing. The constraints are obvious: home-care workers are dispersed across multiple establishments; they work individually; they are low-wage; and while a core portion remains with the same client for many years, a segment of the home-care workforce is highly contingent with rapid turnover. In establishing an "independent provider" system, California has sought not only to meet the needs of clients, but also to avoid taking responsibility for the employment of home-care workers, who perform work previously carried out

---

[3] Average tenure across all United States industries with the current employer was seven years (SEIU Research Department, 1994, p. 345).

in state-funded nursing homes and other institutional settings such as mental hospitals. This abrogation of responsibility has inserted multiple tiers in the employment relation and presented barriers to collective bargaining.

The opportunities are also quite clear. Between 1990 and 2000, the IHSS caseload in LA County grew from 55,064 consumers to 98,211 (DPSS, 2001a, 2001b). At the same time, the workforce also almost doubled. In 1988, there were 40,000 home-care providers (Homecare Workers Union, 1988, p.2); now there are some 74,000, a growth in the workforce of 85 per cent over the period. There is a significant imperative for unions to follow care work into community-based settings as demand for it grows.

Creating a union of independent providers in Los Angeles

In the IP system, home-care providers work alone, with little or no contact with other workers, and no common point at which trainings or cheque pick-ups occur. Workers report that before being contacted by the union, they felt isolated and were unaware of the existence of the many thousands of people in similar circumstances working in home care. Verdia Daniels, who later became President of the LA Homecare Workers Union (also referred to here as Local 434B) reports her response to first being contacted by the union: "At that time, I thought I was the only home-care worker in LA County because...it was just by word of mouth that you would get a job" (reported in Cobb, no date, p. 3). Similar sentiments are expressed by home-care provider Mary Simmons:

Sometimes in this job, you feel like you're all alone. You might be with your client eight hours a day, even longer...I don't think most people understand what that's like. At least here at the union, you get to meet other people who are going through the same thing (Cleeland and Riccardi, 2000).

In part because they are separated from each other across multiple worksites, but also because of the gendered nature of caring work in which women view providing home-care services as part of their family and community duties, home-care workers may initially lack a "worker culture". Indeed, home-care workers may not see themselves as workers at all. Local 434B organizers had to deliberately develop this worker consciousness (Romero, 2000, interview; Barragan, 2000, interview). To do this, the SEIU contacted workers through house visits from a list of the County's home-care workers and developed a neighbourhood-based group meeting structure out of these initial contacts. The union used community sites such as churches and libraries to bring home-care workers into collective relationships with each other, providing an opportunity to share stories, identify common work problems such as injuries, late cheques and sexual harassment, and galvanize around the need for collective action to address these problems (Rolf, 2000, interview).

Working in neighbourhoods across LA, Local 434B signed up almost 20,000 workers to file for an early election, arguing that LA County should recognize the union and bargain. Because the County determined a client's hours and therefore also a provider's hours and processed their timesheets, the union argued that the County could in fact hire and fire, by cutting client hours or programme services (Adams, 2000, interview). In December 1987, Local 434B sued LA County in the Superior Court, seeking to establish the County as the employer of record for the (then) 40,000 IHSS workers in the County and used direct action to support its claim (Adams, 2000, interview; Weinstein, 1988, Metro 1). The approach taken by the County's Board of Supervisors was that the workers were employed by the disabled person, and paid by the State of California, because 90 per cent of the funding came from the State (Weinstein, 1988, Metro 1). The Court found against the union, arguing that County officials were merely administering a State programme, and that home-care workers could not be viewed as County employees (Merina, 1989, Metro 1). In effect, the Court reinforced the three-tiered employment relationship involving the State, County, and home-care recipients. While each of these performed an employment function, there was no single entity that could perform all of the functions of a traditional employer, including collective bargaining.

The Homecare Workers Union now had to maintain its membership without recognition or a union contract over several years as it developed and enacted a new plan to delineate an employer of record. First, it lobbied and won voluntary dues deduction, for those members who had signed up on house visits from the State of California, in April 1989, allowing the SEIU to keep a relatively stable dues base (Adams, 2000, interview; Shulman, 1996). Second, Local 434B developed a series of services for members, non-members and clients to bring workers into contact with the union, and build ties with (and legitimacy in) the consumer community. Some services were available only to union members, most notably a registry that matched clients and providers, benefitting workers and clients alike (Douglas, 2000, interview). Third, the union developed a campaign of direct action and a presence in the political sphere to enable workers to cohere around a common agenda, and also to win direct gains for members, in the absence of the traditional site for collective action – the workplace. Planning and executing direct action, such as marches and rallies, occupation of government offices, street demonstrations and civil disobedience resulting in arrest were essential to bringing home-care workers together to experience power (Rolf, 2000, interview; Adams, 2000, interview).

While all of these strategies were key to maintaining the union, it still lacked formal recognition and could not bargain a contract. It was in the political sphere that this overwhelming constraint needed to be remedied. As the union's General Manager David Rolf explains: "We had to figure out how to leverage the superstructure in order to win" (Rolf, 2000: interview). As home-care workers struggled to maintain their union in LA, SEIU's State Council, which organizes political voice for a range of SEIU locals in California, worked on "the superstructure".

The emergence of the public authority model

In 1992, SEIU's State Council formed an alliance with state-level lobbyists for the Independent Living Centers (ILCs)[4] and the California Senior Legislature to establish an employment relationship for IPs. The challenge for the SEIU was to find a way to negotiate the multi-layered employment relationship in home care and resolve those layers into a single employer of record. For the ILCs and Senior Legislature, the challenge was to protect the rights of consumers to hire, fire and supervise their workers. The result of this alliance was the September 1992 Public Authorities Act which allowed counties to set up Public Authorities, by passing local ordinances, to act as the employer of record for home-care workers. While new public authorities (PAs) would be attached to county governance structures, they would act as the employer for the purposes of bargaining without adding new public workers to the County's payroll. Meanwhile, the State would continue to pay home-care workers and California counties would continue to run their IHSS programmes. Consumers would make two key gains: their voice would be inserted into IHSS either with an advisory committee to the Board of Supervisors which in turn would act as the PA board, or with a PA board directly constituted of a consumer majority; and, they would maintain their right to hire, fire and supervise their attendant.

The next task was to convince individual counties to adopt the PA model. The original legislation, however, did not make any appropriations for PAs, and there existed a zero-sum game between the State and counties over wage increases. Opposition to property taxes in LA in the 1970s had weakened the County's tax base, but meanwhile the State Budget Realignment Process of 1991 had given greater responsibility for funding a range of social services, including IHSS, to the counties. LA County was therefore very resistant to programme improvements (Kealey, 2000, interview; Senate Budget and Fiscal

---

[4] ILCs are non-residential organizations providing advocacy and services for people with disabilities and senior citizens to live more independently (Westside Centre for Independent Living, 2000).

Review, 1998, p.8; Coalition for IHSS Reform, 1996, p.18). The SEIU needed to find state or federal money to cover: a) the start-up costs of the PAs; b) ongoing administrative costs; and, c) wage costs.

Start-up costs were won in April 1993 when, after successful lobbying by the SEIU, California adopted the Federal Government's Medicare Personal Care Option (PCO). The PCO enabled California to pay for more of its home-care caseload with federal Medicare funds; the Federal Government now provided 60 per cent of total programme costs, with the State and counties providing 65 and 35 per cent each of the remainder (Senate and Budget Fiscal Review, 1998, p.7). The savings to the State flowed to a new sub-account of US$3.3 million in the 1993 California Budget which could be mobilized for establishing and running PAs (Senate Bill Analysis Service, 1993). Two million of these savings went to LA for the establishment of a PA there, with remaining funds going to smaller counties. However, while San Francisco, San Mateo and Alameda Counties went ahead with establishing PAs using these funds, LA lagged behind. The ongoing administrative and wage costs that fully functioning PAs would bring were still not provided for within the State budget and these outstanding budgetary challenges, in combination with political opposition on the ground in LA, prevented the county with the largest IHSS caseload from moving to establish a PA.

Establishing a public authority in LA County

In the early years of the organizing drive, the SEIU had failed to win over the consumer community to its plans for unionization and collective bargaining in Los Angeles. While certain understandings between peak bodies (SEIU State Council, the ILCs, the Senior Legislature) had been enshrined in the Public Authority Act, insufficient effort had been put into developing coalitions around PAs on the ground. Disability activists in particular had a number of key concerns, including:

a) their right to hire, fire and supervise their provider would be compromised by unionization;
b) they could be the subject of strikes and grievances;
c) there existed a zero-sum game between wages and hours of service: as the IHSS pie was fixed, wage increases would mean cuts in hours of service;
d) the union would create another layer of bureaucracy for consumers to negotiate, and the union would interfere in consumers' lives in general;
e) the union was powerful, well resourced and disability activists were not; their concerns would never be admitted into union plans and they would be steamrolled; and,

f) the union could not be trusted – it bought off ILCs by making donations to them (Becker Kennedy, 2000, interview; Develyder, 2000, interview; Russell, 1996; Toy, 1996).

A "Consumer Alliance" emerged to articulate these concerns and began to lobby the Board of Supervisors against establishing a PA (Canterbury, 2000, interview; Becker Kennedy, 2000, interview). In 1994, the SEIU began to organize its own alliance with disability activists, working with sympathetic consumers to form IHSS Recipients and Providers Sharing (IRAPS). IRAPS argued that home-care workers needed higher wages and health benefits, in part because inadequate remuneration made it difficult to retain attendants. This in turn contributed to the insecurity of consumers. The establishment of a vehicle for input into IHSS was also very attractive (Navarro, 2000, interview). Despite SEIU's work with IRAPS, in the period after the Public Authority legislation until around 1996, anti-union forces had the loudest voice in IHSS debate in Los Angeles and mistrust of the union was strong (see Russell, 1996).

The coalition was challenged by the lack of fit between the structures and processes of the union with those of the disability community. SEIU organizers contend that disability activists were used to fighting for their rights as individuals, engendering an individualistic rather than collectivist tradition of action, in complete contrast to the union movement and social movements with which unions have tended to build partnerships (the civil rights movement, most notably). The SEIU therefore found itself attempting to build an alliance with a loose collection of individuals who lacked constituencies to which they were accountable, and who were not part of a broader and transparent movement structure that could ratify understandings reached through consultation and negotiation (Canterbury, 2000, interview; Rolf, 2000, interview). At the same time, while the structures of the disability activist community were unclear, in the post-1992 period SEIU's structures were impenetrable to the concerns of the disability community. Consumers and SEIU staff who worked on the coalition agree that the SEIU did not approach the disability community as equal partners, attempting instead to form an agenda and persuade consumers to buy into it (Canterbury, 2000, interview; Toy, 1996; Becker Kennedy, 2000, interview).

As relations with consumers continued to sour, and in an effort to provide a preliminary step forward to a PA, Local 434B lobbied the Supervisors to commission a feasibility study on the establishment of the PA. In the face of opposition from one particularly intransigent Supervisor working with County officials who opposed the PA, the SEIU was forced to mobilize hundreds of providers and recipients to support the study in May 1995 (Toy, 1996, p. 55; Rolf, 2000, interview). The study went ahead to document the extent of problems for both consumers and providers in the IHSS system, but it did not recommend the formation of a fully-fledged PA. It rejected immediate collective bargaining as part of a PA mode, maintaining that "establishing an employer of record will allow an expanded role for organized labor, placing additional pressure to increase County financial participation" (RTZ, 1996, p. vi). As such, while the authors ultimately recommended the formation of a Personal Assistance Services Council (the LA Public Authority) with all the elements of consumer control protected, the report favoured postponing collective bargaining until further state funding entered the system. The report ultimately placed consumer concerns against collective bargaining, instead of outlining a path where consumer and provider needs could both be realized expeditiously through a PA.

As the impending results of the report were filtering through to the union at the end of 1995, union leader David Rolf assessed the situation. Working with renewed funding from SEIU International, and newly endowed with the reins over Local 434B, Rolf judged that the union had to make a renewed effort to work with the disability community, and substantially beef up its political profile after the period of disintegration in 1995.

Home-care workers and consumers emerge as a political force

Once again, the SEIU went to talk with disability and senior citizen activists, trying to make the local coalitions work, overcome long-standing tensions, and find a way forward. From early 1996, SEIU organizers and rank-and-file activists went to senior citizens dances and bingo sessions, Alzheimer's groups, polio groups, and senior citizen housing complexes; it also organized community town hall meetings at which concerns were aired and addressed. The union won strong support from senior citizen activists and growing support from people with disabilities (Canterbury, 2000, interview).

At the same time, Local 434B worked to build its own independent political power. Local 434B became an exemplar of the new American labour movement approach to politics, which aims to be worker- and issue-centred rather than candidate- and party-centred (see Garin and Molyneux, 1998; Rosenthal, 1998). The union educated members about how candidates stood on issues important to working people, encouraged them to vote, mobilized members to walk precincts in campaigns educating other voters, and even ran an election campaign from the Local's office. Rolf argues that with these tactics Local 434B was able to hold candidates accountable to the union's interests more effectively than it could have using the traditional approach of simply donating to candidates. As evidence, he lists more than a dozen current members of the California Assembly and Senate as well as the LA City Council who provided their support in the form of signatures on letters and petitions and their attendance at home-care union (Rolf, 2001, personal communication). By becoming a political force in the city and State, Local 434B developed a cohort of politicians who responded to the union and supported, publicly and in the back rooms, its PA agenda (see Candaele, 1998).

Working with consumer organizations, the union put out its own report on IHSS. *Opportunity Now* outlined a path forward to worker representation within the constraints of the funding system, calling on the County Supervisors to pass an ordinance forming the Personal Assistance Services Council in which consumers maintained control of hiring, firing and supervising attendants, strikes were prohibited, and County budgets protected (Coalition for IHSS Reform, 1996). Working with a sympathetic Supervisor, the union secured advice from State and County lawyers stating that if the County were to follow the feasibility study recommendations, it would create a PA that was ineligible for State money under the PA legislation.

Over the course of the following year, with a renewed union-consumer coalition, a strong political presence, a discredited alternative to the PA, with a series of direct actions and political pressure targeted to the last Supervisor to support a PA, the SEIU won its ordinance. Between July 1997 and the adoption of the ordinance in September, SEIU worked with consumers, Department of Public Social Services bureaucrats, the Auditor-Controller and the County's lawyers to draft the ordinance. On the committee, disability and senior citizen activists and unionists settled key concerns, creating a PA as an employer of record, prohibiting strikes, mandating a consumer-dominated board rather than an advisory board, giving disability activists a more powerful voice in IHSS, and outlining a role for the PA in developing a registry and consumer-directed training for attendants.

It was not until November 1998 that the PA first met. At that meeting, the SEIU delivered 14,000 union authorization cards and petitioned for an election. To win the impending election, the union mounted a sophisticated direct mail, phone and neighbourhood meeting campaign to ensure home-care workers voted for the union. On 21 February 1999, the ballots were mailed out to 74,000 providers. Twenty thousand voted in the election, with 16,250 voting for the union, and 1,925 against (Cleeland, 1999). That is, more than 80 per cent of workers approved the union, in a situation in which only 50 per cent plus one vote was required to approve it by law. When the results of the election were announced John Sweeney, the AFL-CIO (labour federation) President, stated: "I believe the history books will show that their triumph today will play as important a role in American history as the mass organizing drives in the 1930s" (Cleeland, 1999).

Back to the State: Reforming home-care funding in California

As Local 434B worked to pass the PA ordinance in Los Angeles, at the state level it remained for the SEIU to pass legislation that would bring more funding into IHSS to cover the ongoing administrative costs of PAs, as well as the dedicated funding needed to increase the wages of home-care workers. A key part of the plan was an alliance with consumers that was statewide, but took the alliance beyond the level of relationships between lobbyists to one that brought grassroots activists, workers and consumers together (Meyer-Rodriguez, 2000, interview). SEIU's State Council began meeting with consumer groups, developing and enacting a legislative strategy backed by grassroots pressure on the California legislature. The alliance, "IHSS Agenda 97", mobilized worker-consumer teams in electoral districts across the State to write letters, and lobby legislators in their home districts as well as in Sacramento, in order to get bipartisan support for the legislative agenda (Meyer-Rodriguez, 1997; Meyer-Rodriguez, 2000, interview).

In that year, IHSS Agenda 97 introduced and won State legislation to make the State pay for ongoing administrative costs of the PA at the 65:35 rate – the rate at which it shares other IHSS costs with the counties. In 1998, the SEIU State Council designated wage increases for IHSS workers the top legislative priority for the SEIU in the State. IHSS Agenda 98 (now a coalition of 38 senior citizen and disability groups and the SEIU) organized strong mobilization around a bill to get the state share of costs for wage increases. The SEIU won enough Republican sponsors for the bill and bi-partisan support in the legislature for it to pass. However, Republican Governor Pete Wilson vetoed their bill.

In 1999, a Democratic Governor was elected in California. After a series of SEIU worker-consumer local actions at the Governor's local offices, the SEIU won a temporary 50 cent wage increase, which brought home-care workers up from US$5.75 per hour – the California minimum wage – to $6.25 per hour. This was funded on the basis of an 80:20 split between the State and counties, in order to protect county budgets. The agreement was to last until July 2000, but from August 1999, the SEIU pushed to make the increases permanent under the aegis of a "Full State Share for Quality Home Care" campaign. The Quality Home Care Coalition occupied the halls of the Capitol and lobbied the Governor and legislature for six days demanding permanent State funding up to 200 per cent of the minimum wage ($11.50) with health benefits. They supported their demands with street actions every three days. In his 2000–01 budget, the Governor proposed immediate rises to $7.50 per hour, and $11.50 per hour over four years (Meyer-Rodriguez, no date, Quality Home Care Campaign). The legislation reverted back, however, to a 65:35 state-county share of costs, which meant that counties now had to come up with extra funds to cover the increases. In Los Angeles, this proved to be highly problematic.

While LA County had paid its 20 per cent share of the temporary wage increase, in the context of a return to the 65:35 split, the County agreed only to a much smaller wage increase. This took LA workers to $6.75 per hour effective from November 2000. The next increase to $7.00 per hour, in June 2001, was contingent upon a return to an 80:20 split or some other arrangement to cover the County's costs. LA is the only county that has not come up to the standard of $7.50, citing budgetary constraints and caseload size. The County's decision was taken, despite a massive mobilization around the Board of Supervisors organized by Local 434B and the SEIU California State Council. With the budget to be decided on 12 September 2000, 50 workers began a sit-in at the County Administration Office demanding the $7.50. On that day, and over the course of the next week, home-care workers were joined by religious leaders and home-care consumers in the sit-in. By the end of the week, 58 workers, senior citizens, people with disabilities, religious leaders and unionists were arrested without having made their case (fieldwork, 2000).

Conclusions: Security of care, security of work

The organization of home-care work in California during the 1980s and 1990s left thousands of home-care providers performing invaluable care in isolation from each other, and without formal channels for winning recognition, respect and adequate remuneration for their efforts. Home-care places long-term care-givers outside traditional workplace settings, and it places them outside existing frameworks for unionization and bargaining.

To organize home-care workers, the SEIU created a non-traditional union based in neighbourhood contexts. To maintain its union of high-turnover, part-time workers dispersed over thousands of establishments, the SEIU relied on a chapter structure for bringing workers together, automatic dues deduction, the provision of services to give workers contact with the union and some return on union dues, and a programme of direct action that brought providers together to experience their power in the absence of a shop-floor for workplace actions.

To construct its own framework for unionizing and bargaining, the SEIU made two key attempts to identify and pursue an employment relationship that resolved the "multi-employer" problem in home care. The first, a lawsuit seeking determination that LA County was in fact the employer of home-care workers, failed. The second, the passage of legislation enabling PAs, was successful. Having won the legislation, the SEIU turned to finding money in the federal and state budgets to fund the establishment and operation of PAs, and to provide for wage increases and other improvements to IHSS. By September 2000, PAs across California were funded for administrative costs and wage increases, but LA County had baulked at meeting its share of the Governor's wage plan.

On the ground in LA, the fundamental tensions of the home-care employment relation were played out. As workers organized to gain economic security and a voice for themselves, consumers felt railroaded, fearing loss of control over their bodies, homes and relationships with providers, as well as a loss of service levels as wages and hours were traded off. The County's fears for its budgetary security, the intransigence of one supervisor, and the opposition of anti-union senior citizen and disability activists prevented the establishment of the PA.

Key to the success at both state and local levels was the mobilization of workers and consumers and the emergence of one voice that linked worker and consumer issues and identified solutions that enhanced the position of both within the IHSS system. At the same time, home-care workers were mobilized independently in a number of key high-profile political campaigns in 1996 and 1997, which gave Local 434B the ear of a whole cohort of new politicians in California and encouraged incumbents to work with the union.

In agreeing that consumers' homes are not to be the subject of strikes and that consumers can hire, fire and supervise their workers, the SEIU has given up three traditional union rights: the right to fight arbitrary firing, the right to strike, and the right to a grievance procedure to resolve workplace complaints. The SEIU has no ability under the LA ordinance and the subsequent contract to defend the rights of particular workers to particular home-care jobs. This agreement recognizes the specificity of home-care work, the home-care work-place, and the home-care employment relation, and defends the interests of consumers in receiving secure care and control over their lives. Does this, however, mean insecurity for home-care workers?

While not providing security to particular home-care jobs, the SEIU effec-tively provides representational and work security to home-care workers. It has taken 74,000 people spread across the city and working alone and brought them together to speak with a powerful voice that has resulted in fundamental reform of the California and LA social service system – reform that has brought home-care workers respect as well as material gains. The SEIU does not represent home care workers in the workplace, but it makes workplace issues public political issues and represents its members in that sphere, the key sphere in which gains can be made for this constituency. In addition, the union provides work security. Even before winning a PA, the SEIU ran a registry for home-care workers. Now, as part of improvements to IHSS, the Personal Assistance Services Council will work with the union and consumers to run its own registry as well as improve training. While issues remain to be bargained about registry rules, its operation will enable workers to stay in more continuous employment and to be moved out of jobs where there is conflict with consumers.

The SEIU home care model is not without challenges, which include: maintenance of a strong labour-consumer coalition (a rarity in American labour-community politics); the local character of its efforts, which require county by county, state-by-state mobilizations; dependence on political voice, presence and power for material gains for home-care workers, the limitations of which are indicated by LA's refusal to meet wage demands; and, the need to link home-care workers to related and more skilled occupations such as home health work and paraprofessional nursing care if the union is to provide an avenue out of poverty for home-care workers. As the SEIU confronts these challenges, it will continue to suggest a way forward that eschews workplace and job security in favour of organizing entire classes of workers across workplaces (whilst facilitating continuity of employment), and representing those workers with a powerful political voice in alliance with the community, from an independent political base.

BIBLIOGRAPHY

Abel, E.; Nelson, M. 1990. "Circles of care: An introductory essay", in E. Abel, M. Nelson (eds.): *Circles of care work and identity in women's lives* (Albany, New York, State University of New York Press).

Achterhuis, H. 1978. *De markt van welzijn en geluk* [The market of wellbeing and happiness] (Baarn, Ambo).

Adriaansens, H.; Zijderveld, A. 1983. *Vrijwillig initiatief in de verzorgingsstaat* [Private initiative in the welfare state] (Deventer, Van Loghum Slaterus).

Alber, J. 1995. "A framework for the comparative study of social services", in *Journal of European Social Policy*, Vol. 5, No. 2, pp. 131–149.

Alexander, J.D. 1987. *Gendered job traits and women's occupations*, Ph.D. dissertation, (University of Massachusetts, Department of Economics).

Almeida, D; McDonald, D. 2000. *The time Americans spend working for pay, caring for families, and contributing to communities,* paper prepared for the Conference on Work, Family, and Democracy, Racine, Wisconsin, 29 Nov. – 1 Dec.

Almqvist, A-L.; Boje, T. 1999. "Who cares, who pays and how is care for children provided?", in D. Bouget and B. Palier (eds.): *Comparing social welfare systems in Nordic Europe and France* (Paris, MIRE-DREES).

Anandalakshmy, S. 1997. "Early childhood: The years of freedom", in *Fifty years of freedom: Where are the children? Essays in defence of the child* (New Delhi, Mainstream).

Andersen, J. et al. 1999. "The legitimacy of the Nordic welfare states. Trends, variations and cleavages", in M. Kautto et al. (eds.): *Nordic social policy: Changing welfare states* (London, Routledge).

Anderson, E. 1993. *Value in ethics and economics* (Cambridge, Mass., Harvard University Press).

Anheier, H.K.; Salamon, L.M. 1997. *Defining the non-profit sector* (Manchester, Manchester University Press).

Anker, R. 1998. *Gender and jobs: Sex segregation of occupations in the world* (Geneva, ILO).

Anttonen, A. 1997. "The welfare state and social citizenship", in K. Kauppinen and T. Gordon (eds.): *Unresolved dilemmas: Women, work and the family in the United States, Europe and the former Soviet Union* (Aldershot, Hampshire, Ashgate).

—. 1999a. *Lasten kotihoidon tuki suomalaisessa perhepolitiikassa* [Child home care allowances: An innovation in Finnish family policy] (Helsinki, The Social Insurance Institution, Studies in social security and health).

—. 1999b. *Paying for care. Repercussions for women who care: The case of Finland,* paper presented at Meeting of Experts: Paying for care of frail elderly persons: Consequences for women caregivers, OECD, Paris, 12 and 13 Apr. 1999.

—; Sipilä, J. 1996. "European social care services: Is it possible to identify models?", in *Journal of European Social Policy,* Vol. 6, No. 2, pp. 87–100.

—. 2000. *Suomalaista sosiaalipolitiikaa* [Finnish social policy] (Tampere, Vastapaino).

Arber, S.; Ginn, J. 1991. *Gender and later life* (London, Sage).

—; —. 1992. "Class and caring: A forgotten dimension", in *Sociology,* Vol. 26, No. 4, pp. 619–634.

—. 1995. "The mirage of gender equality: Occupational success in the labour market and within marriage", in *British Journal of Sociology,* Vol. 46, No. 1, pp. 21–43.

Atkin, K. 1991. "Health, illness, disability and black minorities: A speculative critique of present day discourse", in *Disability, Handicap and Society,* Vol. 6, No. 1, pp. 37–47.

Badgett, L.; Folbre N. 1999. "Assigning care: Gender norms and economic outcomes", in *International Labour Review,* Vol. 138, No. 3, pp. 311–326 (Geneva, ILO).

Barnes, M. 1997a. "Families and empowerment", in P. Ramcharan et al. (eds.): *Empowerment in everyday life: Learning disability* (London, Jessica Kingsley).

—. 1997b. *Care, communities and citizens* (Harlow, United Kingdom, Addison Wesley Longman).

—. 1999. "Users as citizens: Collective action and the local governance of welfare", in *Social Policy and Administration,* Vol. 33, No. 1, pp. 73–90.

—; Bowl, R. 2001. *Taking over the asylum: Empowerment and mental health* (Basingstoke, Hampshire, Palgrave).

—; Prior, D. 1996. "From private choice to public trust: A new social basis for welfare", in *Public Money and Management,* No. 16, pp. 51–58.

—; —. 2000. *Private lives as public policy* (Birmingham, Venture Press).

—; Shaw, S. 2000. "Older people, citizenship and collective action", in A. Warnes; L. Warren and M. Nolan (eds.): *Care services in later life* (London, Jessica Kingsley).

—; Wistow, G. 1991. *Changing relationships in community care* (Leeds, Nuffield Institute for Health, University of Leeds).

—; —. 1992. "Coming in from the wilderness? Carers' views of the consultations and their outcomes", in Nuffield Institute for Health: *Research evaluation of the Birmingham Community Care Special Action Project* (Leeds, University of Leeds).

—; —. 1993. "Gaining influence, gaining support", in Nuffield Institute for Health: *Working with carers in research and practice* (Leeds, University of Leeds).

—; —. 1995. "User oriented community care: An overview of findings", in Nuffield Institute for Health: *Research evaluation of the Birmingham Community Care Special Action Project* (Leeds, University of Leeds).

Baumol, W. 1967. "Macroeconomics of unbalanced growth: The anatomy of urban crisis", in *American Economic Review,* Vol. 57, No. 3, pp. 415–426.

Becker, G. 1981. *A treatise on the family* (Cambridge, Mass., Harvard University Press).

Bekkering, J.M.; Jansweijer, R.M.A. 1998. *De verdeling van arbeid en zorg: Prikkels en belemmeringen* [The division of labour and care: Incentives and disincentives] (The Hague, Wetenschappelijke Raad voor het Regeringsbeleid).

Bellah, R.N. et al. 1985. *Habits of the heart: Middle America observed* (Berkeley, University of California Press).

—. 1991. *The Good Society* (New York, Alfred A. Knoff).

—. 2000. "Epilogue, meaning and modernity: America and the world", in R. Madsen; W. M. Sullivan and S. M. Tipton (eds.): *Meaning and modernity: Religion, polity and self* (Berkeley, University of California Press).

Bergmann, F. 1977. *On being free* (Notre Dame, Indiana, University of Notre Dame Press).

—. 2000. "Ecology and new work or excess consumption and the job system", in J. Schor and D. B. Holt (eds.): *The consumer society reader* (New York, New Press).

Bettio, F.; Prechal, S. 1998. "Care in Europe", in *A joint report of the gender and employment and the gender and law groups of experts* (Brussels, European Commission).

Bittman, M.; Pixley, J. 1997. *The double life of the family: Myth, hope, and experience* (Sydney, Allen and Unwin).

—,; Craig, L.; Folbre, N. 2001. *Effects of non-parental childcare arrangements on parents' time with children*, paper presented at the meetings of the Allied Social Science Association, New Orleans, Jan.

Blau, F. 1997. *Trends in the well-being of American women, 1970–1995*, National Bureau of Economic Research (NBER), Working Paper No. 6206 (www.nber.org), also published as "Swimming upstream: Trends in the gender wage differential in the 1980's", in *Journal of Economic Literature*, Vol. 15, No. 1 (Jan. 1997), pp. 112–165.

Boeije, H.R. et al. 1997. *Een verzorgde toekomst. Toekomstscenario's voor verpleging en verzorging* [A careful future: Future scenarios for nursing and carework] (Utrecht, NIZW and Vakgroep Verpleging).

Boer, A.H. de, et al. 1994. *Informele zorg: Een verkenning van huidige en toekomstige ontwikkelingen* [Informal care: A study of current and future developments] (Rijswijk/The Hague, Sociaal en Cultureel Planbureau/VUGA).

Boocock, S. 1995. "Early childhood programmes in other nations: goals and outcomes", in *The Future of Children*, Vol. 5, No. 3, Winter, pp. 94–114.

Bradshaw, J., et al. 1996. *The employment of lone parents* (London, Family Policy Studies Centre).

—. 1993. *Support for children: A comparison of arrangements in fifteen countries*, Department of Social Security, Research Report No. 21 (London, HMSO).

Braithwaite, V. A. 1990. *Bound to care* (Sydney, Allen and Unwin).

Bridgman, A.; Phillips, D.A (eds.). 1996. *Child care for low income families: Directions for research, summary of a workshop* (Washington, DC, National Academy of Sciences).

Brody, E. 1981. "Women in the middle: Family help to older people", in *The Gerontologist*, No. 21 pp. 471–480.

Bruijn, J. de.; Verhaar O. 1999. "Waar blijven de financiën voor een nieuwe zorginfrastructuur?", in *Jaarboek Emancipatie '99: Wie zorgt in de 21e eeuw?* ["Where is the money for a new care infrastructure? in *Yearbook of Gender Equality: Who cares in the 21st century?*] (The Hague, Elsevier Bedrijfsinformatie), pp. 40–47.

Bruschini, M.C. 1998. "Trabalho das mulheres no Brasil: continuidades e mudanças no período 1985–1995" ["Women's work in Brazil: continuities and changes in the period 1985–1995"], in *Textos FCC*, No. 17 (São Paulo, Fundação Carlos Chagas).

Bryant, W. K.; Zick C. 1996. "An examination of parent-child shared time", in *Journal of Marriage and the Family*, No. 58, pp. 227–237.

Bubeck, D. 1995. *Care, gender and justice* (Oxford, Clarendon Press).

Bulmer, M. 1987. *The social basis of community care* (London, Allen and Unwin).

Burchardt, T.; Hills, J.; Propper, C. 1999. *Private welfare and public policy* (York, Joseph Rowntree Foundation).

Bussemaker, J; van Drenth, A.; Knijn, T.; Plantenga, J. 1997. "Lone mothers in the Netherlands", in J. Lewis (ed.): *Lone mothers in European welfare regimes: Shifting policy logics* (London, Jessica Kingsley), pp. 96–120.

California Department of Finance. 2000. *California Statistical Abstract* (Sacramento, Department of Finance).

Camarano, A. 1999. "Muito Além dos 60" ["Far beyond the sixties"], in *Os novos idosos brasileiros* [The new Brazilian elders] (Rio de Janeiro, IPEA).

Candaele, K. 1998. "Two for the year 2000", in J. Mort (ed.): *Not your father's union movement: Inside the AFL-CIO* (London, Verso), pp. 127–132.

Cheal, D. 1991. *Family and the state of theory* (Brighton, Harvester Wheatsheaf).

Chhachhi, A. 1998. "Who is responsible for maternity benefit: State, capital or husband? Bombay assembly debates on Maternity Benefit Bill, 1929", in *Economic and Political Weekly*, Vol. 33, No. 22, 30 May, pp. 21–29.

Cleeland, N. 1999. "Homecare workers are expected to join union", in *Los Angeles Times*, 24 Feb., Business 1.

—; Riccardi, N. 2000. "LA county home-care aides still seek 'fair share'", in *Los Angeles Times*, 14 March, A1.

Coalition for IHSS Reform. 1996. *Opportunity now: Ensuring reform to the in-home supportive services programme in Los Angeles County*, document prepared by Keeslar and Associates with assistance from Richard Krolak, Ph.D.

Cobb, R. (n. d.). Background Memo: *Unionizing the homecare workers of Los Angeles County*. Unpublished research note, (Massachusetts Institute of Technology).

Coisineau, M. 2000. *Providing health insurance to IHSS providers (home care workers) in Los Angeles County* (Los Angeles, HealthCare Foundation).

Coleman, J.S. 1988. "Social capital in the creation of human capital", in *American Journal of Sociology*, No. 94, pp. S95–S120.

—. 1993. "The rational reconstruction of society", in *American Sociological Review*, No. 58, pp. 1–15.

—. 1995. "Rights and interests: Raising the next generation", in *American Sociological Review*, No. 60, pp. 782–783.

Commissie Groenman. 1997. *Het vrouwenverdrag anno 1997* [The women's agreement in year 1997] (The Hague, Ministerie van Sociale Zaken en Werkgelegenheid/VUGA).

Commissie Sociaal-Economische Deskundigen (CSED). 1999. *Gezondheidszorg in het licht van de toekomstige vergrijzing* [Health care in the light of the future greying of the population] (The Hague, Sociaal-Economische Raad).

Commissie Toekomstscenario's Herverdeling Onbetaalde Arbeid. 1995. *Onbetaalde zorg gelijk verdeeld* [Unpaid care equally divided] (The Hague, VUGA).

Coote, A. 1981. "The AES: A new starting point", in *New Socialist*, Nov./Dec., pp. 4–7.

Cowan, R. 1980. *More work for mother* (New York, Basic Books).

Creighton, C. 1999. "The rise and decline of the male breadwinner family in Britain", in *Cambridge Journal of Economics*, No. 23, pp. 519–541.

Dalley, G. 1988. *Ideologies of caring: Rethinking community and collectivism* (London, Macmillan).

Daly, M. 1997. "Welfare states under pressure: Cash benefits in European welfare states over the last ten years", in *Journal of European Social Policy*, Vol. 7, No. 2, pp. 129–146.

—; Lewis, J. 1998. "Introduction: Conceptualising social care in the context of welfare state restructuring", in J. Lewis (ed.): *Gender, social care and welfare state restructuring in Europe* (Aldershot, Hampshire, Ashgate).

—; —. 2000. "The concept of social care and the analysis of contemporary welfare states", in *British Journal of Sociology*, No. 51, p. 2.

Deacon, A. 1998. "The Green Paper on welfare reform: A case for enlightened self-interest?", in *Political Quarterly*, Vol. 69, No. 3, pp. 306–311.

Dench, G. 1994. *The frog, the prince and the problem of men* (London, Neanderthal Books).

Department of Health. 1999. *National Strategy for Carers* (http://www.open.gov.uk).

Department of Public Social Services (DPSS). 2001a. *IHSS caseload characteristics: Los Angeles County Totals* (Los Angeles).

—. 2001b. *Persons aided – IHSS* (Los Angeles).

Department of Social, Community and Family Affairs. 1998. *Review of the carer's allowance* (Dublin).

Deutsch, F. 1999. *Halving it all: How equally shared parenting works* (Cambridge, Mass., Harvard University Press).

Donath, S. 1998. *What's feminist about feminist economics,* manuscript, World Health Organization Collaborating Centre for Women's Health, (University of Melbourne, Australia).

Doorn, J.A.A. van.; Schuijt, C.J.M. 1978. *De stagnerende verzorgingsstaat* [The stagnating welfare state] (Amsterdam, Meppel, Boom).

Doty, P. et al. 1994. "Consumer choice and the frontline worker", in *Journal of the American Society on Aging*, Vol. 18, No. 3, pp. 65–70.

—. 1999. *In-home supportive services for the elderly and disabled: A comparison of client-directed and professional management models of service delivery* (Washington, DC, US Department of Health and Human Services and the University of California at Los Angeles).

Dumont, L. 1980. *Homo Hierarchus* (Chicago, University of Chicago Press).

Duyvendak, J.W. 1997. "Waar blijft de politiek?", in *Essays over paarse politiek, maatschappelijk middenveld en sociale cohesie* ["Where are the politics now?", in *Essays on purple politics, civil society and social cohesion]* (Amsterdam, Boom).

Eaton, S. C. 1996. *Beyond unloving care: Promoting innovation in elder care through public policy*, Changing Work in America Series (Cambridge, Mass., Radcliffe Public Policy Institute).

Eisenstein, Z. 1981. *The radical future of liberal feminism* (New York, Longman).

Ellis, K. 1993. *Squaring the circle: User and carer participation in needs assessment* (York, Joseph Rowntree Foundation).

Ellwood, D.; Kane T. 2000. "Who is getting a college education? Family background and the growing gaps in enrolment", in S. Danziger and J. Waldfogel (eds.): *Securing the future: Investing in children from birth to college* (New York, Russell Sage), pp. 283–324.

Elshtain, J. B. 1981. *Public man and private woman* (Oxford, Blackwell).

Emancipatieraad. 1996. "Met zorg naar nieuwe zekerheid. Advies over een geëmancipeerd inkomens", in *Sociale zekerheidsbeleid* ["With care to a new Security", in *Social Security Policy]* (The Hague).

Estin, A.L. 1995. "Love and obligation: Family law and the romance of economics", in *William and Mary Law Review*, Vol. 36, pp. 989–1087.

Etzioni, A. 1993. *The spirit of community* (London, HarperCollins).

Evers, A. 1993. "The welfare mix approach. Understanding the pluralism of welfare systems", in A. Evers and I. Svetlik (eds.): *Balancing pluralism: New welfare mixes in care for the elderly* (Aldershot, Hampshire, Avebury).

—. 1994. "Payments for care: A small but significant part of a wider debate", in A. Evers; M. Pijl and C. Ungerson (eds.): *Payments for care: A comparative overview,* (Aldershot, Hampshire, Avebury), pp. 19–41.

Evers, A. et al. 1997. *Long-term care for the elderly: Britain and Germany compared* (London, Anglo-German Foundation).

Evers, A.; Svetlik, I. 1993. *New welfare mixes in care for the elderly* (Vienna, European Centre for Social Welfare Policy and Research).

Evers, A.; Wintersberger, H. 1990. *Shifts in the welfare mix: Their impact on work, social services and welfare policies* (Frankfurt, Campus).

—; —; Sachsse, C. 1999. *The pattern of social services in Germany: Care for children and the elderly*, paper presented in London, The Finnish Institute, 26–27 Apr.

Feder Kittay, E. 1999. *Love's labour: Essays on women, equality and dependency* (New York, Routledge).

Filgueiras, C. 1994. "A creche comunitária na nebulosa da pobreza 88", in *Cadernos de Pesquisa,* Vol. 18, No. 29, Feb.

Finch, J.; Groves, D. 1983. *Labour and love: Women, work and caring* (London, Routledge and Kegan Paul).

—; —. 1985. "Community care and the family: A case for equal opportunities?", in C. Ungerson (ed.): *Women and social policy, a reader* (Basingstoke, Macmillan).

Finch, J.; Mason, J. 1993. *Negotiating family responsibilities* (London, Tavistock/Routledge).

Fisher, B.; Tronto, J. 1990. "Toward a feminist theory of caring", in E. Abel and M. Nelson (eds.): *Circles of care work and identity in women's lives* (Albany, New York, State University of New York Press).

Folbre, N. 1994. "Who pays for the kids?", in *Gender and the structures of constraint* (London, Routledge).

—. 1995. "Holding hands at midnight: The paradox of caring labor", in *Feminist Economics*, No. 1, pp. 73–92.

—. 1999. "Care and the global economy", paper prepared for the UNDP, New York.

—. 2001a. Forthcoming. "Leave no child behind", *The American Prospect*.

—. 2001b. *Accounting for care in the United States*, ILO Socio-Economic Security Programme, (Geneva, ILO).

—; Nelson, J. 2000. "For love or money or both?", in *Journal of Economic Perspectives*, Vol. 14. No. 4.

—; Wagman, B. 1993. "Counting housework: New estimates of real product in the U.S., 1800–1860", in *Journal of Economic History*, Vol. 53, No. 2, pp. 275–288.

—; Weisskopf T. 1998. "Did father know best? Families, markets and the supply of caring labor", in B-N. Avner and L. Putterman (eds.): *Economics, values and organization* (Cambridge, Cambridge University Press).

Ford, J. et al. 1998. *Creating jobs: The employment potential of domiciliary care* (Bristol, The Policy Press and Joseph Rowntree Foundation).

Forss, S. et al. 1995. *Mistä apua vanhana? Tutkimus vanhusten avuntarpeesta ja eläkeläisten vapaaehtoistyöstä* [Who helps when you are old? A study on need for help and voluntary work among elderly population] (Vaasa, Eläketurvakeskus, Tutkimuksia), p. 3.

Franco, M. C. 1984. "Lidando pobremente com a pobreza" ["Dealing poorly with poverty"], in *Cadernos de Pesquisa* (São Paulo, Fundação Carlos Chagas,), Vol. 51, pp. 13–32, Nov.

Fraser, N. 1993. "After the family wage: Gender equity and the welfare state", in *Political Theory*, Vol. 22, No. 4, pp. 591–618.

Fukuyama, F. 1999. *The great disruption* (London, Profile Books).

Galston, W.A. 1991. *Liberal purposes: Goods, virtues and diversity in the liberal state* (Cambridge, Cambridge University Press).

Garin, G.; Molyneux G. 1998. "Informing and empowering American workers: Ten rules for union political action", in J. Mort (ed.): *Not your father's union movement: Inside the AFL-CIO* (London, Verso), pp.113–126.

Geertz, C. 1975. "On the nature of anthropological understanding", in *American Scientist*, Vol. 63, pp. 57–53.

General Accounting Office (GAO). 1999. "Nursing homes: Stronger complaint and enforcement practices needed to better assure adequate care", in *Report T-HEHS-99-89* (Washington, DC, Government Printing Office).

Gergen, K.J. 1991. *The saturated self: Dilemmas of identity in contemporary life* (New York, Basic Books).

Giddens, A. 1998. "The renewal of democracy", in *The third way* (Cambridge, Polity Press).

—. 1992. *The transformation of intimacy: Sexuality, love and eroticism in modern societies* (Cambridge, Polity Press).

Gilder, G. 1987. "The collapse of the American family", in *The Public Interest*, Fall, pp. 20–25.

Gilligan, C. 1982. *In a different voice* (Cambridge, Mass., Harvard University Press).

Glendinning, C. 1992. *The costs of informal care: Looking inside the household* (London, HMSO).

—; McLaughlin E. 1993. *Paying for care in Europe* (London, HMSO).

Goldani, A.M. 1994. "Retratos de família em tempos de crise" ["Portraits of families in times of crisis"], in *Estudos Feministas* (Rio de Janeiro, CIEC/UFRJ), Special issue, 2nd semester.

Goodman, G. 1996. "Self-other differentiation in India: A cultural perspective" (Ph.D. Dissertation, University of Hawaii).

Gordon, L. 1990. *Women, the state and welfare* (Wisconsin, Madison University).

Gordon, S. 1998. *Life support: Three nurses on the front lines* (New York, Little Brown and Co.).

—. 1999. "Healing in a hurry: Hospitals in the managed-care age", in *The Nation*, 1 Mar., Vol. 268, No. 8, pp. 11–15.

Graetz, M.J.; Mashaw, J.L. 1999. *True security: Rethinking American social insurance* (New Haven, Yale University Press).

Graham, H. 1991. "The concept of caring in feminist research: the case of domestic service", in *Sociology*, Vol. 25, No. 1, pp. 61–78.

—. 1999. "The informal sector of welfare: A crisis in caring?", in G. Allen (ed.): *The sociology of the family* (Oxford, Blackwell), pp. 283–299.

Grant, G.; Nolan, M. 1993. "Informal carers: Sources and concomitants of satisfaction", in *Health and Social Care in the Community*, Vol. 1, No. 3, pp. 147–159.

Griffiths, M. 1995. *Feminisms and the self: The web of identity* (London, Routledge).

Griffiths, R. 1998. *Community care: Agenda for action,* a report to the Secretary of State for Social Services (London, HMSO).

Gupta, D. et al. 2000. *The integrated child development services: Lessons from a pilot study*, Working Paper Series No. 69 (New Delhi, NCAER).

Hakim, C. 1996. *Key issues in women's work: Female heterogeneity and the polarisation of women's employment* (London, Athlone).

Hallberg, D.; Klevmarken, A. 2000. *Time for children? A study of parents' time allocation* (Uppsala, Uppsala University, Department of Economics).

Haq, Mahbub ul; Haq, K. 1998. *Human development in South Asia 1998* (Dhaka, Oxford University Press).

Harkness, S.; Machin, S.; Waldfogel, J. 1996. "Women's Pay and Family Incomes in Britain, 1979–1991", in J. Hills (ed.): *New inequalities: The changing distribution of income and wealth in the UK* (Cambridge, Cambridge University Press).

—; —; —. 1997. "Evaluating the pin money hypothesis: The relationship between women's labour market activity, family income and poverty in Britain", in *Journal of Population Economics*, Vol. 10, No. 2, pp. 137–158.

Harkness, S.; Waldfogel, J. 1999. *The family gap in pay: Evidence from seven industrialised countries*, CASE paper 30 (London, LSE).

Hartmann, H. 1981. "The family as a locus of gender, class and political struggle", in *Signs: Journal of Women in Culture and Society*, Vol. 6, No. 3, pp. 366–394.

Hattinga-Verschure, J.C.M. 1977. *Het verschijnsel zorg. Een inleiding tot de zorgkunde* [The phenomenon of care: An introduction to care knowledge] (Lochem, de Tijdstroom).

Heckman, J.; Lochner L. 2000. "Rethinking education and training policy: Understanding the sources of skill formation in a modern economy", in S. Danziger and J. Waldfogel (eds.): *Securing the future: Investing in children from birth to college* (New York, Russell Sage).

Helburn, S. 1995. "Cost, quality, and child outcomes", in *Child care centers, a technical report* (Denver, University of Colorado).

Held, V. 1993. *Feminist morality: Transforming culture, society and politics* (Chicago, University of Chicago Press).

Hernes, H. 1987. *Welfare states and woman power: Essays in state feminism* (Oslo, Norwegian University Press).

Hersch, J. 1991. "Male-female differences in hourly wages: The role of human capital, working conditions, and housework", in *Industrial and Labor Relations Review*, Vol. 44, No. 4, July, pp. 746–759.

Heymann, J. 2000. *The widening gap: Why America's working families are in jeopardy and what can be done about it* (New York, Basic Books).

Hibbard, J. 1998. "Can Medicare beneficiaries make informed choices?", in *Health Affairs*, Nov./Dec., pp. 181–193.

Himmelweit, S. 1995. "The discovery of unpaid work: The social consequences of the expansion of work", in *Feminist Economics*, Vol. 1, No. 2, pp. 1–19.

Hochschild, A. 1983. *The managed heart: Commercialization of human feeling* (Berkeley, University of California Press).

—. 1995. *Facing up to the American dream: Race, class and the soul of the nation* (Princeton, NJ, Princeton University Press).

—. 1996. "The culture of politics: Traditional, post-modern, cold-modern and warm-modern ideals of care", in *Social Politics*, Vol. 2, No. 3, pp. 331–345.

Homecare Workers Union. 1988. *Homecare – invisible and inadequate: Quality of care in the Los Angeles County IHSS programme* (Los Angeles).

Hooks, B. 1984. *Feminist theory: From center to margin* (Cambridge, Mass., South End Press).

Hooyman, N.; Gonyea, J. 1995. *Feminist perspectives on family care policies for gender justice* (Thousand Oaks, California, Sage).

Horden, P.; Smith, R. 1998. *The locus of care: Families, communities, institutions and the provision of welfare since antiquity* (Routledge, London), p. 2.

Inglehart, R. 1997. *Culture shift in advanced industrial society* (Princeton, Princeton University Press).

International Labour Organization (ILO). 1998. *World Employment Report 1998–99: Employability in the global economy: How training matters* (Geneva).

Jacobs, J.; Gerson K. 1998. "Who are the overworked Americans?", in *Review of Social Economy*, forthcoming.

James, N. 1989. "Emotional labour: Skill and work in the social regulation of feelings", in *Sociological Review*, Vol. 37, pp. 15–42.

Jamieson, A. (ed.). 1991. *Home care for older people in Europe: A comparison of policies and practices* (Oxford, Oxford University Press).

Joel, M-E.; Martin, C. 1994. "Payments for care: The case of France", in A. Evers; M. Pijl; C. Ungerson (eds.): *Payments for care: A comparative overview* (Aldershot, Hampshire, Avebury).

Johnson, F. 1985. "The Western concept of self", in A. Marsella; G. DeVos; F.L.K. Hsu (eds.): *Culture and self: Asian and western perspectives* (London, Tavistock), pp. 91–138.

Joshi, H. 1992. "The costs of caring", in C. Glendinning and J. Millar (eds.): *Women and poverty in Britain: The 1990s* (Hemel Hempstead, Harvester Wheatsheaf).

—; Davies, H. 1992. "Daycare in Europe and mothers' foregone earnings", in *International Labour Review* (ILR), Vol. 6, pp. 561–579.

Jowell, T. 1989. "More care for the carers", in *The Guardian,* 20 Sep., p. 27.

—; Wistow, G. 1989. "Give them a voice", in *Insight*, 28 Feb., pp. 22–23.

Kanter, R. 1993. *Men and women of the corporation* (New York, Basic Books).

Kappel, M. 2000. "As crianças de 0 a 6 anos nas estatísticas nacionais" ["0–6-year-olds in national statistics"], in OMEP workshop: Infància-educacao infantil: Reflexões para o início do século [Childhood-child education: reflexions for the beginning of the century] (Rio de Janeiro, Educação Infantil,) July.

Kaul, V. 1992. "Early childhood education in India", in G.A. Woodill; J. Bernhard; L. Prochner (eds.): *International handbook of early childhood education* (New York and London, Garland).

Keuzenkamp, S.; Hooghiemstra E. 2000. *De Kunst van het combineren: Taakverdeling onder partners* [The art of combining: Division of tasks between partners] (The Hague, Sociaal en Cultureel Planbureau).

—; —; Oudhof K. 2000. *Emancipatiemonitor 2000* [Emancipation monitor 2000] (The Hague, Sociaal en Cultureel Planbureau).

Kilborn, P. 1998. "Nurses put on fast forward in rush for cost efficiency", in *New York Times*, 9 Apr.

Knijn, T. 1998. "Social care in the Netherlands", in J. Lewis (ed.): *Gender, social care and welfare state restructuring in Europe* (Aldershot, Hampshire, Ashgate), pp. 85–110.

—. 2000a. "The rationalized marginalization of care: Time is money isn't it?", in B. Hobson (ed.): *Gender and citizenship in transition* (London, Macmillan), pp. 201–219.

—. 2000b. "Marketisation and the struggling logics of (home) care in the Netherlands", in M. Harrington Meyer (ed.): *Care work, gender, labor and the welfare state* (New York, Routledge), pp. 232–248.

—; Kremer, M. 1997. "Gender and the caring dimension of welfare states: Towards inclusive citizenship", in *Social Politics: International Studies in Gender, State and Society*, Vol. 4, No. 3, pp. 328–361.

—; van Wel, F. 2001. "Careful or lenient: Welfare reform for lone mothers in the Netherlands", in *Journal of European Social Policy* (forthcoming).

Kohner, N. 1993. *A stronger voice: The achievements of the carers' movement 1963–1993* (London, Carers National Association).

Kolehmainen, S. 1997. "Occupational and career opportunities for women in female-dominated occupations", in *Labour Policy Studies, No 173* (Helsinki, Ministry of Labour).

Kotlikoff, L. 1992. *Generational accounting: Knowing who pays, and when, for what we spend* (New York, Free Press).

Kraan, R.J.; et al. 1991. *Care for the elderly: significant innovations in three European countries* (Frankfurt/Boulder, Campus Verlag/Westview Press).

Kramer, S. 1992. "A política do pré-escola no Brasil" ["The pre-school policy in Brazil"], in *A arte do disfarce* [The art of dissimulation] (São Paulo, Ática).

—; Kappel, M.D. 2000. "Educação de crianças de 0 a 6 anos" ["Educating 0–6-year-olds"], in *Pesquisa sobre padrões de vida (PPV): Primeira infância (1996/1997)* [Research on living standards (PPV): The first childhood (1996/1997)]. (Rio de Janeiro, Instituto Brasileiro de Geografia e Estatística/IBGE).

Kremer, M. 2000. *Geven en claimen: Burgerschap en informele zorg in Europees perspectief* [Giving and claiming: Citizenship and informal care in a European perspective] (Utrecht, NIZW).

Kröger, T. 1996 "Policy-makers in social services in Finland: The municipality and the state", in *Scandinavian Journal of Social Welfare*, Vol. 5, p. 2.

—. 1997. "The dilemma of municipalities: Scandinavian approaches to child day care provision", in *Journal of Social Policy*, Vol. 26, p. 4.

Land, H. 1985. "The introduction of family allowances: An act of historic justice?", in C. Ungerson (ed.): *Women and social policy – a reader* (Basingstoke, Hampshire, Macmillan).

—; Rose, H. 1985. "Compulsory altruism for some or an altruistic society for all?", in P. Bean; J. Ferris; D. Whynes (eds.): *In defence of welfare* (London, Tavistock).

Lavinas L. 1997. "Emprego feminino: o que há de novo e o que se repete" ("Women's employment: what's new and what repeats itself"), in *Dados*, Vol. 40, No. 1.

Lebergott, S. 1993. *Pursuing happiness: American consumers in the twentieth century* (Princeton, Princeton University Press).

Le Grand, J. 1997. "Knights, knaves or pawns: Human behaviour and social policy", in *Journal of Social Policy*, Vol. 26, pp. 149–170.

Lefley, H.P. 1996. *Family caregiving in mental illness* (Thousand Oaks, California, Sage).

Lehto, J. 1998. "Muuttuuko pohjoismainen sosiaali- ja terveyspalvelumalli" ["Is the Nordic social and health care in transition?"] in *Yhteiskuntapolitiikka*, Vol. 63, pp. 5–6.

Leira, A. 1992. *Welfare states and working mothers* (Cambridge, Cambridge University Press).

—. 1993. "Concepts of care: Loving, thinking and doing", in J. Twigg (ed.): *Informal care in Europe*, (York, University of York, SPRU), pp. 23–39.

—. 1998. "Caring as social right: Cash for child care and daddy leave", in *Social Politics*, Vol. 5, pp. 362–379.

Levin, E.; Sinclair, I.; Gorbach, P. 1983. *The supporters of confused elderly persons at home* (London, National Institute of Social Work).

Lewis, J. (ed.) 1992. "Gender and the development of welfare regimes", in *Journal of European Social Policy*, Vol. 2, pp. 159–173.

—. 1998. *Gender, social care and welfare state restructuring in Europe* (Aldershot, Hampshire, Ashgate).

—; Astrom, G. 1992. "Equality, difference and state welfare: Labour market and family policies in Sweden", in *Feminist Studies*, Vol. 18, pp. 59–87.

—; Meredith, B. 1988. *Daughters caring for mothers* (London, Routledge).

Lindbeck, A. 1994. *Turning Sweden around* (Cambridge, Mass., MIT Press).

Lister, R. 1990. "Women, economic dependency, and citizenship," in *Journal of Social Policy*, Vol. 19, No. 4, pp. 445–467.

—. 1994. *Dilemmas in engendering citizenship,* paper presented at Crossing Borders Conference (Stockholm, University of Stockholm), p. 19.

—. 1997. *Feminism and citizenship* (London, Macmillan).

Lowe, R. 1993. *The Welfare State in Britain since 1945* (London, Macmillan).

Lundberg, S.; Pollak, R. A. 1996. "Bargaining and distribution in marriage", in I. Persson and C. Jonung (eds.): *Economics of the family and family policies* (London, Routledge).

MacDonald, K. 1995. "The establishment and maintenance of socially imposed monogamy in Western Europe," in *Politics and the Life Sciences*, Feb., pp. 3–23.

Mahoney, R. 1995. *Kidding ourselves: Breadwinning, babies, and bargaining power* (New York, Basic Books).

Marglin, S. 1990. "Farmers, seedsmen and scientists: Systems of agriculture and systems of knowledge", in F.A. Marglin and S.A. Marglin (eds.): *Dominating knowledge* (Oxford, Oxford University Press).

—. Marglin, F.A.; Marglin, S.A. (eds.) 1996. *Decolonizing knowledge: From development to dialogue* (Oxford, Clarendon Press).

McKenzie, H. 1995. "Empowering older persons through organizations: A case study", in D. Thurz; C. Nusberg and J. Prather (eds.): *Empowering older people* (London, Cassell).

Mead, L. 1986. "Beyond entitlement", in *The social obligations of citizenship* (New York, Free Press).

Merina, V. 1989. "Union loses court fight with county to organize", in *Los Angeles Times*, 3 Feb., Metro 1.

Meyer-Rodriguez, J. 1997. *Partnership Plan* unpublished SEIU State Council Document. (Sacramento, Calif.)

—. (n.d.). *Quality homecare campaign* unpublished SEIU State Council Document. (Sacramento, Calif.)

Mies, M. 1986. *Patriarchy and accumulation on a world scale* (London, Zed Books).

Ministerie van Sociale Zaken en Werkgelegenheid. 1992. *Beleidsprogramma emancipatie met het oog op 1995* [Gender equality programme: With an eye on 1995] (The Hague).

—. 1997. *Kansen op combineren: Arbeid, zorg en economische zelfstandigheid.* [Opportunities to combine: Work, care and economic independence] (The Hague).

—. 1999. *Op weg naar een nieuw evenwicht tussen arbeid en zorg.* [On the way to a new balance of work and care] (The Hague).

—. 2000. *Meerjarennota emancipatiebeleid: Van vrouwenstrijd naar vanzelfsprekendheid* [Long-term gender equality programme: From women's struggle to self-evidence] (The Hague).

Ministerie van Volksgezondheid, Welzijn en Sport. 1997. *Verpleging, verzorging en ouderen,* [Nursing, caring and elderly people], 21 Nov.

Morgan, P. 1995. "Farewell to the family", in IEA: *Policy and family breakdown in Britain and the USA* (London).

Morris, J. 1993. *Independent lives: Community care and disabled people* (Basingstoke, Hampshire, Macmillan).

Murray, C. 1985. "Losing ground", in *American Social Policy 1950–1980* (New York, Basic Books).

National Institute on Consumer-Directed Long-Term Services (NICDLTS) 1996. *Principles of consumer-directed home and community-based services: A statement.* (Washington, DC, The National Council on the Aging).

Nelson, J.A. 1999. "Of markets and martyrs: Is it OK to pay well for care?", in *Feminist Economics*, Vol. 4, pp. 43–59.

Nikam, N.A. 1959. "Liberty and community", in N.A. Nikam (ed): *Science and philosophy, individual freedom and community traditional values* (Mysore, International Inst. of Philosophy and Indian Philosophy Congress).

Niphuis-Nell, M. 1997. "Beleid inzake herverdeling van onbetaalde arbeid" ["Policy on re-division of unpaid work"] in M. Niphuis-Nell (ed.): *Sociale Atlas van de Vrouw. Deel 4: Veranderingen in de primaire leefsfeer* [Social atlas of women. Part 4: Changes in the private domain] (Rijswijk, Sociaal en Cultureel Planbureau.), pp. 287–334.

Noddings, N. 1984. *Caring: A feminine approach to ethics and moral education* (Berkeley, University of California Press).

Noro, A. 1998. *Long-term institutional care among Finnish elderly population: Trends and potential for discharge* (Helsinki, Stakes, Research Report 87).

NOSOSCO. 1998. *Social protection in the Nordic countries 1996: Scope, expenditure and financing* (Copenhagen).

Nussbaum, M.; Glover, J. 1995. *Women, culture and development: A study of human capabilities* (Oxford, Clarendon Press).

O'Connor et al. 1988. *Caring for the elderly: Part I: A study of carers at home and in the community* (Dublin, National Council for the Aged).

O'Shea, E. 2000. *The costs of caring for people with dementia and related cognitive impairments* (Dublin, National Council on Ageing and Older People).

Oakley, A. 1974. *The sociology of housework* (Oxford, Martin Robertson).

—. 1986. "Social Welfare and the Position of Women", Richard Titmuss Memorial Lecture, Hebrew University of Jerusalem, 18 May.

Office for National Statistics (ONS). 1998. *Living in Britain: Results from the 1996 General Household Survey* (London, HMSO).

Oliveira, Z. de M.R.; Ferreira, M.C.R. 1986. "Propostas para o atendimento em creche no município de São Paulo" ["Proposals for pre-school attendance in São Paulo municipality"], in *Cadernos de Pesquisa,* Vol. 56, Feb., (São Paulo, Fundação Carlos Chagas), pp. 39–65.

Organisation for Economic Co-operation and Development (OECD) 1991. *Shaping structural change* (Paris).

Orloff, A. 1993. "Gender and the social rights of citizenship: The comparative analysis of gender relations and welfare states", in *American Sociological Review*, Vol. 58, pp. 303–328.

Pahl, J. 1989. *Money and marriage* (London, Macmillan).

Päivärinta, T. 1993. *Jaettu vastuu. Tutkimus sosiaalipalvelujen organisoinnista Suomessa vuosina 1974–1990 (A shared responsibility: A study on the provision of social services in Finland in 1974–1990)* (Helsinki, Suomen Kaupunkiliitto).

Parker, G. 1992. *With this body: Caring and disability in marriage* (Buckingham, United Kingdom, Open University Press).

Parker, R. 1981. "Tending and social policy", in E. M. Goldberg and S. Hatch (eds.): *A new look at the personal social services,* Discussion Paper 4 (London, Policy Studies Institute).

Pateman, C. 1988. "The patriachal welfare state", in A. Gutman (ed.): *Democracy and the welfare state.* (Princeton, Princeton University Press).

Pierce, J. 1995. *Gender trials* (Berkeley, University of California Press).

Plantenga, J.; Schipper, J. 2000. "Arbeid, zorg en inkomen" ["Work, care and income"], in *Long-term equal opportunity policy: From women's struggle to self-evidence* (The Hague, Ministry of Social Affairs and Employment), pp. 7–32.

PNAD. 2000. *Pesquisa Nacional por Amostras de Domícilios* [National Household Sample Survey] (Rio de Janeiro, Instituto Brasileiro de Geografia e Estatística/IBGE, 1999).

Popenoe, D. 1993. "American family decline, 1960–1990: A review and appraisal", in *Journal of Marriage and the Family*, Vol. 55, pp. 527–555.

Prasad, V. 1998. "The politics of child care", in *Seminar,* No. 462, Feb., pp. 48–54.

Princess Royal Trust for Carers. 1995. *Carers in employment* (London).

Prior, D.; Jowell, T.; Lawrence, R. 1989. "Carer consultations: Towards a strategy for consumer-led change", in *Local government policy-making*, Vol. 16, No. 2, pp. 17–25.

Putnam, R. D. 1993. *Making democracy work: Civic traditions in modern Italy* (Princeton, Princeton University Press).

Ramanujam, A.K. 1989. "Is there an Indian way of thinking? An informal essay", in *Contributions to Indian Sociology*, Vol. 23, No. 1, Jan.– June, pp. 41–58.

Rauhala, P-L. 1996. *Miten sosiaalipalvelut ovat tulleet osaksi suomalaista sosiaaliturvaa?* [How have social services become integrated into the Nordic social security model?] (Tampere, University of Tampere, Acta Universitas Tamperensis).

Rissanen, T. 2000. *Naisten ansiotyömallin muotoutuminen* [The development of women's wage work model in Finland] (Tampere, University of Tampere, Research Institute for Social Sciences, Work Research Centre).

Robinson, J.; Godbey, G. 1997. *Time for life: The surprising ways Americans use their time* (University Park, Pennsylvania State University).

Rodriguez, A. 1991. "Molina's anti-union attack is pure Reagan", in *Los Angeles Times*, 15 Feb., Metro 7 (op-ed).

Rogers, B.; Pryor, J. 1998. *Divorce and separation: The outcomes for children* (York, Joseph Rowntree Foundation).

Roland, A. 1988. *In search of self in India and Japan: Toward a cross-cultural psychology* (Princeton, Princeton University Press).

Rosemberg, F. 1991. "Raça e educação inicial" ["Race and early education"], in *Cadernos de Pesquisa,* Vol. 77, pp. 25–34.

—. 1999. "Expansão da educação infantil e processo de exclusão" ["The expansion of child education and the process of exclusion"], in *Cadernos de Pesquisa,* Vol. 107, July, pp. 7–40.

Rosenthal, S. 1998. "Building to win, building to last", in J. Mort (ed.): *Not your father's union movement: Inside the AFL-CIO* (London, Verso), pp. 99–111.

Rostgaard, T.; Fridberg, T. 1998. *Care for children and older people: A comparison of European policies and practices* (Copenhagen, The Danish National Institute of Social Research).

Royal Commission on Long-Term Care. 1999. *With respect to old age,* Report Cm. 41921–I (London, HMSO).

RTZ Associates. 1996. *Bold action for a challenging problem* (Oakland, Calif.).

Rubery, J.; Smith, M.; Fagan, C. 1998. "National working-time regimes and equal opportunities", in *Feminist Economics,* Vol. 4, pp. 71–101.

Russell, M. 1996. "LA County public authority: A zero sum", in *New Mobility,* Nov., pp. 40–53.

Sabóia J.; Sabóia, A.L. 2000. "Condições de vida das famílias com crianças até 6 anos" ["Living conditions of families with children up to six"], in *Sobre Padrões de Vida, 1996–1997* [About living standards, 1996–1997] (Rio de Janeiro, Primeira Infância, IBGE).

Sainsbury, D. 1988. "The Scandinavian model and women's interests: The issues of universalism and corporatism", in *Scandinavian Political Studies,* Vol. 11, p .4.

Salmi, M. 2000. "Analysing the Finnish homecare allowance system: Challenges to research and problems of interpretation", in N. Bruun and L. Kalliomaa-Puha (eds.): *Work and family: Report on new perspectives of equality in the Nordic countries* (Copenhagen, Nordiska Ministerrådet).

Sandel, M. 1982. *Liberalism and the limits of justice* (Cambridge, Cambridge University Press).

—. 1996. *Democracy's discontents* (Cambridge, Mass., Belknap Press of Harvard University Press).

Schor, J. 1991. *The overworked American* (New York, Basic Books).

—. 1998. *The overspent American: Why we want what we don't need.* (New York, Harper Perennial by arrangement with Basic Books).

Schumacher, E.F. 1997. *This I believe and other essays* (Foxhole, Dartington Totnes, Devon, Green Books).

Schweinhart et al. 1993. *Significant benefits: The High Scope Perry Preschool study through age 27* (Ypsilanti, Mich., High Scope Press, monograph).

Secretaries of State for Health, Social Security, Wales and Scotland. 1989. *Caring for people: Community care in the next decade and beyond* (London, HMSO).

Service Employees International Union (SEIU) Research Department. 1994. *Provider turnover: A problem for California's IHSS programme* (Washington, DC).

SEIU President's Committee. 2000 (1999). *Imagine: SEIU's opportunities to change the future* (Washington, DC).

Sen, A. 1999. *Development as freedom* (New Delhi, Oxford University Press).

Senate Bill Analysis Service. 1993. *SB 35* (Sacramento, State of California).

Senate Budget and Fiscal Review. 1998. Subcommittee No. 3 on Health, Human Services, Labor and Veterans Affairs, Senator Mike Thompson, Chair (Sacramento, State of California).

Shariff, A. 1990. *A few cultural concepts and socio-behavioural aspects of human health in India* (New Delhi, NCAER), Reprint No. 17.

Shearer, A. 1993. *The Hindu vision: Forms of the formless* (London, Thames and Hudson).

Shore, R. 2000. *Our basic dream: Keeping faith with America's working families and their children* (New York, Foundation for Child Development).

Shulman, B. 1996. *LA homecare chronology leading to check-off*, unpublished Memorandum to File (Washington, DC, SEIU).

Siim, B. 1987. "The Scandinavian welfare states – towards sexual equality or a new kind of male domination?", in *Acta Sociologica*, Vol. 30, No. 3/4, pp. 255–270.

—. 1993. "The gendered Scandinavian welfare states: The interplay between women's roles as mothers, workers and citizens in Denmark", in J. Lewis (ed.): *Women and social policies in Europe: Work, family and the State* (Aldershot, Hampshire, Edward Elgar).

Sipilä, J. et al. 1997. "A multitude of universal, public services – how and why did four Scandinavian countries get their social service model", in J. Sipilä (ed.): *Social care services: The key to the Scandinavian welfare model* (Aldershot, Hampshire, Avebury).

—; Korpinen, J. 1998. "Cash versus child care service in Finland", in *Social Policy and Administration*, Vol. 32, p. 3.

SMDS/RJ (Secretaria Municipal de Desenvolvimento Social). 1992. *Proposta curricular para creches e pré-escolas comunitárias* [Proposed curriculum for community crèches and pre-schools] (Rio de Janeiro, Prefeitura do Rio de Janeiro).

Smith, R.; West, G. 1985. "The effects of mental illness on the family: Social work practitioner's view", in G. Horobin (ed.): *Responding to mental illness* (Aberdeen/London, Kogan Page).

Sociaal en Cultureel Planbureau (SCP). 1998. *Sociaal en cultureel rapport 1998 (1998 Social and Cultural Report)* (The Hague).

—. 2000. *Sociaal en cultureel rapport 2000* [2000 Social and Cultural Report] (The Hague).

SOTKA Database. 2001. *Electronic database on social and health care* (Helsinki, Stakes).

Spencer, H. 1876. *The principles of sociology*, Vol. I (London, Williams and Norgate).

Spradly, J.; Mann, B. 1975. *Cocktail waitress: Women's work in a man's world* (New York, McGraw Hill).

Standing, G. 1997. "Globalization, labour flexibility and insecurity: The era of market regulation", in *European Journal of Industrial Relations*, Vol. 3, No. 1, pp. 7–37.

Statistical Bulletin. 1998/1999. *Social situation and standard of living of Russian population* (Moscow, Goskomstat).

Statistical Yearbook of Finland. 1997. (Helsinki).

Stephens, J. 1996. "The Scandinavian welfare states: Achievements, crisis, and prospects", in G. Esping-Andersen (ed.): *Welfare states in transition: National adaptations in global economies* (London, Sage).

Stolberg, S. 1999. "Report says profit-making health plans damage care", in *New York Times*, 14 July, 1999.

Stone, D. 1999. "Care and trembling", in *American Prospect*, Vol. 43, pp. 61–67.

Strathern, M. 1992. *After nature. English kinship in the late twentieth century* (Cambridge, Cambridge University Press).

Sudarshan, R. 2000. "The educational status of girls and women: The emerging scenario", in R. Wazir (ed.): *The gender gap in basic education: NGOs as change agents* (New Delhi, Sage).

Sundström, G. 1994. "Care by families: An overview of trends", in *Care for frail elderly people: New directions of care* (Paris, OECD).

Svenhuijsen, S. 1998. *Citizenship and the ethics of care* (London, Routledge).

—. 1999. *Caring in the third way*. Centre of Research on Family, Kinship and Childhood, Working Paper 12 (Leeds, University of Leeds).

Teixeira, N.L. (coord.). 1997. *Perfil das trabalhadoras de creches do município de Nova Iguaçu/Baixada Fluminense* [Profile of pre-school workers in the Nova Iguaçu/Baixada Fluminense municipality] (Rio de Janeiro, Faculdade de Serviço Social da UERJ).

Thair, T.; Risdon, A. 1999. "Women in the labour market: Results from the Spring 1998 LFS", in *Labour Market Trends*, Mar., pp. 103–127.

Thomas, C. 1993. "De-constructing concepts of care", in *Sociology*, Vol. 27, No. 4, pp. 649–669.

Thorne, B. 1982. "Feminist rethinking of the family: An overview", in B. Thorne and M. Yolom (eds.): *Rethinking the family: Some feminist questions* (New York, Longman).

Tiriba, L. 2000a. "Contribuições ao plano de governo" ["Contributions to the government plan"] in *Partido dos Trabalhadores na Área de Educação Infantil: Gestão 2001–2004* [Workers' Party Child Education: 2001–2004 administration].

Titmuss, R.M. 1976. *Essays on the Welfare State* (London, Allen and Unwin, 1st. edn., 1954).

Toy, A. 1996. "LA County Authority: An empowering solution", in *New Mobility*, Nov., pp. 41–69.

Tronto, J.C. 1993. *Moral boundaries: A political argument for an ethic of care* (London, Routledge).

Twigg, J.; Atkin, K. 1994. *Carers perceived: Policy and practice in informal care* (Buckingham, United Kingdom, Open University Press).

—.; —.; Perring, C. 1990. *Carers and services: A review of research* (London, HMSO).

United Nations Development Programme (UNDP). 1995. *Human Development Report* (New York, Oxford University Press), Ch. 4, pp. 97–98.

Ungerson, C. 1987. *Policy is personal: Sex, gender and informal care* (London, Tavistock).

—. (ed.) 1990. *Gender and caring: Work and welfare in Britain and Scandinavia* (Hemel Hempstead, Harvester Wheatsheaf).

—. 1995. "Gender, cash and informal care: European perspectives and dilemmas", in *Journal of Social Policy*, Vol. 24, No. 1, pp. 31–52.

—. 1996. "The language of care: Crossing the boundaries", in C. Ungerson (ed.): *Gender and caring: Work and welfare in Britain and Scandinavia* (Hemel Hempstead, United Kingdom, Harvester Wheatsheaf), pp. 8–33.

—. 1997. "Social politics and the commodification of care," in *Social Politics*, Vol. 4, No. 3 (Fall), pp. 362–381.

—. 1999. "The production and consumption of long-term care: Does gender still matter?", paper for a conference on "Beyond the Health Care State", European University Institute, Florence, Feb.

United Nations Children's Fund (UNICEF). 2001. *The state of the world's children 2001* (New York).

Unni, J. 1998. "Women in informal sector: Size and contribution to gross domestic product", in *Margin*, Vol. 30, No. 3, pp. 73–93.

US Bureau of Labor Statistics. 1999. *Employment and earnings*, Jan. 1999, table 18.

Vaarama, M.; Kautto, M. 1998. *Social protection for the elderly in Finland* (Helsinki, Stakes).

Vanhusbarometri. 1994. [Old Age Barometer 1994] (Helsinki, Sosiaali- ja terveysministeriö).

Vanhusbarometri. 1998. [Old Age Barometer 1998] (Helsinki, Sosiaali- ja terveysministeriö).

Visser, J.; Hemerijck, A. 1997. *A Dutch miracle: Job growth, welfare reform and corporatism in the Netherlands* (Amsterdam, Amsterdam University Press).

Waerness, K. 1984. "Caring as women's work in the welfare state", in H. Holter (ed.): *Patriarchy in a welfare society* (Oslo, Universitetsforlaget), pp. 67–87.

—. 1987. "On the rationality of caring", in A.S. Sassoon (ed.): *Women and the State* (London, Hutchinson).

Wagman, B.; Folbre N. 1996. "Household services and economic growth in the U.S., 1870–1930", in *Feminist Economics*, Vol. 2, No. 1 (Spring), pp. 43–66.

Walby, S. 1997. *Gender transformations* (London, Routledge).

Waldfogel, J. 1997. "The effect of children on women's wages", in *American Sociological Review*, Vol. 62, pp. 209–217.

Walker, A. 1983. "Care for elderly people: A conflict between women and the State", in J. Finch and D. Groves (eds.): *A labour of love: Women, work and caring* (London, Routledge and Kegan Paul).

—. 1987. "Enlarging the caring capacity of the community: Informal support networks and the welfare state", in *International Journal of Health Services*, Vol. 17, No. 3, pp. 369–386.

Ward, D. 1993. "The kin care trap: the unpaid labor of long term care", in *Socialist Review*, Vol. 23, No. 1, pp. 83–106.

Webster, M. 1963. "The forgotten women", in *Federation News*, Vol. 10, No. 2, pp. 13–14.

Weinstein, H. 1988. "Union sues to make county the homecare workers' boss", in *Los Angeles Times*, 1 Jan., Metro, p. 1.

Wenger, C. 1991. "A network typology: from theory to practice", in *Journal of Ageing Studies*, Vol. 5, No. 2, pp. 147–162.

Westside Center for Independent Living. 2000. *Overview of WCIL*, 19 Sep.

Whitebook, M. 1997. *NAEYC accreditation and assessment*, available from National Center for the Early Childhood Work Force, 733 15th St. NW, Suite 1037, Washington, DC, 20005.

Wilson, E. 1977. *Women and the Welfare State* (London, Tavistock), p. 5.

Wilson, W.J. 1987. *The truly disadvantaged: The inner city, the underclass and public policy* (Chicago, University of Chicago Press).

Woldringh, C.; Ramakers, C. 1998. *Persoonsgebonden budget verpleging en verzorging. Ervaringen van vudgethouders en vwaliteit van zorg* [Personal budget nursing and caring: Experiences of budgetholders and quality of care] (Nijmegen/Ubbergen, Instituut voor Toegepaste Wetenschappen/Uitgeverij Tandem Felix).

Wolfe, A. 1989. *Whose keeper? Social science and moral obligation* (Berkeley, University of California Press).

World Bank. 1996. "From plan to market", in *World Development Report* (Oxford, 1996).

Yankelovich, D. 1981. *New rules: Searching for self-fulfilment in a world turned upside down* (New York, Random House).

Young, I.M. 1995. "Mothers, citizenship and independence: A critique of pure family values", in *Ethics*, Vol. 105, pp. 535–556.

INDEX

Note: Page numbers in **bold** refer to major text sections, those in *italic* to figures and tables. Subscript numbers appended to page numbers indicate footnotes. When seeking references under women/gender, it should be borne in mind that virtually every aspect of care provision discussed refers to – or impacts upon – the female experience.

accounting *see* United States (accounting for care)

Acquired Immune Deficiency Syndrome (AIDS) 4, 5–6, 104

active ageing 4

Africa, sub-Saharan 5–6, 96

ageing population 4, 5, 75, 105, 152, 180
  see also elder care

agencies, care provision 20, 22, 23, *23*, 25

AIDS (Acquired Immune Deficiency Syndrome) 4, 5–6, 104

Alameda County, California 226

allowances *see* income security

altruism *see* ethic of care

Ammal (Kerala widow) 79, 80

Anganwadi centres 98–9, 101–2

Anttonen, Anneli xiii, 143–58
  other publications 35₄, 41, 144, 145, 148, *149*, *150*, 155

AOC (Association of Carers), England 8, 198, 199

Association of Carers (AOC), England 8, 198, 199

associations representing care providers/recipients *see* representation

Attendance Allowance (England) 197

Australia 88
  labour market participation *61*
  time-use surveys 181

Austria 45, 46–7
  childcare 42, 43₉, 44–5, *44*
  elder care 42, 45, *46*
  labour market participation *61*

Baixada Fluminense, State of Rio de Janeiro 114

Barnes, Marian xiii, 195–209
  other publications 201, 202, 204, 206, 208, 209

Belgium 45, 46–7, 50
  childcare *44*, 45, 73, 150
  elder care 45, *46*
  labour market participation *61*

Belo Horizonte, Brazil 113

benefits *see* income security

Bergmann, Frithjof 89

birth grants (Russian Federation) 129, *131*

birth weights 96, *97*

boarding homes *see* residential care

Bottomley, Virginia 200

Brasília 119

Brazil
  ageing population 105
  child population 105, 108
  labour market participation (women) 108
  poverty 108–9

Brazil, childcare (pre-schools) **105–24**
  public policies 106–7, **116–23**, 123–4

childcare as a "right to education"
114–16, **117–20**
  tensions and ambiguities **120–23**
as a social good **112–16**
  social struggles **113–16**
supply and demand **107–12**
  management **111–12**
  types of pre-school **109–10**
breast-feeding 101
Bruijn, Jeanne de 161, 169, 170
Bush, George W. 188, 190

California 186, 221–3, **225–6**, **230–31**, 232
  see also Los Angeles
Canada 181
care **1–11**
  definitions 17–18, 34, 36, 69–72, **176–9**
    see also Western Europe
  elevation to mainstream 1–2, 8–9, **15–32**,
    49, 51, *51*, **57–75**
  ethic 24, **69–73**, **162–3**
  marginalization 15–16, 17, 26, 57–8
  quality 3, 47–8, 50, 51, *51*, 52, 53, 54, 94,
    102–3
  social process **19–24**, *23*
  see also individual
    subjects/regions/countries
care gap (supply and demand), Netherlands
  160, 163
care providers 20–21, *23*
  compensation, forms of **24–6**
    see also income security
  fears associated with care provision 21
  right to provide care 1, 18–19, 28, 161–2
  see also individual subjects
care recipients 20, *23*
  fears associated with care provision 21
  right to receive care 1, 18, 19, 28, 161–2
  see also individual subjects
care workers see labour market participation
  (women)
care-provision increments, pensions (Russian
  Federation) 130–32
career breaks *38*, 39
carers see care providers
Carer's Allowance (Ireland) 212, 214–15
Carers Association of Ireland see Ireland
  (representation for informal care work)
Carers Impact (England) 199
Carers National Association (CNA), England
  195, 198, 199, 202, 204

Carers Outreach (Ireland) 216
Carers Resource Centres (Ireland) 216, 217
Catholic Church 113–14
CCSAP (Community Care Special Action
  Project), Birmingham **200–202**, 203, 207
Chayanov, A.V. 29
CHCAs (child home care allowances),
  Finland 147, 148–50, *150*, 151
Cherry, Robert 188
child home care allowances (CHCAs),
  Finland 147, 148–50, *150*, 151
Child-to-Child Programme (India) 100–101
childcare 2–3, 20, 35, *38*, 39, 41–2, **43–7**, *44*,
  73
  note: for larger case studies see Brazil,
    Finland, India, Netherlands, Russian
    Federation, United States
  benefits *38*, 41, 42
  definitions 177, 178
  disabled care (Ireland) 218
  Early Childhood Care and Development
    (ECCD) **91–4**
    India see India
  leave see parental leave
  private sector see private sector
  right to 114–16, **117–20**
children
  education see education (children)
  population (Brazil) 105, 108
  survival/health indicators **96–8**, *97*
children's private care allowance (CPCA),
  Finland 150, 151
China 96, 97, 98
Christian Aid 5
citizenship associations see representation
citizenship rights approach see rights
civil society relationship of care work see
  NGOs
class (social) 6–7
CNA (Carers National Association), England
  195, 198, 199, 202, 204
Collins-Hughes, Eddie xiii, 211–18
Combination Scenario (Netherlands) 74–5,
  161, **163–8**, 169, 170
Community Care Special Action Project
  (CCSAP), Birmingham **200–202**, 203, 207
community organizations 20, *23*
community pre-schools (Brazil) 109, 110,
  119, 121–2
contributions (social security) *38*, 39, 40–41
cost of care (public budget) 49–50, *51*, 52, 53

CPCA (children's private care allowance), Finland 150, 151
crèches *see* Brazil (pre-schools)

Daly, Mary xiv, 1–11, 33–55, 176
  other publications 36, *38*, 41, 143
Daniels, Verdia 223
day-care (children), Finland 147–8, 149, *149*, 150, *150*
decent work strategy (ILO) 1, 19, 22_2
Delhi, India 79, 80
Denmark
  childcare 42, *44*, 45–6, 148, 150
  elder care 43, 45–6, *46*, 152
  labour market participation *61*
  worker-citizen model 74
  see also Scandinavia
developing countries *see* Brazil; India; Russian Federation
disability care 8, 20, 42, 127–8, 208, 218
  California 221, 226–7
  Russian Federation 130–32, *131*, **132–6**, *137*
  see also elder care
domestic helpers *38*, 39, 40
dual breadwinner model *see* gender equality

Early Childhood Care and Development (ECCD) *see* India
earnings models (family) 57–8, **59–65**, *63*, 167, *168*
  see also family structure/roles
ECCD (Early Childhood Care and Development) *see* India
education (children)
  India 97, *97*, 100
  pre-schools *see* Brazil (pre-schools)
  United States 189–90
education (women), India 97, 98
elder care 2–3, 20, 35, 42–3, **45–7**, *46*, 72–3
  note: for larger case studies *see* England, Finland, Netherlands, Russian Federation
  India 79–80, **87–8**
  United States 186–7, **190–91**
  see also ageing population; disability care; home care; residential care
Ellwood, David 188
employer pre-schools (Brazil) 109, 110
employment creation, incentives *38*, 39, 40, 50, *51*, 52, 54
employment-related provisions 20, 22, *38*, 39, 40

England, representation for informal care work 8, **195–209**
  carers' needs from community care **205–9**
  consolidation 202
  elder care **195–9**
  organizations
    Association of Carers (AOC) 8, 198, 199
    Carers Impact 199
    Carers National Association (CNA) 195, 198, 199, 202, 204
    Community Care Special Action Project (CCSAP), Birmingham **200–202**, 203, 207
    King's Fund Informal Caring Unit 199
    National Council for Carers and their Elderly Dependants (NCCED) 197, 198
    National Council for the Single Woman and her Dependants (NCSWD) **195–7**, 199
  and the State **202–5**
  see also United Kingdom
ethic of care 24, **69–73**, **162–3**
Europe *see* individual countries; Western Europe

familial self, India **82–4**
  and childcare **84–7**
  see also individualism
family breakdown, and individualism *see* individualism
family earnings models 57–8, **59–65**, *63*, 167, *168*
  see also family structure/roles
family policy in care provision, Russian Federation *see* Russian Federation
family pre-schools (Brazil) 122–3
family structure/roles, changing 4, 5, 81
  see also family earnings models
females *see* gender equality; women
feminist movement 3, 28, 81–2
  Brazil 113
  Netherlands 161, 163
  Scandinavia 144–5
  see also women
fertility decline (United States) 179
Finland
  ageing population 152
  labour market participation *61*, 145, 151
  see also Scandinavia

Finland, social care **143–58**
  childcare 42, 44–6, *44*, 143, **147–51**, 158
    child home care allowances (CHCAs)
      147, 148–50, *150*, 151
    children's private care allowance
      (CPCA) 150, 151
    day-care 147–8, 149, *149*, 150, *150*
  elder care 42, 45–6, *46*, 143, **151–8**
    home care allowances (HCAs) 147,
      154–6, *157*
    home-based services *46*, 152–4, *155*,
      156, *157*
    residential *46*, 152, *157*
    sources 154, *155*
  employment creation, incentives 40, 50
  and Scandinavian social care regime **144–7**
flexitime 39, 40
Folbre, Nancy xiv, 16$_1$, 175–91
  other publications 31, 64, 70, 175, 177,
    178, 180, 181, 184, 187, 191
FORCES (Forum for Crèche and Child Care
  Services), India 96
Forum for Crèche and Child Care Services
  (FORCES), India 96
France 46–7
  childcare 44–5, *44*, 62, 73, 150
  elder care 42, 45, *46*
  employment creation, incentives 40, 50
  labour market participation *61*

gender bias (general), India 98, 103–4
gender equality (care provision) 3, 34, 35,
  48–9
  and care ethic **69–73**, 162–3
  dual breadwinner model 62–3, *63*
  male breadwinner model 57–8, **59–65**, *63*,
    167, *168*
  policy implications 50, 51, *51*, 52, 53,
    72–5
  see also individualism; labour market
    participation; women
Germany 31, 46–7
  childcare 42, 44–5, *44*, 62, 73, 150
  elder care 42–3, 45, *46*, 72–3
  labour market participation *61*
gift relationship of care work *see* ethic of care
Great Britain *see* United Kingdom
Greece 45, 47
  childcare 43, *44*
  elder care 43, 45, *46*
Griffiths, Roy 204, 205

HCAs (home care allowances), Finland 147,
  154–6, *157*
health care, United States **184–5**, 190–91
Health Maintenance Organizations (HMOs),
  United States 184–5
health services 20
HIV (Human Immunodeficiency Virus) 4,
  5–6, 104
HMOs (Health Maintenance Organizations),
  United States 184–5
home care 42, *46*, 88
  note: for larger case studies *see* Finland,
    Russian Federation
  home helps *38*, 39, 40
  Netherlands 170, 171–2, 173–4
  representation *see* representation
  United States 185, **221–3**, **230–31**
  see also elder care
home-making (United States) 180–82
hospitals
  Finland *157*
  length of stay 4, 185
  United States 184, 185
  see also residential care
Human Immunodeficiency Virus (HIV) 4,
  5–6, 104
human rights *see* rights

ICDS (Integrated Child Development
  Services) programme, India 98–9, 101,
  102
Iceland 33$_2$, 144
  childcare 44–6, *44*
  elder care 42, 45–6, *46*
  see also Scandinavia
IHSS (In-Home Supportive Services),
  California 221–2, 223, 229
  reform of funding **230–31**, 232
IHSS Recipients and Providers Sharing
  (IRAPS), Los Angeles County 227
illness care 20, 42, 127–8
ILO (International Labour Office), InFocus
  Programme on Socio-Economic Security
  v–vi, 19, 22$_2$, 29$_5$
ILO (International Labour Organization) 5
  decent work strategy 1, 19, 22$_2$
  World employment report 1998-99 93$_3$, 95
immunization 96
in-home care *see* home care
In-Home Supportive Services *see* IHSS
income security 21, **26–31**

note: for larger case studies *see* Finland,
Russian Federation
benefits/allowances 31, *38*, 39–41, 50–51,
51, 54
   childcare 41, 42
   Ireland 212, 214–15
   tax-related assistance 30–31, *38*, 39,
   187–8, 189, 190
   United Kingdom 197, 199
   vouchers 29, *38*, 39, 40–41
  right to 1, 2, 24, 27, 28–31
Independent Provider (IP) mode, home care
(California) 221–2, 223, 225
India **79–90**
  childcare/Early Childhood Care and
  Development (ECCD) **91–104**
   dialogue, need for 104
   and familial self **84–7**
   government commitment to 94–5,
   100–102
   indicators **96–8**, *97*
   policy issues **100–104**
   programmes **98–100**, 100–102
  elder care 79–80, **87–8**
  familial self **82–4**
   and childcare **84–7**
  gender bias (general) 98, 103–4
  individualism 80, 82, 88
  labour market participation (women) 95
  modernization 80, 87–8
individualism
  India 80, 82, 88
  industrialized countries **65–9**, **80–82**,
  83
  see also familial self; gender equality
industrialization 80, 89
  see also modernization
industrialized countries **141–91**
  individualism **65–9**, **80–82**, 83
  see also individual regions/countries,
  especially England, Finland, Ireland,
  Netherlands, United Kingdom, United
  States, Western Europe
infants *see* children
InFocus Programme on Socio-Economic
Security (ILO) v–vi, 19, 22$_2$, 29$_5$
institutional care *see* residential care
institutions for supplementary care 22
Integrated Child Development Services
(ICDS) programme, India 98–9, 101, 102
Interforum Movement for Infant Education in

Brazil 119–20
International Labour Organization/Office *see*
ILO
Invalid Care Allowance (England) 197, 199
IP (Independent Provider) mode, home care
(California) 221–2, 223, 225
IRAPS (IHSS Recipients and Providers
Sharing), Los Angeles County 227
Ireland 171
  Carer's Allowance 212, 214–15
  carers, number 211–12
  childcare 41–2, 43, *44*, 45, 47, 218
  elder care 42, 45, *46*, 47
  labour market participation *61*
  market-based care, incentives towards 52
Ireland, representation for informal care work
211–18
  Carers Association of Ireland 7–8, **211–18**
   future 217–18
   lobbying and advocacy 7–8, **213–15**,
   217, 218
   service provision **215–17**
Italy
  childcare 42, 43, 43$_9$, *44*, 45, 47, 73, 150
  elder care 45, *46*, 47
  labour market participation *61*

Japan 60

Kerala, India 79, 88, 98
King's Fund Informal Caring Unit (England) 199
Knijn, Trudie xiv, 159–74
  other publications 28, 36, 161, 167, 169,
  171, 173, 174

LA *see* Los Angeles
LA Home Care Workers Union (Local 434B)
223–5, 227–9, 231, 232
labour market participation 60, *61*
labour market participation (women) 60, *61*,
64, 69, 95, 108
  care occupations 5, 64, 180, **182–4**
  Finland *61*, 145, 151
  Netherlands *61*, 161, **163–70**
   Combination Scenario 74–5, 161,
   163–8, 169, 170
   part-time work 167–9, 170
  part-time work 60, *61*, 167–9, 170
  United Kingdom 60, *61*, 64
  United States *61*, 64, 74, 179–80, **182–4**
  see also gender equality

labour supply/demand 50, 51–2, *51*, 53
Lakunina, Liana 125–39
laws, care provision 22
leave from work *38*, 39, 40, *51*, 52, 54
  childcare *see* parental leave
Lewis, Jane xiv, 31, 57–75
  other publications 36, 58, 60, 63, 64, 70,
    74, 143, 159
literacy 97–8, 100
Local 434B (LA Home Care Workers Union)
  223–5, 227–9, 231, 232
lone carers *see* single women/mothers/
  parents
Los Angeles County (LA), representation for
  formal care work **219–33**
  home care industry and labour market
    221–3
  Service Employees International Union
    (SEIU) **219–20**, 222, 232–3
    and IHSS Recipients and Providers
      Sharing (IRAPS) 227
    and LA Home Care Workers Union
      (Local 434B) **223–5**, 227–9, 231, 232
    and public authorities (PAs) **225–9**, 232
    and reform of home care funding
      230–31, 232
  see also United States
Luxembourg 42, 44–5, *44*, 46–7, *46*$_2$

Macmillan, Harold 196
Maldives 96
males *see* gender equality
malnutrition (children) 96–7, *97*
market-based care, incentives towards *38*, *51*,
  52–3, 54–5
  see also private sector
Marshall, Alfred 15
maternal mortality rates 97, 98
maternity leave *see* parental leave
means-testing 28, 214–15
Meenakshi (Trivandrum carer) 79, 80
Mellor, David 200
men *see* gender equality
migrant workers, as care providers 5
modernization 80, 87–8
  see also industrialization
monitoring care provision 22
mortality rates (India)
  infants/children 96, *97*, 98
  maternal 97, 98
Mysore, India 84

National Council for Carers and their Elderly
  Dependants (NCCED) 197, 198
  see also National Council for the Single
    Woman and her Dependants
National Council for the Single Woman and
  her Dependants (NCSWD) **195–7**, 199
  see also National Council for Carers and
    their Elderly Dependants
NCCED *see* National Council for Carers and
  their Elderly Dependants
NCSWD *see* National Council for the Single
  Woman and her Dependants
Netherlands **159–74**
  care gap (supply and demand) 160, 163
  care and work 161, 162
    Combination Scenario 74–5, 161,
      163–8, 169, 170
    lack of female gains **168–70**
  childcare 43, *44*, 45, 46–7, 163, 165,
    166–7, 170–74
  citizenship rights (to provide/receive care)
    161–2
  elder care 42, 43, 45, 46–7, *46*, 163, 170–73
  ethics of care 162–3
  family earnings models 167, *168*
  home care 170, 171–2, 173–4
  labour market participation *see* labour
    market participation
  substitution of formal by informal care
    161, 171, 173
  welfare state and care 159–60, 163
new work movement (United States) 89–90
NGOs (non-governmental organizations) 26,
  32
  Brazil 106, 109, 110, 118–19, 122, 123
  India 88, 102
Non-Formal Education Programme (India) 100
non-governmental organizations *see* NGOs
Nordic countries *see* Scandinavia
Norway 33$_2$
  childcare 42, *44*, 45–6, 73
  elder care 43, 45–6, *46*
  see also Scandinavia
nurseries *see* Brazil (pre-schools)
nurses 88, 183, 185
nursing homes *see* residential care

old people, as care recipients *see* elder care
Oliver, Judith 198, 207–8
organizations representing care
  providers/recipients *see* representation

parental leave *38*, 41–2, 43–4, *44*, 73
  Netherlands 166–7
  Russian Federation 128, 129, 130, *131*
  United States 187
part-time work (women) 60, *61*, 167–9, 170
PAs (public authorities), home care
  (California) **225–9**, 232
Paternalism Test Principle v–vi
pensions (Russian Federation) 136, *137*
  care-provision increments 130–32
philanthropic pre-schools (Brazil) 109, 110
Philippines 5
Pitkeathley, Jill 204, 205
Portugal 45, 47
  childcare 43, *44*
  elder care 45, *46*
poverty 3, 98, 108–9, 136–8
pre-schools
  Brazil *see* Brazil (pre-schools)
  United States 106
private sector 3, 20, 22, *23*, 25, *38*
  childcare 150, 172, 173, 174
    pre-schools (Brazil) 109, 110, 121, 123
  Netherlands 172–3, 174
  United States 25, 186–7
  see also market-based care
providers of care *see* care providers
public authorities (PAs), home care
  (California) **225–9**, 232
public sector *see* State

Rajasthan, India 95, 98
Rawls, John v
recipients of care *see* care recipients
reciprocity relationship of care work 25
regulations, care provision 22
representation **6–8**, 22–4, *23*, 30, **193–233**
  note: for individual case studies *see*
    England; Ireland; Los Angeles
residential care *38*, 39, *46*
  Finland *46*, 152, *157*
  India 88
  Russian Federation 134–5
  United States 186–7
  see also elder care; hospitals
rights
  income security 1, 2, 24, 27, 28–31
  to provide care 1, 18–19, 28, 161–2
  to receive care 1, 18, 19, 28, 161–2
Rio de Janeiro (State) 114, 114₁₃
Rolf, David 225, 228–9

Russian Federation, social protection for
  home-based care **125–39**
  childcare 127–30, *131*, 132, 137, 138
  efficiency of system **136–8**, *137*
  elder care 128, 130–32, **132–6**, *135*, *137*
  illness/disability 127–8, 130–32, *131*,
    132–6, *137*
  privileges to workers providing care for
    family members **127–9**
  reform **138–9**
  social protection policies, background
    125–7
  system of state support **129–36**
    income benefits **129–32**, *131*
    social-service-related assistance **132–6**,
      135

Sambasivan, Umadevi xv, 79–90
San Francisco County, California 226
San Mateo County, California 226
Sao Paulo, Brazil 114
Sawicky, Max 188
Scandinavia 35, 39, **144–7**
  childcare 41, 73
  elder care 42
  labour market participation (women) 60,
    64
  see also individual countries
school attendance *see* education
Security Difference Principle v–vi
Seear, Nancy, Baroness 196
SEIU (Service Employees International
  Union) *see* Los Angeles
Service Employees International Union
  (SEIU) *see* Los Angeles
services 25–6, *38*, 39, 40, 51–2, *51*, 54
severance pay *38*, 39
Shaw, George Bernard 7, 17
sickness care 20, 42, 127–8
Simmons, Mary 223
single mothers 74, *131*
single parents 165
single women, representation 8, **195–7**
social assistance *see* income security
social insurance *see* income security
social workers 20
Sorj, Bila xv, 105–24
South Asia 97
Spain 45, 47
  childcare 43, *44*
  elder care 43, 45, *46*

Sri Lanka 96, 97, 98
Standing, Guy xv, 1–11, 15–32
    other publications 220$_2$
State involvement in care provision 3, 8–9,
    22, *23*, 25–6
    see also individual
        subjects/regions/countries, especially
        Western Europe
Stepantchikova, Natalia xv–xvi, 125–39
sub-Saharan Africa 5–6, 96
supplementary care, institutions 22
support system, social process of care 22–3,
    23
Sweden 144, 171
    childcare 42, *44*, 45–6, 62, 73, 148, 150
    elder care 43, 45–6, *46*
    labour market participation *61*
    worker-citizen model 63, 74
    see also Scandinavia
Sweeney, John 229–30

tax financing, Scandinavia 145
tax-related assistance *see* income security
Taylor, F.W. 29
Tchetvernina, Tatyana 125–39
teachers (female) 183
Thailand 96, 97, 98
time squeeze (care work) 3, 6
time-use surveys **181–2**
Titmuss, Richard 16
trade unions *see* representation
Trivandrum, India 79–80

UN (United Nations) 165
UNDP (United Nations Development
    Program) 26$_3$
UNESCO (United Nations Educational,
    Scientific, and Cultural Organization) 104
Unicef (United Nations Children's Fund) 93,
    96$_6$, 97, *97*, 98, 104
unions *see* representation
United Kingdom 5, 26$_3$, 34, 53
    ageing population 75
    childcare 41–2, 43, *44*, 45, 47
    elder care 42, 45, *46*, 47
    illness care 42
    individualism 67, 68
    labour market participation 60, *61*, 64
    market-based care, incentives towards 52
    welfare-to-work concept 62–3
    see also England

United Nations Children's Fund (Unicef) 93,
    96$_6$, 97, *97*, 98, 104
United Nations Development Program
    (UNDP) 26$_3$
United Nations Educational, Scientific, and
    Cultural Organization (UNESCO) 104
United Nations (UN) 165
United States 88
    ageing population 180
    childcare 95, 106, 181, **185–6, 187–90**
    civil society relationship of care work 26
    education 189–90
    elder care 186–7, **190–91**
    health care **184–5**, 190–91
    home care industry/workers **221–3,
        230–31**
    individualism 65, 66–7, 68, 69, 82
    labour market participation 60, *61*, 64, 74,
        179–80, **182–4**
    new work movement 89–90
    pre-schools 106
    private care services 25, 186–7
    residential care 186–7
    tax-related assistance 187–8, 189, 190
    welfare-to-work concept 62, 74
    see also Los Angeles
United States, accounting for care **175–91**
    care industries
        childcare **185–6**
        elder care 186–7
        health care **184–5**, 190–91
    care labour force **179–80**
    care occupations, female employment 64,
        180, **182–4**
    home-making 180–82
    public support for care **187–91**
        child rearing **187–8**
        childcare **188–90**
        elder care **190–91**
    time-use surveys **181–2**
unmarried women *see* single women/mothers
Uttar Pradesh, India 98

voice representation *see* representation
voluntary organizations 20
vouchers 29, *38*, 39, 40–41

wages, care workers 64, **230–31**
Walsh, Jess xvi, 219–33
Wazir, Rekha xvi, 91–104
Webster, Reverend Mary 195–6

welfare mix 49, 50, 51, *51*, 52, 171
welfare state and care (Netherlands) 159–60, 163
welfare-to-work concept 62–3, 74
Western Europe, care policies **33–55**
  alternative ways of compensating for care
    47–53
    care as a policy good **47–50**
    policy measures, effects **50–53**, *51*
  childcare 35, *38*, 39, 41–2, **43–7**, *44*
  conceptualizations and definitions of care
    34–9
    evolution as a concept 34
    policy parameters of care **36–9**
    as a social policy analysis tool **34–6**
  elder care 35, 42–3, **45–7**, *46*
  overview **53–5**
  provision for care 37, *38*, **39–47**
    general outline of trends **39–41**
    models in European welfare states **43–7**

  public policies in European welfare
    states **41–3**
  see also individual countries
Wilson, Pete 230
women 3–5
  feminist movement 3, 28, 81–2, 113,
    144–5, 161, 163
  home-making (United States) 180–82
  single 8, 74, *131*, **195–7**
  value of unpaid work 26
  see also individual subjects/countries
    (please refer to the introductory note),
    especially Brazil, childcare, elder care,
    gender equality, India, labour market
    participation, representation
work, alternative models 89–90
worker-citizen model 62–3, 74
working time, reduction *38*, 39
World Employment Report 1998-99 (ILO) 93[3],95